ALLIES AT WAR

ALLIES AT WAR

HarperCollins*Publishers*

HarperCollins*Publishers*
77–85 Fulham Palace Road
Hammersmith
London
W6 8JB

The HarperCollins website address is:
www.**fireandwater**.com

First Published in Great Britain by HarperCollins*Publishers* 2001

1 3 5 7 9 10 8 6 4 2

ISBN 0 00711622 5

Copyright of photographs:
Cover photographs – Courtesy of the Imperial War Museum &
Mary Evans Picture Library.
Other photographs – US National Archive, Washington and
Franklin D Roosevelt Library, Hyde Park.

Set in Sabon, ITC Officia Sans and European Pi by
Rowland Phototypesetting Ltd, Bury St Edmunds, Suffolk

Printed and bound in Great Britain by
Clays Ltd, St Ives plc

CONTENTS

FOREWORD

As I grew up in the 1960s, Charles de Gaulle appeared an ogre. From my father's point of view, it was bad enough that we Huguenots had been chucked out of France by Richelieu nearly four centuries before. Now, for us, a naval family, to watch de Gaulle withdraw French forces from NATO, veto the United Kingdom's first attempts to enter the Common Market, and insult our American allies was altogether too much.

Britain's identity crisis and apparent powerlessness were put into even sharper perspective by Winston Churchill's funeral in 1965. It only drove home the unwelcome truth that we were now a nation without an empire, buffeted by de Gaulle, supplicant to the United States, and all adrift in a changing world. Perhaps not much has changed in succeeding decades.

As I knew more, it began to appear that all these seeds had been sown a full generation before, during the Second World War. The leaders of the three great nations of the West were rather more complicated than they appeared on the surface. Their real relationship had nothing in common with the fine public speeches and protestations of mutual support.

I first wrote a proposal for a television series on Churchill, Roosevelt and de Gaulle more years ago than I would like to remember. Initially I had several fruitful discussions with Brian Lapping but our attempt to launch the project foundered in the frustrating milieu we inhabit. However, a few years on, I found a sympathetic ear in Stephen Segaller and Tammy Robinson at WNET in New York, who put their boundless enthusiasm and commitment into raising the first and most significant part of the budget. They were soon joined by Peter Grimsdale, then at the BBC, who with unflagging energy squeezed enough money from BBC2 to make the series viable. I am also grateful to BBC Worldwide for their further contribution and to Dr. Jonathan Howe and the Arthur Vining Davis Foundations.

Val Hudson at HarperCollins persuaded me that it was too good a story for me not to write a book. Her colleagues in the history section have given great support and I am grateful to Ian Drury for his initial enthusiasm and allowing me that extra little bit of time and to Ian Tandy for seeing the book through to publication.

The television series has been much assisted by three eminent scholars, who have given sound advice and always been available at the end of a phone or email. They are Warren Kimball, famed for his massive achievement in compiling and editing the Churchill / Roosevelt correspondence which has been a vital source for both the television series and this book; François Kersaudy, author of a ground-breaking book on Churchill and de Gaulle and raconteur supreme; and Philip Bell, the master of lucid narrative and Franco – British relations. I recommend anyone to cast an eye on the bibliography and read the books of these three men; it will be worth the time. I owe Philip Bell a special debt for taking on the additional task of reading my manuscript. He has encouraged me, saved me from errors and pointed me towards fascinating details. Of course, I must bear sole responsibility for the final version.

I have also had the great pleasure of getting to know FDR's grandson, Curtis Roosevelt. He has been an inspiring sounding board, a source of excellent stories and a fascinating interviewee. I hope that he does not disagree with too much of what I have written.

At 3BM, I have had a wonderful team. My colleague, Jeremy Bennett, always sings for his lunch when it comes to Churchillian matters. Glynis Robertson has managed the production with her customary élan, fun and attention to detail. Natalia Asheshov did great work with the French sources and literature and found whoever is still living and was close to these events. Beth Salt picked up the pieces that went missing and gracefully kept many wheels turning. Andrew Quigley displayed his customary genius in the editing room and a new directing talent. Polly Pettit and Margaret Johnson in Washington speedily conducted mass raids on the picture and film archives. One name above all stands out in helping me with this book: Marc Tiley did superb work in the British and American archives for both book and films, in the process prompting the Cabinet Office to release some extraordinary new documents. Without him, this book would have been impossible.

Finally, I offer my most heartfelt thanks to my family, in particular my father, with whom the political discussions became more and more lively and interesting, and above all to my beloved wife, Penelope, and our children, Helena and Olivia, for their forbearance and support as weekends, evenings and nights out vanished before the onrush of the deadline.

Simon Berthon
March 2001

PROLOGUE

The British Prime Minister, Winston Churchill, could bear the taunts no longer.

It was 21 May 1943, the tenth day of the 'Trident' conference with President Roosevelt in Washington. Crucial decisions on the future of the war hung in the balance. The Allies had agreed to follow up the final victory against the Axis in North Africa with an invasion of Sicily. The American Chiefs-of-Staff were determined that attention would then be exclusively devoted to the build-up of a massive force in Britain to prepare for the invasion of Europe. Would Churchill be able to persuade Roosevelt to overrule them? Would the President back his own strategy of attacking Hitler through the soft underbelly of Italy?

A further, potentially more significant decision was at stake. The Americans were well advanced in their atomic bomb project, code named 'Manhattan', but their scientists were opposed to sharing data with Britain. Could Churchill persuade the President that his British allies should be trusted partners in the war's deadliest secret?

Yet, in the middle of these vital discussions which would affect not just the future of the war, but the future of mankind, one irritant was infuriating the President above all others. Every day he dropped a damning document about it on Churchill's desk; every day it peppered their discussions.

Now it was time for Churchill to act. He would ask his

cabinet colleagues in London to agree to get rid of the irritant once and for all. He cabled his Foreign Secretary, Anthony Eden: 'I must now warn you very solemnly of a very stern situation developing here about de Gaulle. Hardly a day passes that the President does not mention it to me.'

The irritant was General Charles de Gaulle, the leader of the Free French. Ever since the fall of France in June 1940, when he had escaped from his country to London to continue the fight against the Nazis, de Gaulle had been the symbol to the world of French resistance, the valiant, heroic, unconquerable Fighting Frenchman. Yet the President could hardly stand the thought of him.

Among the many documents Roosevelt heaped on Churchill was one containing his own castigation. De Gaulle's attitude, wrote Roosevelt, was 'well nigh intolerable'. He had 'the Messianic complex'. His staff circulated 'vicious propaganda'. Roosevelt produced intelligence reports that de Gaulle had 'Communist' links. Other American analyses had accused him of being 'Fascist'.

From the beginning de Gaulle had been Churchill's protégé, but their relationship had turned into a roller-coaster of mutual admiration, mutual suspicion and, on Churchill's part, loathing. Now, under the influence of the President, Churchill told Eden that he wanted finally to cast de Gaulle adrift: 'I ask my colleagues to consider urgently whether we should not now eliminate de Gaulle as a political force . . . When we consider the absolutely vital interest which we have in preserving good relations with the United States, it seems to me most questionable that we should allow this marplot and mischief-maker to continue the harm he is doing.'

Yet, at this very moment, de Gaulle was not merely the one

consistent beacon of French freedom, he was also consolidating his hold over the underground resistance in mainland France which American and British commanders hoped would play a vital role in the invasion of Europe.

No such consideration would draw Roosevelt's ire. The stage was set for an arm's length and ruthlessly fought duel between the American President and the French General with the British Prime Minister caught in the middle.

—o0o—

Fifteen years later, de Gaulle would become President of France and hold power for eleven years. He lost no opportunity to chastise the United States. He blocked Britain's early attempts to join the European Common Market. This legacy, which affected both Britain and the United States at crucial stages of their post-war development, is rooted in the extraordinary relationship between three titanic figures who became Allies at War.

CHAPTER ONE
TEN DAYS IN JUNE

It was a relationship that began suddenly and in crisis. On the morning of 9 June 1940, an obscure Brigadier General in the French Army flew into London from Paris. He was forty-nine years old and, it seemed, a political innocent. His mission was crucial to the salvation of France. He spoke limited English, and when he very occasionally did, the result was more comic than diplomatic.

His name was Charles de Gaulle. He had been a politician for all of four days and a general for just over three weeks. On 5 June, the French Prime Minister, Paul Reynaud, had invited de Gaulle to join his cabinet as Under Secretary of State for National Defence. The Battle of France was entering its final, fatal phase. The greater part of the British Expeditionary Force – more than 330,000 men, accompanied by 139,000 French soldiers – had made their miraculous escape from Dunkirk. The German Army's sickle cut to divide the allied armies had brought such instant success that Hitler was breathless, even confused, by his sudden victory. After a few days' rest, he launched Nazi forces at Paris and their spearheads sped across the river Somme. French forces fought hard, their casualties exceeding even the murderous killing rate of the deadliest battles of the First World War. But they were badly led and the tactics of their generals, mired in the outdated glory of the earlier war, were irrelevant to the mechanized might of the *Blitzkrieg*.

As de Gaulle arrived in London, France was in full retreat and the Nazi road to Paris was open. The task given by Reynaud to de Gaulle was to persuade the British Prime Minister, Winston Churchill, to gamble the full strength of the Royal Air Force on the saving of France. As de Gaulle crossed the threshold of Downing Street he came face to face with Churchill for the first time. Immediately he understood that, like himself, the British leader's aggression went to the heart. Later he wrote: 'The impression he gave me confirmed me in my conviction that Great Britain, led by such a fighter, would certainly not flinch. Mr Churchill seemed to me equal to the harshest task, provided it also had greatness.'

Churchill wrote no record of this first encounter with the young French general but the minutes of a British cabinet meeting later that day recorded: 'The Prime Minister described a conversation which he had had that afternoon with General de Gaulle. He had given the Prime Minister a more favourable impression of French morale and determination.'

De Gaulle had made a mark. However, under heavy pressure from his air chiefs, Churchill refused to commit himself to throwing every British fighter squadron into the French maelstrom. As a lover of France, his emotional inclination was to respond to French cries of help, but he understood that the battle across the Channel was effectively lost; the fighters would be needed to protect the homeland. At this first meeting de Gaulle told Churchill that, in his position, he would have done the same thing. In the years ahead, Churchill never forgot the understanding and strategic appreciation that de Gaulle had shown.

That night de Gaulle flew back to France and was summoned to see Reynaud at his home. Reynaud, who had been Prime Minister of France for just three months, was a fighter and for that reason had brought de Gaulle into his cabinet. The two men had come to know each other in the 1930s after de Gaulle, then a middle-ranking officer, had spotted Reynaud as the one French politician who might be sympathetic to his views on modern warfare. In the French Army of that time, de Gaulle was an unusual soldier. A thinker and a theorist, he had given lectures at the Sorbonne on the conduct of future wars and published three books, including 'The Army of the Future' in 1934. While the French High Command was stuck in First World War theories of a static, defensive war based, in France's case, on the allegedly invincible Maginot line, de Gaulle realized that future wars would be fought very differently. He proposed the creation of a new army of manoeuvre and attack, comprising a mass of mechanized, armoured units, which could react fast to any threat. De Gaulle's book, which was only published in English in 1940, became required reading amongst the German High Command and helped to form the tactics of the Blitzkrieg. But at home, apart from Reynaud, his ideas found no support in the military and political establishment. Only on 15 May 1940, five days into the Blitzkrieg, was de Gaulle finally allowed to put his ideas into practice and given command of an armoured division. A fortnight later, at Abbéville, his tanks mounted the one successful counter-attack against the Nazis during the battle of France. However this proved to be far too little and far too late.

Now, as de Gaulle and Reynaud met on the night of 9 June, disaster was apparent. Enemy forces had reached the Seine below Paris. The capital was almost surrounded and the next day the French Government was to begin its retreat southwards. While Reynaud wanted to fight on, he was surrounded by defeatism. On 18 May he had felt compelled to invite the 84-year-old Marshal Philippe Pétain, the soldier's hero of the

3

First World War, to join his cabinet, though both Reynaud and de Gaulle knew that Pétain was the screen for those who desired an armistice. "Better to have him inside than out", Reynaud told de Gaulle, but Pétain would weave an insidious spell of surrender inside the cabinet. Indeed, back in January 1940 the editor of a British news letter, Kenneth de Courcy, had reported to the Foreign Office that Pétain, then French ambassador to Spain, had already reached a private understanding with pro-Nazi French politicians, notably Pierre Laval. De Courcy's report was disbelieved.

General Maxime Weygand, the recently appointed French Commander-in-Chief, was also showing no sign of fight. Weygand, aged 73, had made his reputation as Chief-of-Staff to the brilliant Marshal Foch in the First World War. At the outbreak of war he had been recalled from retirement to command French forces in Syria. On 19 May, after the first disastrous week of the *Blitzkrieg*, he had been summoned back to mainland France to take over as Commander-in-Chief. Weygand retained his vigour and a calculating mind; within days of taking overall command that mind told him France was defeated. Immediately after his success at Abbéville, de Gaulle had seen Weygand and received his congratulations. Weygand was in a pessimistic mood. He foresaw the German attack on the Somme, and lamented his poor prospects of a successful resistance. The day before he had left for London, De Gaulle saw Weygand for a second time. De Gaulle later wrote that their conversation remained engraved on his mind. Weygand said that his prophecy of the German attack across the Somme had proved correct and that he could not stop them.

"All right!" replied de Gaulle, "They're crossing the Somme. And then?"

"Then?" replied Weygand, "The Seine and the Marne."

"Yes, And then?"

"Then? But that's the end!"

"How do you mean? The end? And the world? And the Empire?"

According to De Gaulle, Weygand gave a despairing laugh. "The Empire? But that's childish! As for the world, when I've been beaten here, England won't wait a week before negotiating with the Reich."

Both Weygand and Pétain would have lead roles in the later drama between Churchill, Roosevelt and de Gaulle. But at this point their course of surrender was not the only one; there seemed alternative ways for France to fight on. The first option was to create a redoubt in the rugged terrain of Brittany, based in the town of Quimper, where the Government and remnants of the French Army could retreat, regroup and resist. The second plan, as de Gaulle had hinted to Weygand, was to carry on the war from the French Empire in North Africa, comprising the territories of Algeria, Morocco and Tunisia. They already contained a large army of some 370,000 men – of whom nearly half were French. Reynaud put de Gaulle, the one fighting soldier inside France whom he could count on, in charge of preparations for both options.

On 10 June there was suddenly a new hope that was born of a further shattering blow. The Italian dictator, Benito Mussolini, declared war on Britain and France. He was joining the party late, jumping in only when the outcome was certain. At this time, before her army and navy displayed their inherent feebleness, Italy seemed a powerful nation and the shock of Mussolini's declaration was felt far beyond Europe.

Since the middle of May, both Churchill and Reynaud had

been pleading for help from the American President, Franklin Roosevelt. Indeed, almost as soon as he had become Prime Minister on 10 May 1940, Churchill had been banking on the United States. A few days afterwards his son Randolph happened to call on his father at breakfast time and found him upstairs 'shaving with his old fashioned Valet razor. He had a tough beard and as usual was hacking away.' Father told son to sit down and read the papers while he finished shaving. After further minutes of hacking away Churchill turned to Randolph and said, "I think I see my way through". Astounded, Randolph asked his father whether he meant "avoid defeat" (which seemed to him credible) or "beat the bastards" (which seemed incredible). Churchill flung the razor into the basin and said, "Of course, I mean we can beat them." Randolph replied that he was all for such a proposition but did not see how his father could do it. With great intensity Churchill turned round and said, "I shall drag the United States in."

Churchill never succeeded in his ambition, which would only be fulfilled by Pearl Harbour. It was not for want of trying. On 15 May he had sent a message to Roosevelt, imploring an immediate loan of fighter aircraft and fifty old American destroyers, which were sitting mothballed from the First World War. Roosevelt's reply was non-committal, stressing the difficulties of obtaining the agreement of the United States Congress and the restrictions imposed on him by America's Neutrality Act. At that stage the strong reputation of the French Army also led his administration to assume that the threat of Hitler could be contained within the European continent.

Churchill's pleas to Roosevelt were matched by Reynaud, who wrote to Roosevelt that the French, 'will fight before Paris. We will fight behind Paris. We will lock ourselves up in one of our provinces and if we are driven out we will go to North Africa, and, if need be, to our American possessions.' But for France to fight on, Reynaud told Roosevelt that he required America to supply her with guns, planes and perhaps even men.

The American Ambassador in Paris, William C. Bullitt, then a close friend of Roosevelt, reinforced the French Government's requests but on 1 June, when the crisis was clear, Roosevelt repeated his refusal to send the old destroyers to Britain or France. Ingenuously, he advised Bullitt that 'several American republics have destroyers, which they might be willing to sell and could sell under their laws.' Bullitt felt shamed when the French War Minister, Edouard Daladier, responded "that civilization in the world should fall because a great nation with a great President could simply talk." Bullitt cabled Washington, 'words, unaccompanied by acts . . . are rather sickening.'

This was not quite fair to Roosevelt; there had been one act that, despite the legalities of neutrality, was partial to Britain and France. On 1 June, as the retreat from Dunkirk was awakening America to the realities of the disaster in France, the President ordered his Navy and War departments to draw up a full list of the entire American stocks of guns and ammunition which could be spared for Britain and France. It comprised half a million World War One rifles, which had been stored in grease for twenty years with 250 cartridges apiece, 900 field guns and ammunition, 80,000 machine guns and a few extras. Roosevelt bypassed the neutrality laws by approving the sale of the whole bundle for 37 million dollars to an intermediate agency that would then sell it on to Britain and France. But it was not until 11 June that the first consignment was loaded onto British merchant ships. They would be too late to help in the battle of France.

On the evening of Italy's entry into the war, Roosevelt made a speech at the University of Charlottesville which unexpectedly suggested a dramatic change of attitude and seemed to offer a hope that words might at last turn to something more concrete than the sale of old weapons. The speech was inspired by Roosevelt's fury that Mussolini had rebuffed all his pleas to stay out of the war. His pique spawned what, even watching and listening to it sixty years later, was a magnificent oration.

"On this 10th day of June nineteen hundred and forty, the hand that held the dagger has struck it into the back of its neighbour", declaimed Roosevelt. After great applause among the students in the hall, he continued with a rhythmical and mesmerizing cadence, "On this 10th day of June nineteen hundred and forty, in this university, founded by the first great American teacher of democracy, we send our prayers and our hopes to those beyond the seas who are maintaining with magnificent valour their battle for freedom . . . We will extend to the opponents of force the material resources of this nation."

In London, Churchill and his colleagues sat up late to listen to the speech and the thrilling prospects which Roosevelt seemed to be brandishing. The next morning Churchill cabled Roosevelt, 'We all listened to you last night and were fortified by the grand scope of your declaration. Your statement that the material aid of the United States will be given to the Allies in their struggle is a strong encouragement in a dark but not unhopeful hour. Everything must be done to keep France in the fight.'

According to his private secretary, John Colville, Churchill harboured a genuine hope that 'America will come in now, at any rate as a non-belligerent ally.' This was what Churchill had been seeking since his first plea for help in the middle of May. He understood that an instant American declaration of war was out of the question. This could only be enacted by Congress, which was riddled with isolationism. But Roosevelt himself had already displayed a deeper understanding that the European conflict could, if unchecked, spill over to the Americas. If the President exercised his unparalleled political skills, might he not be able to twist Congress's arm and go beyond the mere sale of old weapons to a clear commitment to unconditional material aid – which the Charlottesville speech seemed to imply? Might not Roosevelt even deliver a latent threat that, in the last resort, America itself would go to war?

Reynaud too, fortified by Roosevelt's speech, sent a further, extravagant appeal. 'It is my duty,' he wrote, 'to ask you for a new gesture of solidarity, even greater than before. At the same time that you tell the men and women of America about our plight, I implore you to declare publicly that the United States extends to the Allies moral and material support of every kind, except the sending of an expeditionary force. I implore you to do this before it is too late.' What Reynaud really wanted was the dispatch of American warships to European waters as an immediate and direct warning to Hitler, an incontrovertible sign that in the end the United States would not allow the Nazis to go unchallenged.

On the afternoon of 11 June, after the messages to Roosevelt had been cabled to Washington, Churchill flew over to France to meet the French cabinet which had now left Paris and was lodging at a chateau near Orleans in central France. The British contingent understood that the meeting was an opportunity for the French High Command to provide the latest battle analysis and for the two Governments to plan further resistance. Churchill did not know that the day before, Weygand had arrived, uninvited, at Reynaud's Paris home to declare that

France had no choice but to seek an armistice. The battle, he stated, was over. De Gaulle, who was with Reynaud, reminded the Commander-in-Chief that there were other prospects. Weygand mockingly replied "Have you something to suggest?" De Gaulle, now a cabinet member, tartly reminded his former superior officer that the Government did not have suggestions to make, but orders to give.

De Gaulle immediately sought out another French general, Charles Huntziger, whom he had suggested to Reynaud as a replacement for Weygand. Huntziger said he would act on any order given to continue resistance from Brittany or Africa. However Reynaud, having appointed Weygand only a few weeks before, fatally backed off from another change. As the British arrived at Briare it was left to Weygand to convey, with his customary precision, the imminence of defeat. To any suggestion from Churchill of alternative, even guerrilla, forms of resistance, Weygand's mind was closed. Churchill turned to Pétain, reminding him how, after the British Fifth Army disaster at the Battle of Amiens in March 1918, he had visited Pétain at his headquarters and the French general had outlined his plan to fight back, re-establishing the line a few days later. "Yes", retorted Pétain, "You, the English, were done for. But I sent forty divisions to rescue you. Today it is we who are smashed to pieces. Where are your fifty divisions?" In fact, even in 1918, Churchill had seen the defeatism in Pétain's eyes; it was his commander, Foch, who had revived the Allies.

The self-justification for France's fall was already emerging among the defeatists. It was the British who had scuttled and run from Dunkirk; the British who were failing to send over their fighter squadrons; the British who wished to resist Hitler with French blood. If the British could not come to the rescue, the only possible saviour was America; and America was dithering. As the British group gathered in melancholy fashion for a late dinner in Briare, only one Frenchman seemed to be unimpeachably opposed to submission.

General Edward Spears, a fluent French speaker and close friend of Churchill, was acting as Churchill's personal liaison to the French Government. His first sighting of the gaunt de Gaulle produced a memorable portrait. 'His bearing alone among his compatriots matched the calm, healthy phlegm of the British. A strange-looking man, enormously tall, sitting at the table, he dominated everyone else by his height, as he had done when walking into the room. No chin, a long, dropping, elephantine nose over a closely-cut moustache; a shadow over a small mouth whose thick lips tended to protrude as if in a pout before speaking, a high receding forehead and pointed head surmounted by sparse black hair lying flat and neatly parted. His heavily hooded eyes were very shrewd. When about to speak he oscillated his head slightly like a pendulum, while searching for words.'

The next morning, 12 June, after a further pessimistic meeting during which Weygand exaggerated German strength and undervalued his own, Churchill prepared to fly back to London. Before he left, he had a last encounter, with the Commander of the French Navy, Admiral François Darlan. His fleet was powerful and modern, the fourth largest in the world. It was now becoming Churchill's dominating fear, as it would become Roosevelt's, that should France give in, her navy would be taken over by the Nazis. Churchill took Darlan aside. "Darlan, you must never let them get the French Fleet." Darlan solemnly promised that he would never do so. This meeting was the last that the British leader would see of the unholy trinity of Pétain,

Weygand and Darlan. But in the years to come all three would be siren voices, tearing at the threads of Churchill's and Roosevelt's relationships with de Gaulle.

Churchill returned in his Flamingo aircraft, which was normally escorted by twelve hurricanes. The morning was cloudy, which made it impossible for the hurricanes to join up. Churchill took the risk to fly alone. As the Flamingo neared the Channel, the weather cleared and its passengers could see the port of Le Havre in flames eight thousand feet below. Crossing the channel, the pilot made a sudden dive to one hundred feet above the sea and skimmed his way back to the coast. Churchill only learned later that they had passed beneath two German fighters, which were attacking fishing boats. The Germans had not spotted the defenceless Flamingo.

Back in London, Churchill reported to the War Cabinet on the enfeeblement of Weygand and Pétain. Of the latter he said, "Pétain is a dangerous man at this juncture: he has always been a defeatist, even in the last war." Churchill also told his colleagues that the young and energetic de Gaulle had made a very favourable impression on him. Indeed he thought it possible that, if the present line collapsed, Reynaud would turn to de Gaulle to take command.

Churchill now understood that there was only one hope of keeping France in the war. Both he and Reynaud had to wring more out of Roosevelt. Churchill wrote to him again, mentioning for the first time the name of de Gaulle: 'The aged Marshal Pétain who was none too good in April and July 1918 is I fear ready to lend his name and prestige to a treaty of peace for France. Reynaud on the other hand is for fighting on and he has a young general de Gaulle who believes much can be done. This therefore is the moment for you to strengthen Reynaud the utmost you can. If there is anything you can say publicly or privately to the French now is the time.'

The next day, 13 June, Churchill sent a further, desperate message. 'French have sent for me again, which means that crisis has arrived. Am just off. Anything you can say or do to help them now may make a difference.' There could be little doubt why Churchill's presence was required. As he left Briare the previous morning, he had formally expressed his wish to be consulted if the French Government reached a point of final decision. Each country was obliged by a declaration agreed only three months before not to seek a separate peace without the permission of the other.

Churchill's destination was Tours, the next stage of the French Government's retreat, which would soon end in Bordeaux. When his party arrived at Tours airport, which had been heavily bombed the previous night, there was chaos everywhere and no-one to meet them. They borrowed a car and headed for the local prefecture. Once again they found no-one of consequence. A hungry Churchill insisted on lunch and a local café was specially opened. During lunch Churchill was visited by the new Under Secretary at the French Foreign Ministry, Paul Baudouin – a man who was becoming increasingly influential. In what Churchill described as a soft, silky manner Baudouin regaled him with the hopelessness of French resistance unless the United States entered the war. Churchill merely responded with the hope that America would come in, and an assurance that Britain would fight on regardless. Baudouin immediately spread a rumour that Churchill had agreed that France should surrender unless the United States declared war.

In the afternoon Reynaud finally arrived at the Prefecture. He explained that his Council of Ministers had asked him to raise the question of Britain's attitude should France seek an armistice. Reynaud implied that only one thing might now prevent this – American entry into the war, even if in the first instance it only meant sending warships over to Europe. Churchill said he realized how terrible the suffering of France had been and that the British, though yet to feel the German lash, were aware of its force. However while he understood France's dilemma and would waste no time on recriminations, he asserted that he would not agree to a separate peace. He promised that, whatever happened, Britain would fight on and urged Reynaud at the very least to send a further message to Roosevelt before taking any irrevocable step.

The conference adjourned as Churchill wished to confirm his colleagues' backing for his response to Reynaud. Meanwhile de Gaulle, still preparing for a transfer of government to North Africa, had arrived in Tours and heard Baudouin's rumour. (The Breton redoubt had been abandoned after Reynaud's decision that the French Government's final destination should be Bordeaux rather than Quimper). When the talks were resumed, with de Gaulle now present, Reynaud raised again the prospect of an armistice with Germany. De Gaulle expected an explosion from Churchill at such thoughts of submission, but instead heard compassionate understanding of France's predicament. De Gaulle felt bemused, even betrayed, by Churchill's apparent lack of firmness.

As, in de Gaulle's words, 'the abominable talks' broke up, Churchill made his way down a passage crowded with politicians and officials. In his memoirs he wrote that he saw 'General de Gaulle standing solid and expressionless at the doorway. Greeting him, I said in a low tone in French: "l'homme du destin". He remained impassive.' De Gaulle's impassiveness was understandable. He had not heard what Churchill said and neither had anyone else. Whether Churchill really said these words, muttered them under his breath, or simply thought he said them, has remained a mystery ever since.

But de Gaulle was also smarting from Churchill's display of sympathy. In fact, because he had not been present at the initial talks when Churchill had clearly turned down Reynaud's request for an option to seek an armistice, he had misinterpreted Churchill's meaning. It was their first misunderstanding, not serious in itself as de Gaulle soon discovered that Reynaud personally intended to continue the fight. But it demonstrated the dangers of nuances.

While Churchill was in Tours, Roosevelt's private reply to Reynaud's plea of 10 June arrived. With noble and generous sentiments the President wrote, 'Your message of June 10 has moved me very deeply. As I have already stated to you and to Mr. Churchill, this Government is doing everything in its power to make available to the Allied Governments the material they so urgently require, and our efforts to do still more are being redoubled. This is so because of our faith in and our support of the ideals for which the Allies are fighting.'

That night Reynaud, buttressed by Roosevelt's declaration and repudiating all diplomatic caution, made a radio broadcast to the world, declaring: "the French Army has been the *avantgarde* of the democracies . . . France has the right to turn toward the other democracies and say to them: 'I have rights on you.'" It was an idea that might have made sense to the French people but it could have meant nothing at all to Americans, apparently safe in their continent three thousand miles away.

Now it seemed to Churchill that private messages were not enough. To keep France in the fight, the President had to go public and commit America to the possibility of war. On 14 June, Churchill sent another transatlantic cable. 'Mr. President, I must tell you that it seems to me absolutely vital that this message should be published tomorrow, June 14, in order that it may play the decisive part in turning the course of world history.'

On that day Reynaud also sent his final, highly loaded appeal to Roosevelt. He wrote that France could not continue to fight without American intervention, which was the only way of ensuring an allied victory. It was also, claimed Reynaud, the only chance of stopping Hitler attacking America, once he had destroyed Britain and France. He concluded: 'I know that a declaration of war does not depend on you alone. But I say to you again, at this grave hour in our history, as in yours, that if you cannot give to France in the coming hours the certainty that the United States will enter the war in a short time, the destiny of the world will change. You will then see France go down like a drowning man and disappear, after having thrown a last look toward the land of liberty where she sought salvation.'

The image of drowning was apt. The language was that of a man whose head was now under the water and Roosevelt knew this. It was as if he had been playing a game with words whose time was now up. With unequivocal language he replied to Churchill's request for publication, 'My message of yesterday's date addressed to the French Prime Minister was in no sense intended to commit and did not commit the Government to military participation in support of Allied Governments. I regret that I am unable to agree to your request that my message be published.' To Reynaud the boot was no less crushing, 'I know you will understand that these statements carry with them no implication of military commitments. Only the Congress can make such commitments.'

On 14 June, the day of Roosevelt's final refusal, Paris fell to the Germans. It had been declared an open city by the French Government. Churchill had tried to persuade Weygand to fight street to street in the capital, arguing that its buildings and ruins would serve as a purpose built barricade of resistance. It was another option that the Commander-in-Chief decided was impossible. Weygand had come to hold a belief, curious in a Commander-in-Chief, that France, having made mistakes, deserved to suffer its humiliation. Four years later, the Germans, despite Hitler's orders, also left the capital intact. The survival of a magnificent city was a permanent symbol of French capitulation.

De Gaulle travelled to Bordeaux where Reynaud told him once more that he would fight on. In that case, De Gaulle said, he must head for London to organize British help for the evacuation to North Africa. Minutes before de Gaulle, cast down by the prospect of surrender, had offered to resign his cabinet post. He was talked out of it by the Minister of the Interior, Georges Mandel, one of the few remaining unwavering fighters. The following afternoon de Gaulle arrived in Brittany and boarded the destroyer *Milan*, which was bound for Plymouth with a party of French chemists carrying France's 'heavy water' for safe storage in Britain.

As de Gaulle set sail, Churchill disconsolately replied to Roosevelt's telegram. 'Reynaud will, I am sure be disappointed at non-publication. This moment is supremely critical for France.' He tried one last plea: 'A declaration that the United States will, if necessary, enter the war might save France.' He added that the successful defence of Britain was now the only hope of 'averting the collapse of civilization as we know it' and asked once again 'as a matter of life or death to be reinforced with these destroyers.'

Churchill spent the night at Chequers, the British Prime Minister's country residence in the Chiltern Hills, 30 miles from London. John Colville recorded that 'dinner began lugubriously. However champagne, brandy and cigars did their work and we soon became talkative, even garrulous.' After dinner Churchill paced up and down the rose garden in summer moonlight with his son-in-law, Duncan Sandys. Colville was constantly on the telephone to London, emerging to search out Churchill among the rose bushes with updates of news. 'I told him that fuller information had been received about the French attitude, which appeared to be slipping. "Tell them," he said, "that if they let us have their fleet we shall never forget, but that if they surrender without consulting us, we shall never forgive. We shall blacken their name for a thousand years !" Then half-afraid I might take him seriously, he added: "Don't, of course, do that just yet." He was in high spirits, repeating poetry, dilating on the drama of the present situation.'

The following day, 16 June, the French government asked the British for permission to explore armistice terms with Germany, claiming that it wished to show the French people that such terms would be unacceptably harsh. Churchill and the war cabinet agreed, but only on condition that the French fleet sailed immediately to British ports. As the events of the next twenty-four hours unfolded, Darlan refused to give the order.

Churchill would never forget this: 'He had only to order the ships to British, American or French colonial harbours . . . He would have carried with him outside the German reach the fourth Navy in the world, whose officers and men were personally devoted to him . . . Nothing could have prevented him from being the Liberator of France.'

There was one extraordinary final card to be played. When de Gaulle arrived at the Hyde Park Hotel in London at dawn on the morning of Churchill's request to Darlan, he was immediately visited by André Corbin, the French ambassador and Jean Monnet of the French Economic Mission. Together with Sir Robert Vansittart, the Chief Diplomatic Adviser to the British Government, they had been concocting a plan for a total union of Britain and France.

De Gaulle was captivated by the drama of the idea, believing that a fusion of the two nations, their governments, armies and peoples, might give Reynaud the *deus ex machina* with which to revitalize his ministers. A day of high drama unfolded as Churchill, initially reluctant, was talked into the idea by his cabinet colleagues and de Gaulle. Once again Colville was there to record the scene. 'De Gaulle has been strutting about in the cabinet, with Corbin too; the Cabinet meeting turned into a sort of promenade . . . and everyone has been slapping de Gaulle on the back and telling him that he shall be Commander-in-Chief (Winston muttering "je l'arrangerai"). Is he to be a new Napoleon? From what I hear, it seems a lot of people think so.'

By afternoon the Cabinet had agreed to adopt the document of union. Its contents were remarkable. Among its key sentences it stated:

'The two Governments declare that France and Great Britain shall no longer be two nations, but one Franco-British Union.

The constitution of the Union will provide for joint organs of defence, foreign, financial and economic policies.

Every citizen of France will enjoy immediately citizenship of

Great Britain; every British subject will become a citizen of France.'

It was unreserved and unequivocal. In high spirits de Gaulle telephoned Reynaud and read it over to him. Reynaud immediately grasped its significance and felt it would sway his ministers to continue the fight. Churchill came on the line to Reynaud and arranged to sail over the following morning to meet him in Brittany. With a plane loaned by Churchill, de Gaulle headed back for France. But his arrival brought only despair. Far from embracing the idea of union, the majority of the French Council of Ministers had preferred to view it as some sort of British plot. "To make a union with Great Britain," declared Marshal Pétain, "was fusion with a corpse." By the end of the meeting, Reynaud felt forced to resign and Pétain was the new leader of France. His first act was to put out feelers to the Nazis for an armistice.

De Gaulle was now in potential danger from Pétain's new regime, which would act quickly to smother the resisters. On the morning of 17 June, he published a schedule of appointments for the day, providing a cover for the flight he was about to make to England. He pleaded with Roland de Margerie, Reynaud's foreign affairs *chef du cabinet*, to send passports to his wife and children who were waiting at Carantec in Brittany. It would at least give them a chance of boarding one of the last transports to Britain. A few days earlier de Gaulle had said goodbye to his sick elderly mother. Within two months she would be dead. With Churchill's envoy, General Spears alongside, he boarded the plane to Britain. He would not see France again for over four years. As they arrived in London, Churchill was awaiting them. 'Winston was sitting in the garden enjoying the sunshine,' recorded Spears. 'He got up to greet his guest, and his smile of welcome was very warm and friendly.' De Gaulle later wrote, 'I seemed to myself, alone as I was and deprived of everything, like a man on the shore of an ocean, proposing to swim across.'

The next day, the swim began. De Gaulle wanted to broadcast a rallying cry to France on the BBC. The British cabinet, uncertain of the outcome of Pétain's armistice approach, debated whether this was wise. If de Gaulle did broadcast, John Colville noted that 'he had better not go back to France just yet.' Ultimately Churchill, against the instincts of his Foreign Office, gave permission for the broadcast to go ahead. *L'Appel* of 18 June 1940, would go down in history. De Gaulle acknowledged that France had been overwhelmed by superior forces and tactics, but continued:

'But has the last word been said? Must we abandon all hope? Is our defeat final and irredeemable? To those questions I answer – no! France is not alone! She is not alone! She is not alone!' After this impassioned repetition, de Gaulle continued: 'Behind her is a vast Empire, and she can make common cause with the British Empire, which commands the seas and is continuing the struggle. Like England, she can draw unreservedly on the immense industrial resources of the United States.

The war is not limited to our unfortunate country . . . This is a world war . . . The destiny of the world is at stake.

I, General de Gaulle, now in London, call on all French officers and men who are at present on British soil, or may be in future, with or without their arms; I call on all engineers and skilled workmen from the armaments factories who are at present on British soil, or may be in the future, to get in touch with me.

Whatever happens, the flame of French resistance must not and shall not die.'

After he delivered *L'Appel* de Gaulle wrote 'As the irrevocable words flew out upon their way, I felt within myself a life coming to an end – the life I had lived within the framework of a solid France and an indivisible army. At the age of forty-nine I was entering upon adventure, like a man thrown by fate outside all terms of reference.'

The following day, 19 June, John Colville noted with disappointment in his diary, 'President R. has turned down our demand for forty destroyers ... We need them badly.' The searing experience of June 1940 was something that Churchill and de Gaulle would share forever and from which Roosevelt would forever be excluded. In the years to come, it would make a difference.

CHAPTER TWO
THREE MEN OF DESTINY

In June 1940, the two leaders of western democracy, Winston Churchill and Franklin Roosevelt, and the man who, after many twists, would become its third, Charles de Gaulle, hardly knew each other. In fact, Churchill's relationship with Roosevelt was even more tentative than his brief encounters with de Gaulle. He had only met the American President once, twenty-two years before, in a less than propitious encounter.

In 1918 a fit and active Roosevelt, then in his first American Government post as Assistant Secretary of the US Navy, toured the French battlefields and on his way home made a fleeting visit to London. He gave a speech at a dinner at Gray's Inn, bastion of the British legal establishment and Churchill, then a far more famous public figure, was among the audience. Joseph Kennedy, who by 1940 had become Roosevelt's ambassador to London, claimed that Roosevelt later told him that Churchill behaved like a 'stinker . . . lording it all over us.'

By the 1930s Roosevelt, despite being struck down by polio and losing the use of his legs, had fought back to become President of the United States. At the same time Churchill was in his wilderness years, preaching two gospels: preservation of the British Empire and resistance to Hitler. The first would have been anathema to Roosevelt who was a rigid anti-imperialist; his long-term aim was the disbandment of all of Europe's empires, including the British and French. The second would have struck a chord.

Unlike Churchill, the American leader disliked committing himself to paper, making his motives and private thoughts often difficult to interpret. However one recipient of them was Margaret "Daisy" Suckley, a distant cousin with whom Roosevelt had the most significant emotional relationship of his last ten years. His marriage with Eleanor Roosevelt, also a cousin, had become a remarkably successful public and political relationship, but the love had drained from it after Eleanor's discovery of Roosevelt's affair with Eleanor's social secretary, Lucy Mercer. That affair was long past but from September 1935, after one particular encounter which has remained a mystery, Roosevelt's friendship with Margaret became something much deeper. It was always secretive and only became public knowledge after the publication in 1991 of Margaret's own diaries and the letters she received from Roosevelt. Many of these displayed an almost adolescent swooning; in one Roosevelt wrote, 'I have *longed* to have you with me'. Some contained valuable insight into Roosevelt's political thinking.

The day after Hitler's troops had marched into the Rhineland, on 17 March 1936, Roosevelt wrote to Margaret, 'The news from Germany is bad & though my official people all tell me there is no danger of actual war I always remember their saying all the same things in July 1914 (before you can remember, my blessed infant).' Roosevelt went on to bemoan the lack of any strong leadership in France, 'The Tragedy – deepest part of it – is that a nation's words and signatures are no longer good – If France had a leader whom the people would follow their only course would be to occupy all Germany quickly up to the Rhine – no further – They can do it today – in another year or two Germany will be stronger than they are – and the world cannot trust a fully rearmed Germany to stay at peace.'

In September 1939, at the outbreak of war, Churchill, with his and indeed Roosevelt's prophecies of Nazi aggression now fully justified, had been invited to join Neville Chamberlain's cabinet as First Lord of the Admiralty. Roosevelt immediately initiated a correspondence with him, silkily complimenting him, at the end of his first letter, on his literary achievements even if he Americanized the spelling of Churchill's illustrious ancestor: 'I am glad you did the Marlboro volumes before this thing started – and I much enjoyed reading them'. In December 1939, Joseph Kennedy, back home from London for the Christmas holiday, asked Roosevelt why he was having these private exchanges with Churchill. According to Kennedy, the President replied "I have always disliked him since the time I went to England in 1918 . . . I'm giving him attention now because there is a strong possibility that he will become Prime Minister and I want to get my hand in now."

The events of June had shown that Roosevelt could not as yet be counted on, despite all the fine words. In his memoirs Churchill expressed understanding for Roosevelt's refusal to publish his message to Reynaud but it had, in fact, deeply depressed him. Roosevelt faced a difficult predicament. In the latter half of the 1930s, with Hitler on the march in Europe and Japan invading China in Asia, few Americans could have failed to notice that there were dangers in the world. However the reaction of most was to retreat within the safety of their own continent, believing that it was possible to isolate themselves from any outbreak of war. As the Nazis invaded Poland and Britain declared war, Roosevelt had done nothing to disillusion the American public, stating on 8 September: 'There is no thought in any shape, manner or form, of putting the Nation, either in its defences or in its internal economy, on a war basis. That is one thing we want to avoid. We are going to keep the Nation on a peace basis.' He further assured his people that his Government would make every effort to keep America out of the war. Even by 1940, the idea that America might declare war or even threaten such a declaration was unreal; an opinion poll in the late summer of 1940 showed that three-quarters of Americans would have preferred Britain and France to make peace with Hitler.

Yet Roosevelt himself understood that Nazi aggression could ultimately threaten America. Rather than going to war himself, he instead wanted to provide the weapons with which France and Britain could do their own fighting – thereby becoming America's shield. Supplying arms to any foreign country was politically sensitive in America but Roosevelt insisted, against isolationist opposition, that a large part of America's arms pro-duction, particularly aircraft, should be made available for sale to France and Britain. When war was declared, this policy faced a further hurdle, as arms could not be sold to belligerents. After several weeks Roosevelt persuaded Congress to lift this embargo but it was done only on the basis that arms should be made equally available for sale to every nation. Happily Germany was perforce excluded because of the Allies' blockade on her ship-ping; in any case the Nazis hardly had need of foreign arms. But everything had to be paid for in cash and what Churchill had been imploring in May and June was the loan of destroyers – this Roosevelt had failed to provide.

On 18 June, as de Gaulle made L'Appel, Churchill's relation-ship with Roosevelt was therefore in the balance. There had been strong words and a willingness to sell arms, but nothing more.

There was no personal bond. Roosevelt's advisers regaled him with stories of the British Prime Minister's legendary drinking habits, though Roosevelt indicated that he preferred a drunken fighter to a sober appeaser. The two men also knew that a fundamental political difference stood between them. Roosevelt viewed Churchill as an old-fashioned Victorian Tory, with outmoded views about empire. Churchill knew that Roosevelt stood for self-determination for all peoples, although, as the war progressed, it became clear that Roosevelt intended to see that the world was reordered to American taste. There was a final difficulty – 1940 was American election year.

Whether, as his foremost chronicler has put it, he decided 'from hubris, overweening ambition, or conviction' it was clear by mid-summer 1940 that Roosevelt was going to ignore American convention and stand for a third term. Domestic politics meant that he had to go easy on any signs of war-mongering. The first hurdle was cleared in July when, by carefully orchestrated acclamation, he received, in his absence, the Democrat Party's nomination. But the election itself was not until November.

With all these tensions, the summer of 1940 saw the longest lull in the Roosevelt-Churchill correspondence. Between 15 June (the date of Churchill's final unsuccessful appeal) and 31 July, only one letter passed between them – a minor one from Churchill on the movements of the troublesome Duke of Windsor. Churchill knew that for the moment he and Britain were truly alone. Roosevelt was receiving a stream of advice that Britain could not fight on and would be forced to sue for peace with Hitler.

Roosevelt had been shattered by the rapid submission of France, a country that he knew and liked. Indeed he spoke

French well and had family connections there. One embarrassment was only just avoided when his ageing Aunt Dora, who lived in Paris, had refused to leave the capital after the German invasion, arousing fears that a relation of the American President would fall into Nazi hands. Fortuitously, she died a few days before the German Army entered Paris. But France's fall, preceded by the constant and chaotic changes of French Governments and civil strife during the inter-war years, had removed all of Roosevelt's faith. He believed that France could and would never sit at the high table of nations again, an indelible view that in the coming years would bring great tension to his relations with his Allies. What guarantee could he have that Britain might not go the same way? Churchill had no choice but to sit it out and prove that his words of no surrender meant just that. As he looked around in his isolation there must have seemed a glow about Charles de Gaulle.

De Gaulle was starting with little except his own determination. Beyond his initial meetings with Churchill, he was virtually unknown. During a visit to France in 1938, Churchill had the chance of meeting de Gaulle but, at that point, the French colonel's theories of warfare had little interest for Churchill who still believed in the invincibility of the Maginot Line and the quality of France's military leadership. In May 1940, he would be the first to see the error of both beliefs. Alexander Cadogan, the permanent secretary at the British Foreign Office, told colleagues, "I can't tell you anything about de Gaulle except that he's got a head like a pineapple and hips like a woman." There were a few clues. De Gaulle was clearly brave; he had been wounded five times in the First World War. His books had shown that he was an intellectual soldier, a strategist and a theorist. *The Times* newspaper judged that he was 'rather aggressively right wing . . . but also clear-minded, lucid, and a man of action as well as a man of dreams and abstract ideas".

Shortly after de Gaulle's arrival in London, an American State Department analysis made a more brutal assessment: 'The de Gaulle pre-war outlook was rightist, with semi-Fascist tendencies in its approach to internal politics, and traditional imperial view of foreign policy. He was convinced of the instability of the political, social and economic order of the Third Republic and looked for a reaction in favour of a more disciplined and controlled society.' Such ideas would have primed every hostile trigger in Roosevelt's anti-imperialist and democratic armoury. However it was a crude analysis. In part, de Gaulle was simply sharing Roosevelt's own weariness with French interwar politics. In his memoirs he recorded that between 1932 and 1937 he served under fourteen different French Governments. Certainly de Gaulle was authoritarian; after all he was an officer trained in one of the world's most rigidly hierarchical armies. But his politics would turn out to be more complex than knee jerk labels like 'semi-Fascist' or 'rightist' allowed. American and indeed British, failure to appreciate de Gaulle's intensity of passion for his country and how its genius could be harnessed, would later be a cause of much misunderstanding and hostility.

That was in the future. Now, despite Churchill's go-ahead for *L'Appel* of 18 June, it was neither his nor the British Government's intention that de Gaulle would become the leader of French resistance. On 21 June, a committee, chaired by Sir Robert Vansittart, was set up to co-ordinate plans dealing with the continued resistance of France. At its first meeting it was decided that 'no further manifestations of General de Gaulle should be permitted for the time being'. Two days later, the War cabinet authorized de Gaulle to set up a provisional French

National Committee but did not yet promise recognition. Indeed minutes of the Vansittart committee, on 23 June, recorded 'the desire of H. M. G. to keep the committee and General de Gaulle in the background for the time being.' But later that day there was a change in British thinking. In the evening de Gaulle was allowed to broadcast to France, announcing the establishment in agreement with the British Government of a French National Committee to continue resistance.

Churchill was still assuming that at least one leading French politician would cross over to London and head the Committee, perhaps Reynaud himself or George Mandel, the courageous Interior Minister in Reynaud's government. Mandel and other resisting French politicians had left France for North Africa on the French ship *Massilia*, intending to continue the fight. But when they arrived at Casablanca on 25 June, they were arrested on the orders of General Auguste Nogues, the French military commander in North Africa. After *L'Appel* De Gaulle had contacted Nogues, offering to serve under him if he would carry the fight from North Africa; but Nogues had sided with Pétain. Mandel was eventually returned to France where he would be murdered by French Fascists in 1944. Surprisingly, De Gaulle had also written to Weygand, who was now Minister of Defence under Pétain, offering to serve under him, 'I must tell you very simply that I desire for France and for you, General, that you recognize and are able to escape disaster, reach overseas France and pursue the war.' The letter was eventually returned to de Gaulle with a typed notice: 'If retired Colonel de Gaulle wishes to enter into communications with General Weygand, he must do so through regular channels.'

While Churchill waited for a more recognized Frenchman to arrive, the Foreign Office was anxious that any indelicacy from de Gaulle would upset whatever chance remained of constructing a relationship with France's new regime. France had signed its armistice with Germany in the famous railway carriage at Rethonde in the forest of Compiegne, the scene of German surrender twenty years before. Hitler had his revenge and imposed terms that were onerous, but acceptable to the defeatist mood of France's new leaders. Two thirds of France was to be occupied by the Nazis, the remaining third would be governed by Pétain's new state based at the spa town of Vichy. The geography hid a less palatable split of population – three quarters of the French people had their homes in the occupied zone. Hitler had not demanded that France hand over her fleet, the one condition that might have made even Pétain blanche. Instead French warships were to be disarmed in their home ports, which for some two-thirds were in the German-occupied zone, and supervised by German and Italian monitors – a condition that quickly struck fear into Churchill and, as would soon become apparent, Roosevelt.

The spirit of the Pétain state's observance of the armistice was yet to be tested and the Foreign Secretary, Lord Halifax, was particularly anxious that diplomacy should be given the first chance of repairing relations with Pétain. Halifax's caution produced the first small brush with de Gaulle, a tiny indication that he was not merely a junior French general who would consent to obey British orders. On 26 June, de Gaulle was due to broadcast at 8.30pm but only on the condition that his words were vetted by the Foreign Office. An official, Gladwyn Jebb, was given the task of reading the speech and decided some changes were required. He rushed round to the Rubens hotel where de Gaulle was staying and was told to wait until the General had finished dinner. De Gaulle appeared just after 8pm in a bad mood and, in

French, inquired of Jebb, "Who are you?" Jebb explained that he was a mere subordinate but, with de Gaulle's text having arrived late, he had the task of suggesting certain small modifications. De Gaulle asked to be given them and then declared, "I find them ridiculous . . . perfectly ridiculous." The deadline was fast approaching and Jebb boldly declared that if the General could not accept the changes, he would not be able to broadcast. De Gaulle responded, "I accept. It's ridiculous, but I accept". He would soon learn not to be so biddable.

On 27 June, the uncertainties of de Gaulle's position were resolved. Either because they were unwilling or because they had been forestalled by the Vichy authorities, no other French leader promised to continue the resistance. Most of the commanders and governors of the many territories of the French Empire had fallen in line with Pétain. Those who refused to do so had been sacked. Churchill met de Gaulle and told him, "You are alone – well! I shall recognize you alone."

The next day Churchill approved a statement that: "His Majesty's Government recognizes General de Gaulle as leader of all Free Frenchmen, wherever they may be, who rally to him in support of the Allied cause." De Gaulle would never forget his debt, recalling it later in almost poetic language; 'This exceptional artist could certainly feel the dramatic character of my mission . . . Washed up from a disastrous shipwreck upon the shores of England, what could I have done without his help? He gave it to me at once.' Even the Foreign Office sceptics like Cadogan were resigned. On the day of Britain's recognition he noted, 'De Gaulle came to see Halifax this afternoon and I was present. I am still not impressed . . . Anyhow he is the only hope – I see no other.'

Two Frances had now emerged; the Vichy France of Pétain

and the Free France of de Gaulle. For these two men, it was an extraordinary outcome for they had once been close. After he graduated from military college as a second lieutenant in 1912, de Gaulle's first regiment had been the 33rd infantry. One of its attractions was its commander, Colonel Philippe Pétain, already fifty-six years old but still a sprightly and youthful figure, who had risen from peasant origins to be famed in social circles as a lady's man and in military circles as an advanced thinker. Pétain had understood that the next war should be fought not with wasteful displays of offensive spirit, but with the highest possible concentration of fire-power and had preached this gospel at the Ecôle Supérieure de Guerre, the French Army staff college.

De Gaulle later wrote that Pétain taught him the gift and art of command and after the war, with Pétain now the famous Marshal and hero of Verdun, they resumed their acquaintance-ship. In 1925 Pétain, now the Vice-President of the Supreme War Council, invited de Gaulle to join his staff. Pétain was working on a massive study of the history and future of the French Army and military tactics to be published under his name, but written by his staff. De Gaulle was asked to write the chapters on the First World War and was increasingly seen by Pétain as his most promising protégé and heir apparent. However, the two men fell out after de Gaulle criticized the tactics of static defence which Pétain still believed in, but de Gaulle thought had been super-seded by the future war of movement. His chapters were shelved and de Gaulle's career stifled. De Gaulle would later say that the real Pétain "died" in 1925. A decade later de Gaulle reworked and expanded his early chapters, turning them in to a book called *La France et son Armée*. Before its publication in 1938, he apprised Pétain of the book and suggested he should include a dedication to Pétain. Pétain was furious, believing that de Gaulle had stolen his property and the whole episode resulted in an irretrievable split.

Now, in June 1940, the odds between them were hardly even. Pétain controlled one third of the French mainland and the entire French Empire in North, West and Equatorial Africa, Indo-China, Syria and Lebanon, and various islands scattered around the world's oceans. De Gaulle had a temporary office in London, no money, no arms and a handful of volunteers. Politically Pétain's regime was unattractive. For several years he had flirted with far right elements in France and now sought to reinvent the French nation, founding it upon his own personality cult and old-fashioned sounding values of work, family and country which covered a pernicious and viciously anti-Semitic police state. There was no need for the Nazis to ask Pétain to bring in harsh laws discriminating against Vichy's Jewish population – he and his ministers embraced the prospect.

The most graphic description of the debasement of the French nation was sent to Roosevelt by his Ambassador to France, William Bullitt, on 1 July. His report was later described by the American journalist and historian, William Shirer, as giving 'better than any contemporary record I have seen the state of mind and heart and soul of the tattered men who controlled the French Government at this hour of adversity and trial.' In the light of the attitude towards Vichy which Roosevelt would strike within just a few months, it is worth recording some of Bullitt's portrayal. He began by summarizing conversations he had held that day with the new French leadership, among them Pétain himself, Darlan, who had been appointed Minister of Marine, and Weygand. 'The impression which emerges is the extraordinary one that the French leaders desire to cut loose from all that France has represented during the past two generations, that their physical and moral defeat has been so absolute that they have accepted completely for France the fate of becoming a province of Nazi Germany. Moreover in order that they may have as many companions in misery as possible they hope that England will be rapidly and completely defeated by Germany and that the Italians will suffer the same fate.' At the end of a long report there was only one touch of optimism. 'The simple people of the country are as fine as they have ever been,' wrote Bullitt. 'The upper classes have failed completely.'

This was the moving spirit of the New France and, for the moment, it seemed as if among Frenchmen de Gaulle alone stood against it. He did have one consolation. His wife and three children had managed to escape to Britain on one of the last transports from Brittany on 19 June. They were lucky. Another British ship, the *Lancastria*, with five thousand soldiers on board, had been set on fire by Nazi planes. In one of the war's most appalling losses, three thousand died. Churchill, believing that there was only so much pain the people could take at any one time, ordered a news black-out on the *Lancastria* disaster. In the turmoil of the coming weeks he forgot to lift the ban and the news only emerged much later.

De Gaulle was also solidifying his position with the British Government. After tortuous negotiations he obtained a British agreement that the full restoration of 'the independence and greatness of France' should be a British war aim. He showed that he stood apart from governments in exile like Poland, Belgium, Holland and Norway, who had quickly accepted that their soldiers, sailors and pilots who had made it to Britain should fight under British colours. De Gaulle insisted that he should form his own army and navy, whose officers and men would come under his direct command. Even on British soil they would come under his discipline. But so far he hardly had any men. One obstacle was Britain's military leaders. The country was awash with French officers and men who had retreated from Dunkirk and Norway. De Gaulle wanted open access to recruit them but British commanders viewed these men as a nuisance. In the exigencies of Hitler's threatened invasion they were happier to see them out of the way and returned to France. The great majority of Frenchmen obliged.

Then, a second obstacle suddenly confronted de Gaulle. Viewing the conditions of the Compiègne armistice, Churchill became consumed by the reasonable obsession that the French fleet could be grasped by Hitler at any time, despite the assurances of Pétain and Darlan. On 3 July, he took ruthless action. French ships in Portmouth and Plymouth were seized by the British navy. Most crews came over peacefully, despite a frequent lack of sensitivity by the naval boarding parties. On the French submarine *Surcouf* fighting broke out and a British and French sailor were killed. More significantly, Churchill launched 'Operation Catapult'. Its target was a significant part of the French navy which was lying at the naval base of Mers-el-Kebir in French Algeria, three miles west of Oran.

While British forces under Admiral Somerville patrolled outside the harbour, a French speaking officer, Captain Holland, was sent to convey Churchill's ultimatum to the French commander, Admiral Gensoul. In essence Gensoul was given three options: sail to Britain, sail to the other side of the Atlantic, or scuttle your ships. As the deadline of 6pm approached Gensoul had given no clear response though there was some indication that, with more time, he might have consented to render his ships unusable. Captain Holland's launch sailed back beyond the boom of the harbour and on a sultry Mediterranean evening

Somerville, with a heavy heart, opened fire. The action lasted all of nine minutes, during which more than 1,250 French sailors were killed. Two French battleships ran aground and another, the *Bretagne*, blew up. When Churchill heard the news that battle had begun Colville noted, 'Winston said the French were now fighting with all their vigour for the first time since war broke out. He did not see how we could avoid being at war with France tomorrow.'

Tragic though it was, Oran immediately became a symbol and a turning point for Churchill. When he reported on it to the House of Commons, he had, for the very first time since he became Prime Minister seven weeks before, the House's unequivocal support. Colville noted, 'When the speech was over all the Members rose to their feet, waved their order papers and cheered loudly. Winston left the House visibly affected. I heard him say, "This is heartbreaking for me."' The action at Oran reverberated throughout the world. In Rome the Italian Foreign Minister, Count Ciano, noted a report from Italy's former Ambassador to Britain which confirmed Britain's fighting spirit: 'The morale of the British is very high . . . Everybody – aristocracy, middle class and the common people – are embittered, tenacious, and proud.' More importantly, in Washington Roosevelt let it be known to the British Ambassador, Lord Lothian, that he approved of Churchill's action. It was concrete proof of British aggression and determination to fight on, even if it meant attacking the forces of a country which only two weeks before had been an ally.

For one man, Charles de Gaulle, Mers-el-Kebir could only seem a wreckage. In the previous days he had been having some success recruiting French soldiers who had ended up in Britain. But this 'lamentable event', as de Gaulle described it in his memoirs, threatened to ruin everything by placing him in the impossible position of siding with his country's attacker. He was cool enough not to rush into public criticism. General Spears, who was now the British Government's main liaison with de Gaulle noted his attitude on the day after the attack: 'De Gaulle's calmness was very striking, the objectivity of his view astonishing. He had evidently done a lot of thinking. What we had done, he said, was no doubt inevitable from our point of view. Yes, it was inevitable, but what he had to decide was whether he could collaborate with us or whether he would retire from the scene and withdraw to private life in Canada. He had not yet made up his mind but would do so before morning . . . I then went to tell the Prime Minister of the magnificent dignity displayed by de Gaulle.'

Within France, Mers-el-Kebir served only to fan the flames of burgeoning Anglophobia. Pétain wrote a letter of bitter complaint to Roosevelt asserting that 'nothing could justify this hateful aggression.' Pétain was also embarking on a long term play to win American backing for Vichy. His implied threat was that, if America could not help her, France would have no choice but to move closer to Hitler's camp. 'It is with confidence,' wrote Pétain, 'that I lay the case before you, Mr President, whose active friendship for France will not, I am sure, fail my country in the cruel misfortune from which I have undertaken to extricate it.' Bullitt sent a message to Roosevelt that, after Mers-el-Kebir, 'several members of the present Cabinet advocated immediate acts of war against England . . . Pétain was resolutely opposed to anything more than a break in diplomatic relations with England.' This message too contained the seed of a view that would begin to be consistently conveyed to Roosevelt by American diplomats dealing with France: Pétain was the one bulwark preserving the neutrality of France, even harbouring a subterranean desire eventually to rejoin the Allies.

By 8 July, de Gaulle had put aside thoughts of retirement. The British Government had the sense to allow him to broadcast uncensored to France and he responded in remarkable fashion. He acknowledged the grief and anger all Frenchmen felt at the British action and asked the British "to spare us, as well as themselves, any portrayal of this hateful tragedy as a direct naval success." But he then pleaded with his countrymen to see the tragedy from the only point of view that really mattered, "ultimate victory and the deliverance of our country." He argued that in the end there was no doubt that the Nazis would have used these ships which had been placed at their mercy by the conditions of the armistice and that it was better for French ships to be stranded rather than manned by Germans. In such difficult circumstances, he gave a bold rallying call: "Come what may, even if for a time one of them is bowed under the yoke of the common foe, our two peoples – our two great peoples – are still linked together. Either they will both succumb, or they will triumph side by side."

De Gaulle's speech convinced Churchill that he was a man whom he could trust unconditionally, a trust he had no such reason to vest in Roosevelt as yet. De Gaulle was soon committed beyond recall. Two days after his speech the French Senate and Chamber of Deputies combined into one Constituent Assembly in Vichy. They voted, by a majority of just over two-thirds, to abolish the French Third Republic which was established in 1875 and bring in a Constitutional Law which gave Pétain the powers of an absolute monarch. The Law had been drafted by the calculating pro-Nazi former Foreign Minister, Pierre Laval, whom Pétain had appointed as his deputy. Laval believed that the only future for France lay in full alliance with Germany and deputies were effectively blackmailed by the threat that, if they did not vote for Laval's Law, the Nazis would soon occupy the rest of France. Nevertheless many abstained and eighty voted against, of whom a large number were soon arrested by Pétain's police state.

One of the regime's first acts was to try de Gaulle in his absence for 'refusals to obey orders in the presence of the enemy and inciting members of the armed forces to disobedience.' He was sentenced to death, the execution ordered by Marcel Peyrouton, Vichy's interior minister. On 16 July, de Gaulle's mother died in France. Condemned as a rebel, he could not attend her funeral. Despite the knowledge that they too would be viewed by their own Government as traitors, some Frenchmen continued to join up with de Gaulle's movement. Only 7,000 of the 115,000 servicemen on British soil stayed but others somehow found a boat across the Channel to Britain. They had to be a special breed and many of them were very young, liberated by having no family to look after back home.

One recruit was Pierre Messmer, a future Prime Minister of France, who finally arrived in London at the end of July. Like most Frenchmen he had been unable to listen to L'Appel of 18 June: 'French people were uprooted and on the move, very few were in a position to know about de Gaulle's appeal. Radios in those days were large, heavy things that you had in your home and plugged into an electrical socket. There were none of the small transistors you have today. But the following day I read his speech in the Marseilles newspapers and it made a forceful impression on me. I was anyway intending to continue the war effort but when I read it in the papers, I at once decided to follow the orders of General de Gaulle.'

Another volunteer was Claude Bouchinet Serreulles who soon became de Gaulle's ADC. In an interview just before his death in December 2000, Serreulles described what drove him to take such a risk: "When this old man (Pétain) said 'I am asking for an armistice' I said I will have to desert. I shall not remain with a country behaving like this. We had an empire, we had some good planes, we had gold, and we had the Mediterranean which was the best protection we could dream of." Serreulles had also not heard *L'Appel* of June: "I was not aware of the fact that de Gaulle was in London, I decided to join the ones who were fighting." Claude Serreulles kept a wartime diary that was published just before his death. It contains an evocative description of what it was like for a young Frenchman to meet their future leader: 'The general got up, he had his back to the window. A shadow emerges; an enormous silhouette, out of proportion and with a tiny head. The man is very thin, belted in tight in his green tunic. My first impression was how young he was. He's 49 and seems a lot less. What a contrast with all the portly and elderly generals you see in France. Another surprise: his distance. Not a hint of having shaken too many hands. His face: he has above all a piercing look.' To all of his colleagues and recruits, de Gaulle baldly stated his single article of faith: 'We are France'. It would take a long while for the implications of that simple statement to emerge.

De Gaulle's recruiting and Churchill's support continued to build. The British Government hired the services of a 1940s spin-doctor called Richmond Temple, to make the world familiar with the name of de Gaulle. De Gaulle was unused to the attention and complained of being sold like 'a bar of soap'. He insisted on preserving his family's privacy. Even the Englishman closest to de Gaulle at this time, General Spears, when asked by

Richmond Temple to supply a profile, could write no more than: 'General de Gaulle is extremely reticent about his private life and a phrase he often uses in his conversations with his staff officers is "I do not want to be made a film star by the press". So we only know that he is married, that he has three children, one girl and two boys aged respectively: 16, 14 and 12. His wife and his children are now living somewhere in England and take no part in his public life.' Throughout the war De Gaulle wrote frequently to his family but never discussed them with his followers or friends. When his son, Philippe, published his notes and letters fifteen years after his death his erstwhile colleagues were astonished at his displays of affection and sensitivity. Claude Serruelles remarks, 'we discovered another man, who was affectionate, who called his wife 'Ma Chère Petite Femme'. For us it was almost unbelievable, he had what we call a cover and under his cover there was a great sensibility, which he never showed.' Though few knew it, de Gaulle's youngest daughter, Anne, was mentally and physically disabled, a further reason in less enlightened times to keep a veil over his family and home.

De Gaulle was also invited into another family – the Churchills. He was a frequent visitor to Chequers and, during an early weekend in August, had a conversation with Churchill about the expected German bombing campaign against Britain which suggested a touching familiarity between the two men. De Gaulle recalled in his memoirs how Churchill, 'raising his fists towards the sky, cried "So they won't come!" "Are you in such a hurry", I said to him, "to see your towns smashed to bits?" "You see," he replied, "the bombing of Oxford, Coventry, Canterbury will cause such a wave of indignation in the United States that they'll come into the war!"' I expressed some doubt about that, reminding him that two months earlier the distress of

France had not made America emerge from her neutrality. "That's because France was collapsing!" stated the Prime Minister. "Sooner or later the Americans will come, but on conditions that we here don't flinch. That's why I can't think of anything but the Fighter Air Force."' The two men then went on to debate whether the full British air support might have helped to save France. They agreed to disagree. 'Mr Churchill and I agreed modestly in drawing from the events which had smashed the West this commonplace but final conclusion; when all is said and done, Great Britain is an island; France the cape of a continent; America, another world.'

While the two men were solidifying their alliance, there had been two significant moves in that other world. The United States, driven by the over-riding concern to stop the spread of war, had called a conference of North and South American nations which convened in Havana on 20 July. The countries agreed that no aggression by any European nation would be allowed in the Western hemisphere. The greatest danger was that the existence of European possessions dotted around the Americas might attract German interest. Some of these possessions, like Martinique, where much of France's gold reserves had been shipped, and the tiny islands of Miquelon and St. Pierre off the coast of Newfoundland, belonged to France. The United States did a deal with the Vichy commander in charge of these territories, Admiral Robert, that they would stay neutral and any attempt to engage them in hostilities would be rebuffed. In doing this, the United States effectively struck its first bargain with Pétain's Vichy Government.

While he presided over this sinuous connection with Vichy, Roosevelt stretched a tentative hand towards Britain. All the evidence suggests that on 31 July, he privately made the decision to send Churchill the destroyers for which he had been so desperately pleading since 15 May. Roosevelt's political position was easing. He had secured the Democrat Party's nomination as Presidential candidate. In addition, the Republicans chose as his opponent Wendell Willkie, who was against isolationism and agreed in principle that America should supply material aid to Britain. On 31 July, Churchill had resumed his correspondence with Roosevelt, urging him again to hand over the First World War destroyers, along with motor boats and flying boats. The President, now more persuaded by British prospects of survival, came up with the politically ingenious solution that the destroyers could be swapped in exchange for the granting to America of the rights to use a number of British possessions in the Western hemisphere as naval bases. This enabled Roosevelt to bypass Congress and satisfy the American public that he had struck a winning bargain that could only benefit American security.

Roosevelt still required assurances that, should Britain ever seek peace with Germany, her navy would be first sent across the Atlantic. While Churchill recoiled at Roosevelt's innuendo that peace-feelers were even a possibility, his gratitude to Roosevelt was heartfelt. On 15 August he wrote to him: 'I need not tell you how cheered I am ... or how grateful I feel for your untiring efforts to give us all possible help.' It was a tentative beginning and Churchill's relationship with the President was still impersonal by comparison with his reflective discourses with the French general. But de Gaulle, much as though he might have wished it, had no connection to the President. He understood as deeply as Churchill that only with America could the war be won and from the very first he peppered references to American might in his public statements. In June 1940, he talked of 'the gigantic possibilities of American industry' which would lead to the defeat of Germany; in August he said 'No sensible man conceives the victory of liberty to be possible without the contribution of the American continent'; he spoke of an 'irresistible current' carrying 'the New World to the assistance of liberty'. But in Roosevelt's eyes de Gaulle was a nothing. Even Churchill's flattering references had brought no response from America. De Gaulle had to put himself on the map.

CHAPTER THREE
ADVENTURES IN AFRICA

On 10 August 1940, Charles de Gaulle wrote a note laying down his creed for the British publicist, Richmond Temple. 'I am a Free Frenchman', he stated, 'I believe in God and the future of my country. I am owned by nobody. I have a mission and one only; that of the pursuit of the fight for the liberation of my country. I declare solemnly that I am attached to no political party nor to any politician, not to the right or the left or the centre. I have one goal: to set France free!' It must have seemed a far-fetched ambition for a man who, at this precise point, commanded forces comprising an army of 140 officers and 2,109 men and a navy of 120 officers and 1,746 ratings.

At the suggestion of one of his naval officers, de Gaulle had adopted an intriguing symbol for the Free French, the Cross of Lorraine, the banner under which Joan of Arc had raised resistance against the English five centuries before. However there was no chance of de Gaulle raising his standard on the soil of the motherland. Instead he began to eye the French Empire on the continent of Africa, where he had tried in June to persuade his former colleagues in the French Government to fight on. French North Africa was in the grip of Vichy; so too was French West Africa. But French Equatorial Africa, right in the middle, gave de Gaulle cause for hope. Félix Eboué, the governor of the remote and sparsely populated colony of Chad, had sent an early message indicating that he would defy Vichy. Eboué, who was born in another French colony, Martinique, was an intriguing character, the only black governor in the French Empire. Perhaps for that reason, he understood, more than any, the vice of Hitler's and Vichy's racism. There were also more practical motives; Chad was dependent on the British territory of Nigeria for trade and had much to gain by backing Britain's ally.

With the help of the British Government, whom he had no choice but to turn to for money and arms, de Gaulle dispatched an elite and tiny band of Free Frenchmen to this hostile region of Africa. They were sent under the leadership of a hardened soldier, Colonel Edgard de Larminat, who had escaped from the custody of Vichy forces in Syria. In late August, de Larminat, three other Free French officers and de Gaulle's diplomatic emissary, René Pleven, met in Lagos. On 26 August, the coup unrolled. Eboué declared for de Gaulle in Fort-Lamy, the capital of Chad. The next day, de Larminat and his handful of men set out in native canoes for Duala, the main port of French Cameroons. In his memoirs, de Gaulle claimed that a thousand African sharp shooters, whom he had discovered by accident in a camp in England, were supposed to join the expedition. But when they were landed en route on the Gold Coast, the local British officers were so impressed that they immediately incorporated them into British units. Nevertheless, de Larminat entered Duala that night and with the help of a few local Gaullists, simply walked into the *Palais du Gouvernement* and took it over. The next day they travelled by train to Yaounde, where the local French authorities obligingly handed over their powers. The following day de Larminat arrived in Brazzaville, the capital of French Congo and administrative headquarters of the whole of French Equatorial Africa. Again with the help of local supporters, he installed himself in de Gaulle's name as High

Commissioner with full civil and military powers. The entire operation had been bloodless.

There was one disappointment. On 29 August, the governor of the colony of Gabon had telegraphed that he too would come over. But the Vichy authorities immediately sent orders to the naval commander at Gabon's capital, Libreville, to resist, saying that his squadron would be reinforced by Vichy forces. The governor quickly changed his mind, claiming that the decision to join Free France had been the result of a misunderstanding, and arrested all Gaullist supporters. Nevertheless de Gaulle held all the rest of French Equatorial Africa, giving him a base in the French Empire. The size of the territories outweighed the resources of people and material they contained but they were of some, if limited, strategic importance, affording an unmolested route for British aircraft to be flown across Africa to the Middle East. Later General Jacques LeClerc, who would achieve fame as the liberator of Paris, also led a remarkable Free French march northwards from Chad and across the African interior to meet up with British troops fighting Rommel in the desert.

The most precious jewel to be prised from Vichy was the port of Dakar, a strategic base of immense value in the French West African colony of Senegal. Dakar jutted out into the Atlantic and was a potential platform from which Nazi U-boats could easily venture to Central and South America. Churchill understood its importance. He had eyed Dakar since early July but his Chiefs-of-Staff had told him that they were too stretched to attempt a takeover. So too had Roosevelt, who, since his days as Assistant Navy Secretary, prided himself on his powers of maritime analysis. In American propaganda films of this time Dakar is portrayed as the epicentre of how near the war could come to America. Therefore, to render Dakar safe beyond doubt was attractive to all. If de Gaulle could come to command it, he would suddenly be elevated to a man who mattered in Washington.

De Gaulle's initial plan was to land a small column at a point along the coast well away from Dakar. His idea was that this column would then march towards the port, rallying support along the way. In order to succeed, it would have to be covered by a British naval expedition which would blockade Vichy's ships inside Dakar so that they could not sail along the coast to snuff out any signs of support for de Gaulle. However this would require the presence of a British fleet for much longer than practicable at this critical stage of the war, when the Battle of Britain was yet to be won.

Instead Churchill outlined an alternative scenario to de Gaulle, dependent on a lightning strike by a fast moving and massive armada. In his memoirs de Gaulle recorded the alluring picture which Churchill painted for him. 'Dakar wakes up one morning, sad and uncertain. But behold, by the light of the rising sun, its inhabitants catch sight of a sea covered with ships in the distance. An immense fleet! A hundred war or transport vessels! From this Allied squadron comes forth an inoffensive little ship bearing the white flag of truce. It enters the port and sets ashore the envoys of General de Gaulle. The governor is to be convinced that, if he lets you land, the Allied fleet will retire, and there will only remain for you and him to settle the terms of his co-operation. On the contrary, if he wants to fight he is very likely to be crushed.'

His imagination fired, Churchill broached his Chiefs-of-Staff with his plan. John Colville noted a distinct lack of enthusiasm. 'I went back to No. 10 and found Winston rending the Chiefs-of-Staff who are being unenthusiastic.' The same day de Gaulle himself entered his own reservations to the Inter Service Planning Staff. Its minutes recorded: 'General de Gaulle stated quite definitely that, if he meets opposition from French sea, air or land forces, the whole operation will be impossible and he would in fact not consider continuing it.'

Not to be thwarted, Churchill made it an order, informing within twenty-four hours those same Chiefs-of-Staff: 'It would seem extremely important to British interests that General de Gaulle should take Dakar at the earliest moment. If his emissaries report that it can be taken peacefully so much the better. If their report is adverse an adequate Polish and British force should be provided and full naval protection given. The operation, once begun, must be carried through. De Gaulle should be used to impart a French character to it, and of course, once successful, his administration will rule. But we must drive him and provide the needful balance of force.' There was still scepticism. Air Marshal Sir John Slessor later wrote that during the planning meeting on that day: 'Tempers got rather frayed. We made him (WSC) angry by saying we thought it was an operation which could only succeed with the hearty co-operation of the enemy, which we did not think was a sound basis for planning.'

Over the next three weeks, a lack of available ships combined with a residual lack of enthusiasm by the British Chiefs resulted in a whittling down of Churchill's vision. The Free French managed to gather three sloops, two armed trawlers and two Dutch liners which would carry a battalion of the Foreign Legion, and an assortment of marines, fresh recruits, and tank personnel, in all a couple of thousand men. They were to meet up with a British fleet of two old battleships, four cruisers, an aircraft carrier, and some destroyers. If the local Vichy Government fell into line, the force was plenty; if there was a fight, it looked borderline.

In addition to the reduction in scale, there was an assortment of hitches before departure. A bizarre row broke out between de Gaulle and the British over what would happen if de Gaulle gained control of a stock of French, Belgian and Polish gold, which had been evacuated to Senegal before the *Blitzkrieg*. De Gaulle assured the Polish and Belgian Governments in exile in London that he would return their share, but the British Government suggested that some might be used to pay for American weapons as they were for the joint benefit of the allied coalition. De Gaulle was unimpressed, even threatening to break off the Dakar expedition before it was conceded that the gold would only be used for Free French purchases.

There was also a quaintly amateurish attitude to security. Though it was hardly a precise giveaway, de Gaulle himself, while being fitted out for his tropical kit in Simpsons in Piccadilly, had let it slip that he was going to West Africa. There were more serious breaches by both British and French. A case burst open at Euston station scattering leaflets emblazoned with the French tricolour and calling for the liberation of Dakar. A naval officer wrote to the First Lord of the Admiralty, complaining that troops waiting to depart in Liverpool and clothed in obviously tropical gear were visible to any passers-by including unreliable neutral ships. He opined that: 'The Germans must know by now of the existence and composition of this expedition and they must further know that its destination is in the tropics . . . I was told of our destination by a man on Liverpool docks. I have since been told by a Marine Officer that he was not only told of our destination by a docker hand but was also told of the precise composition of our escort. So much for secrecy.' The officer said he understood that, in writing such a letter, he was committing a court-martial offence. It was forwarded to

Churchill who wearily noted: 'No action is possible except to make sure that the faults alleged by the writer do not occur next time. The writer is granted protection by me and must not be proceeded against in any way.'

French indiscretions were reported by General Spears, who was to sail with de Gaulle on the expedition. The British Security Board wrote to him that, 'on a certain date between the 4th and 10th of August, a French officer attached to the *Service des Armements* of General de Gaulle stated openly to a friend that the Free French Forces were earmarked for an expedition to French West Africa, where a landing would be made at Dakar.' He went on to say that, 'the Expedition was due to set out about the end of August. This officer is alleged to be very free in his confidences to the opposite sex.' The truth was that gossip flourished everywhere. Pierre Messmer, who had been assigned to the French squadron recalls, 'secrets were very, very badly guarded. As always in this kind of situation everyone accused each other. The English accused the French for their lack of secrecy and the French accused the English. When we left Liverpool it was obvious that we weren't heading for the North Pole, but for Africa. There was nothing very secret about that!'

Despite the hitches, 'Operation Menace', as it was now called, sailed from Liverpool on 31 August and the Dakar enterprise was underway. Spirits were high. On 4 September, Spears noted in his diary, 'There is much to be thought of and prepared in this unforeseeable adventure. All aboard gay and lighthearted.' De Gaulle too was flushed with optimism. Just before sailing, he had received news of de Larminat's lightning coups in Chad and the French Cameroons and Congo. He left a letter to await the arrival in London of General Georges Catroux, the most senior Frenchman to rally to his cause, who had been sacked from this post as Commander in French Indo-China after opposing the armistice. 'When you receive this letter I shall have left for Dakar with troops. I have full confidence in final victory. The English have gone all out for it and, luckily for them and for us, Mr Winston Churchill is "the man for this war". The game is between Hitler and him.' Pierre Messmer remembers, "we were very happy to be leaving for Dakar and we all believed that we would be welcomed there. All we had to do was show that we were strong; just the sight of this naval force was going to convince the people of Dakar to side with us."

De Gaulle's transports lumbered south to Africa. They were already well behind the heady schedule envisaged in early August. Originally they had been due to reach the British port of Freetown, south of Dakar, by 8 September for final refuelling and restocking before heading back north to Dakar. They would not reach Freetown until 17 September.

A few days after sailing, there was a quite separate disappointment emanating from the United States. Though small in itself, it was a significant symbol of American attitudes. De Gaulle was interested in the colony of French Guiana where, although the authorities were Vichyite, the people had shown signs of sympathy with the Free French. Respecting the edicts of the Havana conference, de Gaulle had decided against sending a ship to foment a coup. However in early September, Admiral Emile Muselier, the head of the Free French navy who had been left behind in London and was deputizing for de Gaulle, approached the American Ambassador, Joseph Kennedy, to seek American blessing for a popular insurrection. Time was tight as the Vichy Government had just dispatched a clipper to French Guiana, carrying two senior officials on board with orders to quell anti-Vichy sentiment. Muselier argued that, if the Free

French action was purely an internal matter rather than external aggression, it did not contravene American policy. Kennedy forwarded Muselier's request to the United States Secretary of State, Cordell Hull. Hull responded the next day that 'any overt insurrectionary movement in French Guiana . . . would in the opinion of this Government be unfortunate.' The message was clear; Free French hands were to kept off America's hemisphere. The arrangement with Vichy must not be challenged.

The American decision only added to the pressure for success at Dakar. But disturbing news now reached London. On 11 September, a powerful squadron of Vichy French ships, three heavy and three light cruisers, had broken through the Straits of Gibraltar into the Atlantic and put in at Dakar. British ships had failed to intercept them by a series of mischances and mistakes. Most seriously, on 10 September, the British naval attaché in Madrid had been officially informed, by the Vichy Admiralty, of the ships' passage the following day. He reported this to Admiral North, who was based at Gibraltar in command of the Atlantic station. However North was not in the Dakar loop and saw no special significance. A signal also reached the Admiralty just before midnight and was passed on to the Director of Foreign Operations Division (Foreign) who was in the loop. He failed to take instant action. For this error, as Churchill later wrote, 'he received in due course the expressions of their lordships displeasure'. That such an error should occur at this time was hardly surprising. London eyes were on the Channel and the skies above Britain where the Battle of Britain was reaching its climax. But its consequences were devastating.

Churchill and his war cabinet had no doubt that the presence of the French ships at Dakar meant that 'Operation Menace' had to be called off. Churchill remarked that 'a fiasco had undoubtedly occurred, and it was hoped that it would not too much engage public attention.' He was hoping to get out of it lightly and on 16 September the War Cabinet signalled the expedition: 'His Majesty's Government have decided that presence of French cruisers at Dakar renders the execution of Dakar operation impracticable.' It suggested that the expedition should sail on to Duala, from where de Gaulle could consolidate his hold over his new territories in French Equatorial Africa and try to take over Gabon. But the British commanders – Admiral Cunningham and General Irwin and de Gaulle now had the bit between their teeth. De Gaulle had a further worry. He had judged, correctly as it very soon turned out, that the purpose of the Vichy Squadron was to sail down to Duala and recapture the territories he had only just liberated. If they were not tackled now, they would have a free run.

On 17 September, as the 'Menace' ships regrouped at Freetown, de Gaulle protested to London, insisting that if the existing plan was called off he still intended to land troops to advance to Dakar from the interior and would require British air and sea cover. Admiral Cunningham reported that the presence of French cruisers had not sufficiently increased the risks to justify abandonment. General Irwin said that the new risks were 'worth accepting in view of the obvious results of success'. The next day Churchill reversed his decision and gave the go-ahead. In his own words, his instinct was 'to let things rip.' On 19 September, the Vichy ships put out from Dakar and headed south. They were intercepted by the British and, after a chase, three of them agreed to head back up the African coast to the port of Casablanca and a fourth scuttled herself. However, two escaped in a heavy rainstorm and made it back to Dakar. Already in the harbour was the Vichy battleship, *Richelieu*, which had been damaged by a British submarine after the Mers-el-Kebir operation in July. Her guns were intact.

On 20 September, the day before setting forth from Freetown, de Gaulle roused his men with stirring words: 'You are my soldiers, my friends, my companions. I have confidence in you and I love you all. At the moment, we are the only ones representing France.' On 22 September, anxious to impress America with a offensive military success to follow the heroic defence of the Battle of Britain, Churchill wrote to Roosevelt: 'Combined Franco-British force is now on way to Dakar with object of capturing that place with as little bloodshed as possible and establishing General de Gaulle there.'

On 23 September, the fleet, whose very sight was once supposed to make every onlooker shiver, drew near to Dakar. At 5.50am two small unarmed French planes from the aircraft carrier *Ark Royal* landed at Dakar airfield. For the moment they were unmolested. Overhead, British aircraft dropped leaflets on the town. As news filtered back to London, John Colville noted: 'During the morning the Admiralty telephoned the messages from Dakar as they came in. So far (12.30pm) all seems to be going according to plan.' Five and a half hours later he recorded a changed mood in London 'Cabinet at 5. Rather gloomy, 'Menace' going none too well and 'Cumberland' hit.'

It had all gone wrong. The spectre of the armada was obliterated by fog. Churchill claimed that Admiralty meteorologists had checked years of records and declared fine weather was certain. In fact, sea mists were not uncommon at this time of year. At 6am, de Gaulle broadcast an appeal to the people of Dakar. General Spears noted in his war diary that this was one hour earlier than expected : 'This was never contemplated in the plan . . . it is difficult to estimate the psychological effect this may have on the whole future happening.' Three Free French emissaries entered the port on a sloop and landed. They demanded to see the Vichyite governor, Pierre Boisson, but their proposals were rejected by his troops. On returning to their boats they were fired on. Two were wounded and they rapidly retreated to rejoin the fleet.

In order to show that there was a proper fleet, the British warships were forced to move to within three thousand yards of the shore to be visible through the fog. Immediately Vichy's shore batteries opened fire. Admiral Cunningham radioed to the Dakar Admiral that, if the shelling continued, he would be forced to return fire. To this he received the reply: 'To avoid being fired at, British ships must keep 20 miles to sea.' Major disaster now struck. The cruiser, *Cumberland*, was the last in the line. By the time it passed by the shore batteries, they had found their range and were dropping shells all around the ship. One struck it amidships, putting all the boilers out of action and blowing the electricity. Seven men were killed. The stoker was hit while reading a book; his head was blown off and later found in a locker. Gerry Harper, a seaman on the *Cumberland*, recalls: 'We were lucky still to be there because if the shell had entered just a little further in one direction it would have ignited the magazine and blown the bottom out of the ship and we would all have been swimming.' As well as the *Cumberland*, two British destroyers were hit.

With a landing at Dakar itself clearly impossible, de Gaulle and Cunningham agreed an alternative plan to land Free French troops ten miles down the coast at the small port of Rufisque which was out of range of Dakar's guns. The *Westernland* was unable to beach there so troops would have to be transferred to sloops for landing. British ships were intended to provide cover against any attack by French cruisers. However, the fog was thickening and there was a breakdown in communications between Cunningham and de Gaulle's ships. As the first Free French troops landed they were welcomed by natives but almost immediately fired on by Vichy troops. Several were killed. Pierre Messmer recalls, "We arrived in Dakar just as naïve as when we left and we were not even in uniform for our arrival, instead we were dressed as if for a parade with our medals if we had them and our guns unloaded. We were not dressed for war."

Vichy cruisers were now approaching the sloops and, owing to the communications breakdown, there was no British cover. De Gaulle and his men were forced to withdraw to sea again. As the grim news reached London, Churchill remained robust. John Colville noted: "'Menace' proceeding less favourably. The French had opened fire and all prospects of a peaceful landing had had to be abandoned. I told the PM who said cheerfully, "Let 'em have it. Remember this: never maltreat your enemy by halves. Once the battle is joined, let 'em have it."' Just after 10pm Churchill signalled: 'Having begun, we must go on to the end. Stop at nothing.'

The next day, again in poor visibility, the British bombardment was renewed. It seemed to have little effect on the shore batteries although two Vichy ships were damaged and one submarine, forced to the surface, surrendered. The British battleship *Barham* was hit four times but lightly damaged. It was increasingly clear that the Vichy governor, Boisson, would fight to the end. That evening, de Gaulle and the British Commanders held a conference. The attempt at a peaceful coup had failed and the British bombardment of itself would not bring submission. De Gaulle said he must avoid a pitched battle between Frenchmen. He generously proposed that Cunningham should announce that, at de Gaulle's suggestion, the bombardment would be called off. General Irwin's later report into the fiasco noted that 'the bearing of General de Gaulle was remarkable for its brave acceptance of a great disappointment.'

There was a peculiar irony. On this day, when the news reaching the world was prematurely reporting prospects of a Free French triumph, Richmond Temple, the publicist hired to promote de Gaulle, submitted his final report. He remarked: 'The *amount* of publicity received by General de Gaulle in today's press in connection with the operations at Dakar demonstrates the cumulative value of the gradual "building up" of his name during the past sixty days ... As a direct result of two months' work, General de Gaulle has become an actual living and *tangible* person to the general public.'

All was not yet over. Churchill was unimpressed by his commanders' apparent weakness. The following morning, 25 September, the Spears Mission war diary noted: 'The day opened with an extremely terse reply from the Prime Minister stating that, with the information at his disposal, he failed to understand why the commanders wished to call off the operation.' The fog had now lifted and Cunningham decided to rescind the previous evening's agreement and resume the attack. Soon after 9am the battleship *Resolution* was hit by a torpedo from a Vichy submarine. That spelt finality. General Spears recorded in his diary. 'The *Resolution* was torpedoed and badly damaged – The submarine which did it was sunk with all hands – This is an awful blow from every point of view.'

In the heat of the moment Spears even cast doubt on de Gaulle, whom up until this point he had admired without reservation. 'De Gaulle is considerably shaken and this worries me. He is so hypnotized by the fear of being accused of attacking

Frenchmen that it is entirely vitiating his judgement. I told him he knew the risks before he started and must not give London the impression of vacillation. He answers that he never envisaged a pitched battle which is true, but that is only half the truth. He is brave but he is more a gambler than a resolute man it turns out. For the moment he cannot see his way . . . I am sad to think of this flat failure and that I pressed for the expedition.' Spears's allegation of a lack of resolution would turn out to be ridiculously wide of the mark; the suggestion that de Gaulle was a gambler, in the sense that he would become a master of psychological bluff and blackmail, was more acute.

Churchill immediately reported the humiliation to Roosevelt: 'I much regret we had to abandon Dakar enterprise. Vichy got in before us and animated defence with partisans and gunnery experts. All friendly elements were gripped and held down. Several of our ships were hit and to persist with landing in force would have tied us to an undue commitment when you think of what we have on our hands already.' The timing could not have been worse. Despite the breakthrough on the loan of the destroyers, these were still early and tentative days in the long process of negotiating American aid. The American people would not go to the polls until November and the election was not a foregone conclusion. Until then Roosevelt, ever the politician, was inherently unreliable.

For the soldiers on the ground the disappointment was savage. Pierre Messmer and his compatriots felt that they had been led into a failed coup. 'That didn't give one much confidence in either de Gaulle or Churchill.' For Seaman Gerry Parker, on board the *Cumberland*, the whole exercise was pointless. Because of the intended peaceful nature of the operation, his ship had kept its guns quiet and, it seemed, had simply waited to be hit. "Two of the guys who were killed came from the same town as I did. I was very friendly with them. We didn't fire a shot, that was the most galling thing, we could have fired several shots because they fired and fired and fired and nobody fired back."

In London the news began to sink in. John Colville recorded: ''Menace' has proved a miserable fiasco, with what results it is only too easy to prophesy. This may be the end of de Gaulle; it will at any rate give his cause a serious setback.' The British Government feared that the attack might provoke war with Vichy France. Vichy ordered a retaliatory bombing of Gibraltar, dropping around 150 bombs and damaging the dockyard. However observers noted that the French pilots did not seem particularly eager to press home their attacks and the action was little more than a gesture. More seriously newspapers in both Britain and America were, in Colville's words, 'stigmatizing Dakar as a major blunder. It will be difficult for Winston to escape criticism.' In the Daily Mirror of 28 September, Cassandra wrote: 'The Dakar *debacle* is worse than appeasement. It has the unmistakable imprint of weak and frightened men.'

The impact in the United States was devastating, compounded by a clever piece of Vichy news management. On 17 August, America announced that it would be opening a new consulate in Dakar, an indication of the importance Roosevelt attached to preventing its use as a U-boat base. The dispatch of Vichy ships to Dakar in September had aroused alarm and news of the operation by Britain and de Gaulle was applauded. However, during the operation, American newspapers were receiving information only from Vichy sources in New York and Washington. The British, according to the London correspondent of the *New York Times* were 'reticent, the Admiralty said it knew nothing, and the Foreign Office was snappish.' The Vichyites spread a story of a rapid British and Gaullist victory, resulting in American headlines saying that Dakar had surrendered on the afternoon of 25 September (at the exact time that the operation was being called off). When London was forced to make its announcement of withdrawal, the defeat seemed all the greater, suggesting Anglo-Gaullist muddle and Vichy triumph against the odds. Victory now turned to 'blunder' and the *New York Times* concluded: 'The authority of General de Gaulle as the spokesman of "Free France" has been discredited.' Nothing could have been more satisfactory to Vichy's aim of appearing to the United States as the only French authority worth dealing with.

A further dispatch to the State Department compounded the wound. The Free French had high hopes of following the Dakar operation with a coup in Syria and Lebanon, countries which had been mandated to France after the First World War and which were controlled by Vichy. On 28 September, Claude Serreulles noted in his diary: 'Terrible week. Before this, there were many reasons to think that Syria would be easy to rally and that all we had to do was go and pick the fruit.' On the same day, the United States Consul General in Beirut cabled the Secretary of State in Washington: 'Developments of the past week have effectively broken up previously widespread and growing support here for de Gaulle and have indefinitely set back the local movement to join forces with the British that gave some promise of action earlier in the month.' Dakar, which had promised to make de Gaulle a figure of substance in Washington's eyes, had left him a man of straw.

The man himself was hardly feeling good. In his memoirs he recalled that ' the days which followed were cruel for me. I went through what a man must feel when an earthquake brutally shakes his house and he receives on his head the rain of tiles falling from the roof.' Three days after Dakar he wrote to his wife: 'As you saw, the events in Dakar were unsuccessful . . . At the moment, all the debris is falling on my head . . . I don't think I'm coming back to London for a while. We have to be patient and firm . . . I think that the battle of Britain is now won . . . I think that American intervention is a certainty. It is the biggest drama in history and your poor husband has been thrown into the front of the stage with all the inevitable ferocity against those who are directing the play. Hold on! No storm lasts forever.'

Even to his wife, there was an element of bravado. According to Claude Serreulles, Dakar was, for de Gaulle, 'terrible and dramatic'. In its immediate aftermath 'he very sincerely thought about forgetting the whole business. He was prepared to retire from being head of the Free French. He would have renounced his dream.' When he arrived at Duala and met up with de Larminat his first question was, "Well, do we go on?" Maurice Schumann, de Gaulle's close colleague and the voice of Free France on the BBC, believed that after Dakar, de Gaulle was never entirely happy again. Another colleague, Alain Peyrefitte, said de Gaulle told him he had contemplated 'blowing his brains out.' Whether he was being serious or metaphorical remains unclear.

Within a few days, de Gaulle had picked himself up. His colleagues all wanted to fight on. And in his new territories in French Equatorial Africa, he found himself greeted as a hero. He issued a communiqué to the Free French office in London committing himself to the long play: 'France's recovery in the war is a game in several sets. The Free French have won the first by rallying twelve million men in the empire. The Germans have won the second by forcing Vichy to fight at Dakar. The game continues. We shall see how it turns out.' Dakar also demonstrated, to Claude Serreulles, a vital part of de Gaulle's will: "Something that never changed in de Gaulle was his refusal to consider the past; he was only interested in the future. He always considered what force he still had with him, however weak. Even if he had a hundred tanks with him and two thousand in front, he was thinking what his counter attack would be."

Above all, de Gaulle continued to have Churchill's unstinting backing. Churchill had been the prime mover behind 'Menace' and was besieged by harsh criticism from the press and Parliament. To some extent, on this particular operation, he and de Gaulle sank or swam together. But, in general, de Gaulle's position was fragile while Churchill's was unshakeable. A lesser leader might have passed the buck and cast de Gaulle as the scapegoat. Churchill went out of his way to do the opposite, telling the House of Commons: "Our opinion of him has been enhanced by everything we have seen of his conduct in circumstances of peculiar and perplexing difficulty. His Majesty's Government has no intention whatever of abandoning the cause of General de Gaulle until it is merged, as merged it will be, in the larger cause of France." Two days later de Gaulle sent from Africa what amounted to a letter of thanks: 'Once again, the storm has arrived. Once again you are at the centre. I am, if I am permitted to say so, more certain than ever of your destiny which is victory.' Some MPs continued to raise questions on Dakar. One called it a 'disgraceful incident' and asked for a fuller report. Churchill instructed the Deputy Prime Minister, Clement Attlee, simply to tell the Commons that the Prime Minister did not think it in the national interest that the matter should be discussed further at the present time.

In his memoirs Churchill acknowledged that to the world at large Dakar seemed 'a glaring example of miscalculation, confusion, timidity, and muddle.' However, both and he and De Gaulle rightly judged that it had served a purpose, even if was not the intended one. The Vichy squadron sent to recover de Gaulle's territories in French Equatorial Africa was repulsed and 'Free French activities in these regions played their part not only in halting the penetration of the Vichy virus' but also in the later development of the air transport route across Africa. However, these were subtle benefits, visible to very few. Not only did Dakar discredit de Gaulle in America, it also stirred an undercurrent of suspicion against the Free French in London. From now on they would be considered irredeemably leaky and chaotic.

In a curious footnote a senior Foreign Office official, Harold Mack, wrote on 2 October that Major Sinclair (MI5) 'has given me an appalling account of the de Gaulle organisation.' In de Gaulle's absence the London Free French headquarters, now in Carlton Gardens, was being run by Admiral Muselier, who was viewed as a 'stormy petrel' by the Foreign Office, though more fondly by British naval chiefs. At the end of Sinclair's note a Foreign Office official attached a hand-written comment 'the mice will play all the more now that the cat's away.' But Sinclair also made an extraordinary allegation that was more serious than mere chaos. 'He is particularly suspicious of a Professor Labarthe', recorded Mack. Labarthe had been an early appointment of de Gaulle and put in charge of military supplies for the Free French. He had since been sacked and was now trying to start up a French magazine. Major Sinclair pointed to Labarthe as the source of the Dakar leak, and stated that his secretary, Mlle. Lecoutre 'is a Polish national and a Soviet agent.' The implication against Labarthe was clear at a time when Soviet Russia was in cahoots with Hitler.

The next day an official at the Ministry of Information wrote to Mack that he was 'inclined to think' that Labarthe 'is the victim of an Anglo-French Blimp offensive.' As it turned out, Major Sinclair's innuendo was justified. Fifty years later Oleg Gordievsky, the British KGB mole who escaped from Moscow to London, confirmed that Labarthe had been a full-time Soviet agent during the war, passing on political and military intelligence to a Soviet controller whom he knew as 'Albert'. In his book *Spycatcher*, the renegade M15 agent, Peter Wright, confirmed the story. Wright wrote that a decrypt, broken in 1964, confirmed that Labarthe had been working as a spy during the period of Hitler's pact with Stalin. Major Sinclair had no evidence and none has since emerged to suggest that Labarthe had leaked any secrets on Dakar; but the story served to show the extent to which the Free French were under the suspicious and watchful eye of British Intelligence and the Foreign Office.

These were merely furtive dangers, the inevitable games of wartime intrigue. A much greater threat to de Gaulle was in the offing; a flirtation towards the men who were now his greatest enemies by the two leaders whom he needed to be his friends.

CHAPTER FOUR
DANGEROUS LIAISONS

In late September 1940, as the Dakar fiasco unfolded, Robert Murphy, the American Charge d'Affaires in Vichy, was unexpectedly recalled to Washington. He had no idea why. Murphy, a career diplomat in his mid-forties, had served in Paris for ten years. Before that he had spend most of the 1920s in the mounting chaos of inter-war Germany. On the night of 9 May 1940 he had attended a dinner given by the American ambassador to France, William Bullitt, in honour of the French Prime Minister, Paul Reynaud. Bullitt had assembled a glittering guest list combining politicians, service chiefs and a favoured journalist or two. A lively argument developed over the dinner table as to whether the Nazis would attack late in 1940 or delay any offensive in 1941. At dawn the following morning Hitler launched the *Blitzkrieg*.

Murphy had watched as the shattering events of May and June unfolded – the chaos of refugees, the muddle of government, the terrible death toll of the French Army. He had stayed on in France after the armistice, ending up as the senior American diplomat in Vichy after Bullitt's return home. He probably had more experience of European politics than any other American and would play a vital role in the triangular relationship between the leaders of the West. He was smart, genial, articulate and sociable. It was later said by de Gaulle, that the France Murphy knew was defined by the Frenchmen he had dinner with. But he had one fault in a diplomat – an occasional failure to remain cool and dispassionate, a certain lack of judgement. His enthusiasm for a cause could allow him to exaggerate.

Murphy, unaware of the reason for his summons to Washington, arrived with his cause of the moment. After Mers-el-Kebir, the Vichy Government had broken off diplomatic relations with Britain. It never occurred to the American Government or indeed Murphy to do anything other than recognize Vichy as the legally constituted French State. For that matter, British interests also continued to be represented by the Canadian minister, Pierre Dupuy, whom Churchill described as "my little window on Vichy."

In an attempt to take some form of offensive action against Germany, Britain had set up a blockade, sporadically enforced, of all supplies including food. The blockade included France, as Churchill believed that any supplies sent there would simply be passed on to the Nazis. With genuine distress Murphy watched the suffering and hunger of the French people. Germany had taken nearly two million Frenchmen prisoners of war; they were only to be released upon a final peace settlement. Many of these were farmers in what was still essentially a peasant country. Millions more refugees were crammed into the unoccupied zone.

In addition to his sympathy for the people, Murphy was generous minded towards France's new leaders. He had had no first hand contact with Pétain or Weygand during the fall of France and did not understand how eager they had been to seek an accommodation with Hitler. When he arrived in Washington, Murphy was therefore bearing a report which argued that America should persuade Britain to allow, at the very least, supplies of food to France: 'abandonment of the French population by their ally Britain and their oldest friend the United States would compel the French to consider making new friends,' he stated. 'If the winter is severe and the situation desperate, they will turn to Germany or anywhere . . .' This was an early sounding of the siren voice that would shape America's attitude to Vichy. Go soft on them, or Pétain and his men will end up with Hitler.

Murphy was also carrying the seeds of an intriguing possibility. In the late summer of 1940 the naval attaché at the American Embassy in Paris had made a quick tour of Morocco and Algeria. He was startled to find that the Nazis appeared to have left French North Africa largely to its own devices, apart from the presence of a few German consuls and Italian members of the Armistice Commission. From Hitler's point of view this was entirely deliberate. Why tie down good German soldiers on distant French territory when the Neo-Fascist Vichy regime was perfectly happy itself to repress any outbreaks of opposition? Behind this lay a secret to which only Hitler and his High Command were privy. The next goal for Nazi Germany was Russia.

On 28 October, Hitler gave the rationale of his Vichy policy to the Italian dictator, Mussolini. 'It is in the interest of the Axis,' said the Führer, 'to see to it that the Vichy Government maintains control of the French Empire in North Africa. If Morocco were to come under the orders of de Gaulle, we should have to carry out a military operation in which success would be difficult, since it would have to be based entirely on the successes of the air forces. The best way to keep this territory is to see to it that it is the French themselves who defend it against the English. This is possible since the Air Force and the Navy are in the hands of anti-British commanders and the Army, too, if it feels that it can save something, will be faithful to Pétain.' Of course, none of this was known outside Hitler's circle but it was an analysis that would have intrigued both the British and the Americans for several reasons.

Firstly it showed that a Free French insurrection in Morocco, which Churchill and de Gaulle had always intended to follow the takeover of Dakar, would not have attracted a full German onslaught in retaliation. Secondly, it demonstrated Hitler's perception of Pétain. Just four days before, on 24 October, Pétain had been summoned to see the Führer at Montoire. At the end of the meeting, Pétain announced that he was embarked on a policy of 'collaboration' with the Nazis. Some believed that Pétain was only saying this to keep Hitler off his back. From his conversation with Mussolini, Hitler clearly believed that Pétain was his tool. Thirdly, and, had the Americans known it, most importantly, Hitler's remarks cast an important light on the state of French North Africa.

That region contained over three hundred thousand men at arms. After his visit, the American naval attaché reported that they had not lost their traditional French fighting spirit: 'If France is going to fight anywhere in this war, I believe North Africa will be the place,' he reported. This optimistic assessment was reinforced in American eyes when, on 9 September, General Weygand was appointed Vichy's 'Delegate-General' in French North Africa, with plenipotentiary powers. This cannot have disturbed Hitler. His statement to Mussolini demonstrated his belief that Weygand would keep the region under strict and collaborationist Vichy control. But Roosevelt had noted Weygand's appointment with interest and saw quite different prospects in it. It was at this point, quite out of the blue, that Murphy was summoned to see the President.

'There is no official record, so far as I know,' Murphy later wrote, 'of that hour-long conversation.' One thing is certain; although Murphy's is the only account and he was not always objective, the conversation showed a marriage of minds. Before the meeting Murphy was informed that Roosevelt had carefully read the naval attaché's reports describing the fighting spirit in the French North African Army. The President now told Murphy of his hope that the appointment of Weygand would be the prelude to anti-Nazi action in North Africa. Of course, like Murphy himself, Roosevelt had not witnessed Wegand's supine set of mind during May and June. He preferred to believe that 'this honourable old soldier', once Chief of Staff to the great Marshal Foch, would not tolerate indefinitely French sub-servience to Germany. As he spread out a large map of North and West Africa, the armchair strategist of the White House believed that this was where resistance might start.

Roosevelt paid no heed to the French resistance already underway with de Gaulle. According to Murphy, he barely mentioned him: 'the President's only reference to him was to say that the ill-fated attempt to capture Dakar confirmed his poor opinion of de Gaulle's judgement.' This assessment was, of course, unfair, reflecting the abuse of the American press, which had placed the blame for the fiasco almost entirely on de Gaulle's shoulders. In Roosevelt's eyes, Weygand, the general who surrendered, was the prospective leader of resistance, not de Gaulle, the general who fought on. This was entirely rational. Roosevelt's chief concern remained to stop Hitler's war spreading to America. The main bulwarks were Britain, whom he was trying to help, and, potentially, Vichy which controlled most of the French Empire. If Vichy could somehow keep the Nazis out and, one day, be induced to counter attack, the war would retreat back towards the middle of Europe and further away from America.

So began the United States's Vichy policy and Murphy's record of the meeting shows that it was the President's own. Roosevelt told Murphy that he wanted him to return to Vichy and obtain passes to visit French North Africa. Once there, he was to cosy up to Weygand. Roosevelt told Murphy that one reason why he had selected him was that he was a Catholic. 'The President', Murphy recalled, 'seemed to have exaggerated ideas of the bond between Catholics because of their religion.' He told Murphy with a wink 'You might even go to church with Weygand!'

Curiously, despite Roosevelt's anti-imperialism, there seemed to be one empire in the world which he would do everything to prop up, that of Vichy France. Back in June he had displayed a remarkable appreciation of French colonialism. Replying at a press conference to a journalist who questioned his sympathy towards France and its colonies, he said: "Martinique is a French colony and they have a very interesting form of government for nearly all Negroes. They get on extremely well with the small number of white people who are down there. They never have any trouble. They have a low standard of living but that is so all through the West Indies. They are a happy, cheerful people and, surprisingly, they have a much better education among the Negroes of Martinique than we have in most of the states in the south. Now that is an interesting fact and that is a French colony." Martinique was now ruled by the particularly repressive Vichy authority of Admiral Robert, with whom the American State Department had struck its deal after the Havana conference in July.

As the meeting drew to a close, Roosevelt casually told

Murphy: "If you learn anything in Africa of special interest, send it to me. Don't bother going through State Department channels." Later Murphy asked Sumner Welles, Under Secretary of the State Department, whether the President really intended this. Welles replied that he often operated that way, as Welles himself knew full well. He was Roosevelt's man in the State Department with a direct line to the President that was not shared by the Secretary of State, Cordell Hull, whom the President kept in post for mainly political reasons.

While Roosevelt hatched his plans and Murphy prepared for his new mission, there was also intrigue on the other side of the Atlantic. Churchill was indulging in a flirtation with Vichy, which was threatening to cause embarrassment with de Gaulle.

Much as though Churchill had backed him, the Dakar disaster could not help but cause many in the British Government to reflect on their relationships with the two Frances of de Gaulle and Pétain. Vichy's Foreign Minister was now Paul Baudouin, who in June had spread the false rumour that Churchill was allowing France to seek an armistice. Baudouin had risen quickly under Pétain and throughout September was putting out feelers, conveyed by the British Embassy in Madrid, implying that Vichy's resolve against Germany might be strengthened by a British relaxation of the blockade against France. The approach struck a chord with the Foreign Secretary, Lord Halifax, a natural appeaser who, back at the end of May, had advocated exploring the possibility of peace terms with Hitler. According to John Colville's diary of 2 October, Halifax's instincts were resurfacing, this time towards Vichy: 'Halifax comes perilously near advocating appeasement, saying that all we require is an assurance that the French Colonies are "healthily anti-German and anti-Italian". If they are, it does not matter whether they are nominally under Vichy or de Gaulle. We must be careful not to let de Gaulle down, I feel very strongly; but perhaps there is no harm in our flirting with M. Baudouin, through the embassy at Madrid, about questions of interest to both countries.'

In a message to Roosevelt two days later Churchill put a somewhat different gloss on Baudouin's messages, smoothly moving from British failure to the benefits of stout resistance. 'In spite of the Dakar fiasco the Vichy Government is endeavoring to enter into relations with us which shows how the tides are flowing in France now that they feel the German weight and see we are able to hold our own.' In fact, despite Mers-el-Kebir, Churchill had always wanted to keep a door open to Vichy. At the end of July he had written to Halifax that he wanted to promote 'a collusive conspiracy in the Vichy Government' to encourage some of its members to decamp to North Africa and steel resistance to Hitler from there. He too had noticed the appointment of Weygand and saw similar prospects to Roosevelt, though with less optimism and not as a replacement for de Gaulle.

The British were also having problems with the Free French. De Gaulle had asked that his representative in New York be included in discussions about security in the Pacific where the remote French possessions of New Caledonia and Tahiti had declared for him. A Foreign Office official, Somerville Smith, told the Free French that 'they were trying to run before they could toddle.' The Free French were also keen to be involved in resistance operations inside France. These were being organized by the Special Operations Executive, set up by Churchill in the summer 'to set Europe ablaze.' On 11 October, S.O.E.'s Chief wrote to his head of French section that while he had no objection to a 'close collaboration on the surface with the de Gaulle intelligence', he held the opinion that 'any bases which we establish in France in collaboration with the de Gaulle staff would be dangerous and liable to dissolution by betrayal at any moment.'

De Gaulle himself was in better spirits. He had undertaken a three week tour of his territories in Africa and was greeted everywhere with acclamation. The ghosts of Dakar were being buried. However life and death in wartime was an arbitrary thing. Where Churchill's Flamingo aircraft had luckily made it back to Britain in June, de Gaulle was almost killed when his Potez 540 plane had an engine failure and crash landed in an African swamp. It would make him vigilant to the point of near paranoia about his future travel arrangements. On de Gaulle's return to Brazzaville on 20 October, General Spears, whose mission was now based there, cabled to London: 'De Gaulle back from Fort Lamy. Enchanted with all he has seen and by high morale of troops. Only disadvantage of trip is previous tendency to assume role of absolute monarch increased but will be dealt with.' Two days later de Gaulle wrote to his wife: 'I am writing to you after a very long plane journey all over Cameroon and Chad. The spirit is great. While everything is going well, the load is materially and morally heavy. We must accept – and I do – all the consequences of this drama which, due to certain circumstances, have made me one of the principal actors . . . I haven't received anything from you since my departure and it bothers me so much. I want to know everything that's going on with you and the babies.' The letters to his wife are constant evidence of the wall de Gaulle had erected between his private and public personas.

These were confusing days as the different camps set out their stalls. De Gaulle was beginning to assert his independence. Roosevelt was making his approaches to Vichy. Churchill was trying to straddle the two Frances. Then, after Pétain's meeting with Hitler at Montoire on 24 October, in which he had promised 'collaboration', rumours spread that his Vice-Premier, Pierre Laval, and the Minister of Marine, Admiral Darlan, were offering France's naval bases and ships to the Nazis. Churchill reacted with justifiable fury, threatening to bomb Vichy. Such rumoured threats also gave reason for regular contact with Roosevelt whom he asked on several occasions to send warnings to Pétain against any further accommodation with Hitler. Roosevelt was happy to pass these on via his diplomats, but had to be pushed to send them in his own name. He retained a benign view of Pétain, seeing him as the hero of the First World War rather than the defeatist of the second and as a sincere French patriot now doing his best for his fallen country.

On 27 October there was one of several coincidences, which would cross these many-sided relationships. The rumours of a hand-over of the French Navy had subsided and in London a Professor Rougier, who was acting as Pétain's unofficial envoy, agreed a protocol with Churchill. Vichy gave assurances that it would never allow its fleet or African Empire to fall into Nazi hands and also would not seek to re-conquer de Gaulle's territories. In return, Britain would neither physically attack Vichy territories, nor verbally attack Pétain. It would also relax its blockade if France were to assist, even passively, in a British victory. Though it was never signed, the document was taken seriously at the time. Churchill immediately wrote to Weygand asking him to 'raise the standard of rebellion' in North Africa. Weygand showed no interest whatsoever.

On the same day that London agreed the protocol with Vichy, de Gaulle issued his own clarion call, the *Brazzaville Manifesto*. Pétain's debasement before Hitler three days before at Montoire had given him his cue and he now declared that the

Vichy Government was 'unconstitutional and in subjection to the invader . . . It is necessary therefore for a new authority to assume the burden of directing the French war effort. Events are imposing this sacred duty upon me. I shall not fail in it.' He announced that he was setting up an 'Empire Defence Council' of men 'who symbolise the highest intellectual and moral values of the nation' to represent the French nation and empire. There was dismay in the Foreign Office, which had received no warning and wanted to avoid treading on Vichy's toes. One official plaintively noted, 'General de Gaulle might have awaited his return to London and consulted us here before issuing it.' The same day, again without consulting London, de Gaulle sent a telegram to the American State Department via its consul in Leopoldville, capital of the neighbouring Belgian Congo. He suggested that his forces, backed by the American Fleet, should take over all French colonies in the American hemisphere. He even offered to negotiate an agreement with the American Government whereby it could use French air and naval bases on the same basis of its agreement with Britain. The implication was that de Gaulle too would like some old destroyers in return. Neither Washington nor London was amused and the only reply was a stony silence.

De Gaulle also came up with the cheeky idea that Weygand should cross over to his command, bringing North Africa with him. Alexander Cadogan was enraged: 'A ridiculous telegram from Brazzaville, showing that that ass de Gaulle is contemplating "summoning Weygand to declare himself". Just exactly what de Gaulle should not do at this moment. Drafted a reply to that effect and sent it to P.M. (whose faith in de Gaulle – and Spears – is, at last, I think, shaken).' But Churchill's heart remained with de Gaulle. As Colville recorded, he was finding Vichy's bowing before Hitler more disgusting than ever: 'Speaking of Vichy, and their recent negotiations with the Germans, the P.M. said, "Owing to our unexpected resistance they have been able to market their treachery at a slightly higher rate than otherwise would have been possible." He referred to them with loathing and said that while he could understand people being wicked he could not understand their being so contemptible.' The ten days of June coloured everything.

Yet Churchill knew that, while there was any prospect of steeling Vichy, the effort had to be made. He was also beginning to feel guilty that de Gaulle was being kept out of the loop. The feelers from Baudoin via the Spanish Embassy had been passed on, but the protocol with Rougier had not. Churchill decided that it was time to level and wrote to de Gaulle on 10 November, 'I feel most anxious for consultation with you. Situation between France and Britain has changed remarkably since you left . . . We have hopes of Weygand in Africa, and no one must underrate advantage that would follow if he were rallied. We are trying to arrive at some modus vivendi with Vichy . . . You will see how important it is that you should be here.'

De Gaulle was not ready to travel. His forces were attacking Gabon, the one element still missing in French Equatorial Africa. In London Colville noted: 'The Free French forces seem to be making a successful attack on Libreville in Gabon, but their activities are rather an embarrassment in our relations with Vichy.' On 10 November, the Free French captured Libreville after a firefight, which killed twenty men. Three days later the whole territory was under Gaullist control. Governor Masson, who had declared for de Gaulle in August and then reneged under Vichy force, hanged himself.

On 17 November, de Gaulle issued a fuller declaration,

amplifying the *Brazzaville Manifesto*. With complicated and detailed legal arguments, it asserted that de Gaulle was now the only legitimate heir to the French third republic. He was, in effect, declaring that he was France. On reading the declaration, Churchill wrote to his Foreign Secretary: 'This is a very remarkable document, and it is bound to have a great effect on the minds of Frenchmen on account both of its scope and its logic. It shows de Gaulle in a light very different from that of an ordinary military man.' The same day, de Gaulle left Africa for London. There could now be no misunderstanding about his intentions or his declared status.

Forewarned by Churchill's letter, de Gaulle's mission was to persuade London to have no truck with Vichy. Cadogan attended a long conversation between Halifax and de Gaulle on 28 November: 'De Gaulle . . . made a better impression. Less pompous, and talked rather well, firmly but with restraint. We drew him on Weygand, but he would have none of him. He thinks there is nothing to be done with Vichy. He says Darlan is the root of evil, and determined to produce a clash with us.' But de Gaulle was powerless to stop the Vichy flirtation.

These various intrigues had led to an ambivalence towards de Gaulle at the heart of British diplomacy. Two Englishmen, who had now seen more of him than any other, believed that the arm's length dance with Vichy was mistakenly preventing a whole-hearted commitment to de Gaulle's leadership. One was General Edward Spears, some of whose observations about de Gaulle have already been noted. Spears was a pivotal figure in Churchill's relationship with de Gaulle. He seemed the typical British officer; hair brushed flat, close moustache, strong jaw, and a pipe permanently lodged in his mouth. However he was exceptional for two reasons. He was a fluent French speaker and a brilliant descriptive writer, married to another literary figure, the American novelist Mary Borden. He was also a close and long-term friend of Churchill. In the First World War he had been a liaison officer with the French Army. When Churchill had resigned from the Admiralty, after the failure at Gallipoli and went to command an infantry battalion in France, he had asked for Spears to be his adjutant. His request was refused because Spears was doing such an outstanding liaison job.

Spears was returned in 1931 as the Conservative Member of Parliament for Loughborough and became an influential figure in the anti-appeasement group which coalesced around Churchill. He loved France and his wife later wrote that during the 1930s he was known among the anti-French block in the House of Commons as 'the Member for Paris.' In 1940, Churchill brought him out of retirement to be first his personal representative to Reynaud and then to head what became known as the Spears Mission to de Gaulle. Despite his occasionally caustic remarks, he had become a passionately partisan supporter. After he and de Gaulle had together escaped from Bordeaux in June, de Gaulle presented him with a photograph of himself, inscribed: 'To General Spears, witness, ally, friend'. Spears had shared the heartbreak of Dakar and later wrote that, immediately after the fiasco, de Gaulle's path 'appeared to stretch, arid and ill-defined, in no particular direction. I watched his lonely figure stalk off down it, and I can only be sure of one thing: that as he observed its steepness and the number of boulders that strewed it, the motive that impelled him was not personal ambition. I am certain that when he started the Free French movement it did not occur to him that one day he would lead his nation . . . His duty was to attempt to free France.'

Spears's future relations with de Gaulle would evolve into a bitter and very personal tragedy, but at the end of November 1940 he believed that he was seeing France's man of destiny. He wrote a long memorandum arguing that Britain should unequivocally back him: 'The obscure personality of last June, whom so many considered a hopeless figure to back because he was so little known, is a world figure today. That position he could not have obtained without British support, but it has been achieved principally by his own efforts. He has made his mistakes and I for one have deplored them, but he is nevertheless a very great man . . . To give any support to General Weygand, who in an ever-growing degree is bound to bear part at least of the odium for France's defeat is to undermine the position of General de Gaulle. We must, I submit, choose between these two men, but if we choose General de Gaulle, we should give him constant and unfailing support. If he feels that we remain faithful to the ideal of a Free France his loyalty can be relied on. He will always be a loyal ally if we are ourselves loyal to the ideals we professed when he threw in his lot with us.'

Spears's arguments were supported by a second Briton, Robert Parr, a career diplomat who had spent many years in Morocco and who was also a fluent French speaker. In appearance, Parr was an eccentric Englishman abroad. Spears wrote that, in the central African heat, Parr, 'side-whiskered and rotund, would even, to the bewilderment but genuine if concealed admiration of the group of officials and soldiers in shorts and sun helmets, await the arrival of all VIPs on the landing ground in a morning coat and black top hat.' However this belied a lucid mind, trained in the cool and dispassionate ways of the Foreign Office, an institution Parr revered above all others. Spears recalled that, although Parr had an excellent sense of humour, he would never joke about 'the Office'.

Parr went to Brazzaville, in late October, as Consul General and spent his first fortnight in Africa observing de Gaulle at close quarters. He emerged with an analysis that was remarkable for its foresight. Parr wrote to London that, 'General de Gaulle is the leader of a people and we must sooner or later recognize him as the head of a state unless his work is to fail of its real achievement. Moments and occasions must be chosen, but the principle can be established at once.' Parr accompanied this with a warning, which, if it had been heeded, might have saved much later agony. 'Until his mind – indeed I should say, until his soul is reassured on this score, he will never be really at ease . . .' This shrewd insight was followed by a further warning of the dangers that would ensue if the British Government allowed any impression that it viewed the Free French like a 'colonial adventure', whose actions were to be dictated by London. This would 'result in bitter discouragement that can only weaken the movement and prejudice our relations with France after the war.' Given the attitudes that de Gaulle would strike as France's President in the 1960s, Parr was some prophet.

At the root of it all was de Gaulle's complex psychology and birthright, which could never have been easily understood by British or American minds. His father, a descendant of minor aristocracy who had fallen on hard times, scraped a lowly living as a teacher and raised his family in genteel poverty. He had fought in the war of 1870 when France was overrun by Prussia and had wanted to continue as a soldier but could not afford it. But he retained a near fanatical commitment to order, tradition, patriotism and the Catholic Church, all values inherited by his son. As a boy in the last decade of the 19th century, Charles de Gaulle had also been brought up to believe that the one nation which stood in the way of the greatness of France and its imperial ambition was Britain. The incident at Fashoda in the White Nile in 1898, when a French expedition was forced to give way to Kitchener's British Army, stuck long in his memory. After de Gaulle's response to Mers-el-Kebir, Churchill believed that he would always be able to rely on him as a loyal ally and a friend of Britain. Despite many vicissitudes, the first turned out to be true; but the idea of some sort of emotional friendship was not merely optimistic, it also misunderstood de Gaulle's very being.

Spears wrote that, when de Gaulle arrived back in London, he said to Lord Halifax, 'I am France.' Such a statement must have sounded preposterous, but it actually conveyed a precise thought, and also a clue to the split personality that de Gaulle was deliberately adopting. Politically it was another way of expressing the manifestos that de Gaulle had issued from Brazzaville. The Vichy State was illegitimate; Free France was the real France. Behind it also lay de Gaulle's perception that he as an individual was an entity and the state was something into which his public persona must be subsumed. This had all sorts of disconcerting consequences. One, as Spears wrote, was that de Gaulle 'soon developed a dislike of being liked as if it were a weakness.' This would be felt not just by the British and Americans, but by his own followers. His refusal to discuss his family and children with his staff, or indeed ever to inquire about theirs, was one symptom.

More seriously, it precluded him from forming ties that went beyond *raison d'état* with those of his allies who would have wished also to become his friend. Most notable was Churchill, himself an emotional and passionate man, who would have liked nothing better than a real friendship with de Gaulle, albeit on the basis that he was his protégé. This was impossible for de Gaulle. The most wounding of all the allegations made against him was Vichy's constant trumpeting that he was Churchill's poodle. This was calumny on the grandest scale. De Gaulle was not only mortified by the abject surrender of his beloved nation, whose burden he had elected to take on his own shoulders; he had also found himself with no alternative but to accept charity from a nation about whom he was historically suspicious. It meant nothing now to say that he would repay every penny borrowed from Britain, as indeed he did in 1946. De Gaulle's answer, as he would later tell his colleagues was an unremitting 'intransigence in defending the rights of France.' That often meant biting the hand that fed him, even if apparent British arrogance often provoked it.

This was all perceived by Spears and Parr. Churchill claimed to understand it too. In his memoirs he wrote that de Gaulle 'felt it to be essential to his position before the French people that he should maintain a proud and haughty demeanour towards 'perfidious Albion', although an exile dependent upon our protection and dwelling in our midst. He had to be rude to the British to prove to French eyes that he was not a British puppet. He certainly carried out this policy with perseverance. He even one day explained this technique to me, and I fully comprehended the extraordinary difficulties of his problem. I always admired his strength.' This judicially phrased passage was written at a time when de Gaulle was a political force in post-war France. However, the furies that would soon track Churchill's relations with de Gaulle suggest that such comprehension might not have been as contemporaneous as he implied.

In November 1940, those furies were yet to break. Indeed, it almost seemed that de Gaulle was becoming a part of the British establishment. On 12 December that august institution, the Royal Thames Yacht Club, invited de Gaulle to become an honorary member for the duration of the war, but only after its secretary had checked personally with Lord Halifax that he was a suitable sort of chap. But while no row had come between Churchill and de Gaulle, the stirrings and mutterings persisted in the undergrowth. The British Government had drawn a veil of silence over the *Brazzaville Manifesto*; to be seen to pay it any attention might upset the delicate game being played with Vichy. This had provoked one member of Parliament, sympathetic to the Free French, to put down a question in the House of Commons. The MP was politely asked to withdraw his question and admitted that he had 'been put up to it by someone in General de Gaulle's headquarters'. A Foreign Office official noted that 'this is yet another example of the dirty work in which Carlton Gardens is at present engaging.' Rows over publicity, propaganda and the right to broadcast uncensored would become a running sore.

Arms and supplies would be another. Spears, despite his unambiguous support, kept a weather eye on Free French housekeeping. Hearing of a request from de Gaulle that one hundred lorries be sent to his African territories, Spears wrote to General 'Pug' Ismay, at the War Cabinet: 'I gather they have been promised, but I could have told you from the evidence of my own eyes that the French have far more lorries in Equatorial Africa than they could possibly use.'

Distrust of the Free French by the British intelligence services was now axiomatic. De Gaulle believed that the Free French should be in on undercover operations on the French mainland. SOE needed them for their language and contacts but the suspicions first displayed in October had hardened. On Christmas Day 1940, the Chief of SOE wrote that he wanted his French section 'to keep in the closest and most friendly contact with their opposite numbers in the de Gaulle Intelligence.' Such friendliness was not quite what it seemed. He went to state with brutal finality: 'This co-operation however – to put it quite brutally – must be one-sided; i.e., I should wish our F section to be fully cognisant of everything that the de Gaulle people are doing, but I do not wish the de Gaulle organisation to be in the least cognisant of anything that SOE are doing.' A few days later SOE's Chief gave another reason for maintaining discretion with the Free French. He told the Foreign Office that he had received information that de Gaulle was unilaterally planning subversive activities in France. He warned that they must not be allowed to commit acts 'which might prejudice our relationship with Vichy . . . it is by no means improbable that some kind of reconciliation will follow shortly.'

While the British intrigued, President Roosevelt was making a crucial move in his campaign to cultivate Pétain's Government. In mid-November Admiral William Leahy, a retired naval commander and now the governor of Puerto Rico, received a confidential message from the President, 'a complete surprise', Leahy later wrote. Leahy and Roosevelt went back a long way. During 1915–1916, Leahy had commanded the Secretary of the Navy's official boat, the *Dolphin*. Roosevelt, whom Leahy describes at that time as 'a handsome, companionable, athletic young man of unusual energy, initiative and decision,' made several cruises and the two men became good friends. Roosevelt saw Leahy as dependable, straightforward, and uncluttered by political baggage or intellectual prejudice; in other words, a rock. In 1937, he had appointed him as his Chief of Naval Operations, before sending him to comfortable semi-retirement in Puerto Rico. Roosevelt's grandson, Curtis Roosevelt, who as a child, listened in to dinner table conversations in the White House during the latter part of the war when Leahy was back in Washington as Roosevelt's Chief of Staff, recalls: 'I once had lunch with Leahy and FDR in FDR's office, the Oval office, just eating from trays, and he was a very stiff man. But I remember my grandfather making references – well, Bill says this and Bill says that, and he obviously took this first-hand advice. He trusted Leahy's perception of things.'

Roosevelt now wanted Leahy to become his Ambassador to Vichy. His letter outlined his particular concern that France 'may actually engage in war against Great Britain' and that the French Fleet might come under German control. 'We need in France', wrote Roosevelt, 'an Ambassador who can gain the confidence of Marshal Pétain, who at the present moment is the one powerful element of the French Government who is standing firm against selling out to Germany.' This interpretation of Pétain's stand was idiosyncratic as Roosevelt was receiving regular messages from Churchill about Pétain's fawning before Hitler. Roosevelt continued: 'I feel that you are the best man available for this mission. You can talk to Marshal Pétain in language which he would understand, and the position which you have held in our own Navy would undoubtedly give you great influence with the higher officers of the French Navy who are openly hostile to Great Britain'. Leahy would have a strong starting point for another reason; he too disliked Britain.

Like Murphy, Leahy was expected to report directly to the President, bypassing the State Department. While the British Government wavered, Roosevelt was set upon a clear course. His two key envoys were in place and his motive remained to keep America out of the war. As far as France was concerned, the best tactic was to make friends with Vichy so that it would stand up to the Nazis. Pétain was pleased with the new possibilities of playing off America against Germany. On hearing about Leahy's appointment he sent a message to Roosevelt: 'The Marshal is delighted that the choice of the US Government is a personality that combines distinguished service with the privilege of being close to the President and personally approved by him. He is furthermore very sensitive to the mark of sympathy towards his person that the choice represents." Pétain and Roosevelt genuinely concurred on one matter. Charles de Gaulle, whom Churchill had recognized as the leader of all Frenchmen who continued the fight, was a non-person.

CHAPTER FIVE
AN END TO FLIRTATION

On New Year's Day 1941, Charles de Gaulle, who was taking a short break with his family in Shropshire, was summoned urgently back to London. The next morning he was ushered into the Foreign Office to see Anthony Eden, the new British Foreign Secretary, who had just succeeded Lord Halifax, recently appointed as Britain's Ambassador to Washington. De Gaulle was in for a jolt.

Eden told him that 'something lamentable had happened.' The British Security Service, M.I.5, had incontrovertible proof that Admiral Emile Muselier, head of the Free French navy, was a spy acting for Vichy. Documents emanating from the French Consulate in London, which was still occupied by a Vichy French official, showed the extent of Muselier's treachery. He was in secret touch with Vichy; he had tried to pass on details of the Dakar expedition to Admiral Darlan, Vichy's Minister of Marine; and he was planning to spirit away the Free French submarine *Surcouf* to Vichy. British Intelligence had concluded that the documents were genuine (in fact the words used by M.I.5. in a memorandum to Churchill's personal assistant, Major Desmond Morton were, 'we feel fairly reasonably certain that the documents are genuine') and Muselier had been arrested on the Prime Minister's direct orders.

The Foreign Office had bridled at Churchill's peremptory action, Sir Alexander Cadogan noting in his diary: 'Talked to A.

(Eden) about Muselier. P.M. of course wants to hang him at once. I pointed out possible effect on de. G. movement and suggested we must consult de. G. first, who is away in the country. A. agreed.' However Churchill insisted on instant action before de Gaulle could be found. Muselier was thrown into prison along with two other Free Frenchmen and two women, whose arrest caused high excitement. One had been found in bed with a doctor attached to the Free French; the other was found at home with a naked Brazilian diplomat.

Eden showed de Gaulle the documents and regretfully admitted that the British had 'no illusions about the impression this dreadful affair will make on your people and on ours.' Though dumbfounded, de Gaulle felt either that there must be some mistake or that it was a Vichy plant. Muselier, who had presided over the mounting chaos at Free French headquarters in Carlton Gardens during de Gaulle's absence, was hardly a favoured comrade. However the idea that he was a Vichy spy seemed far-fetched. For years Muselier had felt only rivalry and hatred towards Darlan; indeed that was a prime motive for establishing a rival French navy. And the allegations seem to de Gaulle to be 'laid on a bit too thick.' De Gaulle asked Eden for Muselier to be released from Pentonville prison where he was languishing in a cramped cell. Eden refused.

Further investigation over the next few days produced the truth. At its root was the constant intrigue at Carlton Gardens. In some ways this was not surprising. The early Free French were bound to be a motley crowd, embracing political views of every colour and not a few malcontents and rascals. During de Gaulle's absence an industrialist called Antoine, who changed his name to Major Fontaine (noms de guerre were all the rage), had become prominent and decided to oversee a security clear out. With de Gaulle's approval, Fontaine had sacked Labarthe, the man who turned out decades later to be a Soviet agent, and brought in a man called Meffre, who adopted the pseudonym 'Howard'. Howard introduced an elaborate security regime involving secret searches of offices and inspection of imprints on blotting paper. This began to cause untold friction and on de Gaulle's return, Muselier, who had opposed both Labarthe's sacking and Howard's appointment, campaigned for Howard's removal. De Gaulle agreed and sacked him, but not before Howard had taken his revenge by getting a certain Collin to forge the deadly documents which appeared to convict Muselier.

It was a pack of trouble de Gaulle could have done without. On 6 January, as the investigation continued, he wrote to his wife, 'I am busy at the moment and have some grave difficulties. The English are valiant and solid allies but at the same time, very tiring.' Two days later he told Spears that he was giving the British Government twenty-four hours to set Muselier free; otherwise all relations between Free France and Great Britain would be broken off, whatever the consequences. Fortunately the same day M.I.5 was forced to admit that it had bungled. The documents were crude forgeries and there was egg on many faces. The Admiralty, which had grown rather to like Muselier, took a certain pleasure in seeing its security colleagues taken down a peg or two. It was difficult to protest against the decision to arrest Muselier as this had been done on Churchill's orders, but that still left room to criticize the way he had been treated. Admiral Dickens, the principal liaison officer with Allied navies, wrote: 'So far as we can make out, he was placed in a prison cell and treated certainly no better than a prisoner serving a sentence . . . M.I.5 are much too inclined to think that security at any cost is the only thing that matters.' After an investigation by the Attorney-General, Morton reported to Churchill his conclusion that 'certain members of M.I.5. cannot escape censure on the grounds of inefficiency, and especially a lack of that astuteness which is to be expected from officers employed in their special type of work. There has also been a failure of junior officers to report action to seniors.' These remarks were an early adumbration of future decades of M.I.5. bungling and treachery.

Churchill and Eden offered profuse apologies to de Gaulle and he was even granted an audience with the King. But, despite the embarrassed climbdown, the episode confirmed de Gaulle's predisposition to mistrust the British, particularly its intelligence services. He immediately banned all British employees at Carlton Gardens, right down to the tea ladies. Only after much persuasion by Spears was the ban rescinded. De Gaulle also used the Muselier arrest to manoeuvre for further independence. At this time S.O.E. was planning its first raid on German forces in France, code-named 'Savanna'. The idea was to parachute in agents to ambush an elite squadron of German pilots, based in Brittany, who were acting as pathfinders for the Luftwaffe's night bombing raids on Britain. S.O.E. wanted eight Free Frenchmen to join the operation but were not willing to divulge its exact nature to de Gaulle. De Gaulle refused S.O.E.'s request, provoking S.O.E. to send a memorandum to Hugh Dalton, the Minister for Economic Warfare, stating that, in view of the importance attached to 'Savanna', 'it is earnestly desired that General de Gaulle be persuaded to revoke his decision.'

Spears was despatched to mollify de Gaulle. Although their conversation was polite, de Gaulle insisted that he needed to know the full details of the operation so that he could decide whether he sufficiently approved of it to allow participation of his men. Spears reported back to Dalton: 'I felt bound to tell him that I feared the impression would be deplorable if it was realized that, when we had asked his co-operation in an operation which might be of maximum importance to this country, he had refused it. This argument did not move him, his feeling being, I believe, that this was an excellent opportunity to force us into accepting him as a co-equal authority in all matters connected with the conduct of the war in which he has any interest . . . It must be taken into account that General de Gaulle is extremely nervy on all questions connected with Intelligence since the Muselier case . . . This has led him to take some extreme measures, such as forbidding any of his officers to have even social relations with any British Intelligence officers.'

While the first real chill descended on the relationship between de Gaulle and the British, a warm front was moving across the Atlantic. On 5 November, Roosevelt had been elected as President for the third time. Though his Republican opponent, Wendell Willkie, was not an isolationist, Roosevelt was terrified of appearing to succumb to isolationist allegations that he was a warmonger. These had been reinforced by Roosevelt's introduction of selective conscription for the Army. In a climactic campaign speech in Boston he used Rooseveltian repetition to allay his audience's fears. 'While I am talking to you mothers and fathers', he said, 'I give you one more assurance. I have said this before, but I shall say it again and again and again: Your boys are not going to be sent into any foreign wars.' He kept to his word; it was only when war came to America at Pearl Harbour that the boys were sent out. The day after his victory, Churchill sent Roosevelt a message of congratulations: 'I did not think it right for me as a Foreigner to express any opinion upon American policies while the election was on, but now I feel you will not mind my saying that I prayed for your success and that I am truly thankful for it.' Roosevelt failed to send any reply, which Churchill found hurtful. Four years later, when Roosevelt won his fourth victory, Churchill also sent him a note, including a reminder that he had not answered the message of 1940. That time Roosevelt did reply.

The strong currents of isolationism had made for an exhausting election campaign; when it was over, Roosevelt relaxed. It seemed to some onlookers that he had rather lost interest in the war; certainly it was creating no urgency. There were a couple of communications with Churchill over British fears about the movements of French warships. Roosevelt seemed happy to rely on Pétain's repeated assurances that they would never be used against Britain. In December Roosevelt went for a holiday on the Presidential ship *Tuscaloosa*, playing poker or watching movies with his cronies. Then on the morning of 9 December, he received a four thousand word message which may have been 'the most carefully drafted and redrafted message in the entire Churchill-Roosevelt correspondence.' The first draft had been written on 12 November and, after it had criss-crossed the war cabinet, the Ambassador in Washington, Lord Lothian, and Churchill himself, it was finally ready to go four weeks later. Among all the finer details of the state of the war and future British strategy and requirements, Churchill gave a simple message. Britain was out of cash and needed America to provide her with planes, ships and arms.

Roosevelt, refuelled by his cruise, soaked in every word of the message. In fact, before going off, he had given the go-ahead to a British arms order, although he knew that there was no cash to pay for it. He was therefore already committed to the idea of some sort of loan. By the time he returned to Washington he had rationalized how he would present it to the American people and Congress. On 17 December he told a press conference, 'there is absolutely no doubt in the mind of a very overwhelming number of Americans that the best immediate defence of the United States is the success of Britain in defending itself.' Rather few Americans would have seen it like that; they just wanted nothing to do with a war. But when, in his folksy way, Roosevelt began to explain the idea that the way not to have to fight yourself was to supply others with the means to do it for you, it all began to sound more attractive. "Suppose my neighbour's home catches fire and I have a length of hose . . .' continued the President and everybody could understand that you would not insist on selling your garden hose to your neighbour, rather you would lend it until the fire was put out. He forbore to mention that this partic- ular hose of planes, ships and munitions might be rather badly shot up or spent during the fire.

For a fireside chat, his special adviser, Harry Hopkins, sug- gested a sentence that he had spotted in a newspaper editorial: 'We must be the great arsenal of democracy.' The policy came to be called lend-lease and, after nearly three months of debate and isolationist abuse, the legislation to enact it was passed by the United States Congress. In his broadcast Roosevelt, safely back in the White House, was also free at last to say what he really felt about the folly of appeasing Hitler: 'A nation can have peace with the Nazis only at the price of total surrender . . . Such a dic- tated peace would be no peace at all. It would be only another armistice, leading to the most gigantic armament race and the most devastating trade war in history . . . All of us, in all the Americas, would be living at the point of a Nazi gun – a gun loaded with explosive bullets, economic as well as military.' Roosevelt had consistently believed this with a passion. And yet he would continue to ignore the fighting Frenchman, Charles de Gaulle.

Roosevelt was now keen to know rather more about the British leader to whom he was proposing to donate this American largesse. Harry Hopkins offered himself as the emissary and, after some hesitation at being parted from his most trusted adviser, Roosevelt agreed to send him. It was a happy decision. Hopkins was closer to the President than anyone. He had run the Federal Emergency Relief Programme in 1933 at the height of the Depression and ended up as Roosevelt's Secretary of Commerce. But his career in the cabinet had been soured by internecine feuds among Roosevelt's senior colleagues – he was also castigated by the right wing business lobby as the liberal devil incarnate. At the end of Roosevelt's second term Hopkins had resigned from the cabinet which now left him free to carve out a new role as Roosevelt's Second World War troubleshooter. It would become an arduous role. Hopkins, tall and untidy looking, seemed always to bear a pale pallor. He hated travelling by plane, an unfortunate fear for a putative globetrotter. In the latter years of the war, he was constantly ill and would die in 1946 at the age of fifty-six.

As de Gaulle was embroiled in the Muselier affair, Hopkins arrived in Britain, bearing a letter of introduction to the King from Roosevelt and a distrust of Churchill. Before leaving Washington he had taken advice from the French businessman, Jean Monnet, who was now working with the British Purchasing Commission in America. Monnet advised him to go straight to the top in London. There was no point in bothering with mere ministers for "Churchill *is* the British War Cabinet, and no-one else matters." Hopkins responded sardonically, "I suppose Churchill is convinced that he's the greatest man in the world!"

Hopkins was warned by a friend, "Harry – if you're going to London with that chip on your shoulder, like a damned little small town chauvinist, you may as well cancel your passage right now."

Churchill's first reaction on hearing of Hopkins's mission was to ask "Who?" His own trusted servant and Parliamentary Private Secretary, Brendan Bracken, filled in the gaps and Churchill understood that the red carpet was to be rolled out. Bracken was despatched to Poole airport to meet the plane. Hopkins did not descend and Bracken boarded the plane to find 'Hopkins still sitting, looking sick, and shrunken and too tired even to unfasten his safety belt.' He perked up on the train to London, which on Churchill's orders, had to be the best that could be found. Later the general manager of Southern Railways wrote that, 'arrangements were made for the most modern Pullman cars to be formed in the train. The conductors wore white gloves; a good meal, with liquid refreshment, was available, together with papers, periodicals etc. Mr Harry Hopkins was obviously impressed.' There was an even more striking display as the train passed through Clapham Junction. Hundreds of German incendiary bombs showered down through the dark winter sky, blocking the tracks into Waterloo. That evening Hopkins saw the American correspondent, Ed Murrow, who had been broadcasting the horrors of the blitz across the Atlantic. Hopkins would say only of his mission, 'I suppose you could say that I've come here to try to find a way to be a catalytic agent between two prima donnas.'

The following morning, Hopkins met prima donna number one at 10 Downing Street. They hit it off. Churchill later described Hopkins as 'a soul that flamed out of a frail and flaming body. He was a crumbling lighthouse from which there shone the beams that led great fleets to harbour . . . He could also be very disagreeable and say hard and sour things. My experiences were teaching me to be able to do this too, if need be.' Hopkins wrote to Roosevelt that 'a rotund – smiling – red faced gentleman appeared – extended a fat but none the less convincing hand and wished me welcome to England.' Their meeting cleared some air. Hopkins told Churchill that there was a feeling in some quarters that he did not like America, Americans or Roosevelt. This provoked Churchill into an attack on the malicious anglophobia of the American ambassador, Joseph Kennedy, whom he assumed to be the source of any such impression. Churchill produced in evidence the telegram he had sent to Roosevelt, to which he had received no response, congratulating him on winning the election. Hopkins then gave Churchill the assurance he wanted above all. According to Churchill Hopkins told him, 'The President is determined that we shall win the war together. Make no mistake about it. He has sent me here to tell you that at all costs and by all means he will carry you through, no matter what happens to him – there is nothing that he will not do so far as he has human power.' In fact Roosevelt was not yet in a position to make this promise; the lend-lease legislation had yet to pass through Congress and it was not a foregone conclusion. But this time, unlike the 'dagger in the back speech' back in June, Roosevelt was in a stronger political position to make his words count.

Hopkins's intended two-week trip stretched to six, of which he spent some ten days with Churchill. They travelled to Scapa Flow to see Britain's new ambassador, Lord Halifax, off to the United States on the latest battleship, *King George V*. A few days later, at a dinner in Glasgow, Hopkins said that on his return to Washington he intended to quote to Roosevelt a verse from the

Book of Books: 'Whither thou goest I will go; and where thou lodgest, I will lodge; thy people shall be my people, and thy God my God.' And then he added very quietly, 'Even to the end.' On hearing this, Churchill wept.

After the trip to Scotland, Hopkins accompanied Churchill on a tour of naval bases on the South Coast. As Churchill moved among the crowds, Hopkins could see his popularity at first hand. He also admired Churchill's stoical reaction to the reality of war as news came in of German dive-bombers appearing in the Mediterranean and sinking British ships with great loss of life. A particular suspicion about Churchill was also resolved; Hopkins witnessed at first hand his Olympian drinking but, observing Churchill's ability to remain on his feet in the small hours and out-think any colleague in the argument, decided that it could not really matter.

Hopkins wrote to Roosevelt, 'The people here are amazing from Churchill down and if courage alone can win the war – the result will be inevitable. But they need our help desperately . . . I cannot believe that it is true that Churchill dislikes either you or America – it just doesn't make sense.' Churchill wrote to the President, 'I am so grateful to you for sending so remarkable an envoy, who enjoys so high a measure of your intimacy and confidence.' The goodwill was multiplied by a letter from Roosevelt carried by another influential American visiting London, Wendell Willkie, who had been Roosevelt's Republican opponent in the election. Roosevelt wrote, 'Wendell Willkie will give you this. He is truly helping to keep politics out over here. I think the verse applies to your people as it does to us:

> "Sail on, O ship of State!
> Sail on, O Union, strong and great!

> Humanity with all its fears,
> With all the hopes of future years,
> Is hanging breathless on thy fate!"'

Churchill wrote that these 'splendid' lines from Longfellow were an 'inspiration'.

In all of this emerging unity, only one matter contained the seeds of divergence between Churchill and Roosevelt. At this point it seemed insignificant and certainly not worthy of any conversation between Churchill and Hopkins. The matter was France. On 6 January, Churchill drew up for his Chiefs-of-Staff his appreciation of the general state of the war. He still held out hopes for resistance by Pétain and Weygand, believing that German pressure might finally force the Vichy Government to move to North Africa and resume the war from there. He had promised the Vichy French leaders that, if they did this, he would send them strong British forces – six divisions, and substantial air and naval power. In the meantime it was only possible to wait and see what Vichy would do.

De Gaulle and Spears viewed the waiting game as a waste of time. Spears wrote a note of passionate opposition to the continuing flirtation: 'Our painstaking attempts to propitiate the Vichy Government might, conceivably, make a dispassionate observer conjure up the picture of a well-meaning person bent on feeding a lettuce to a rabbit while it is being chased around its cage by a stoat. Vichy is completely at the mercy of the Germans. Who can doubt it?' De Gaulle told Claude Serreulles that Pétain was 'clever enough to look like he's resisting but in fact he always lets himself be walked over.'

By February, Churchill himself had also run out of patience. On 12 February he wrote the Foreign Office: 'We have made

Weygand great offers, to which we have had no reply. Not one scrap of nobility or courage has been shown by these people so far, and they had better go on short commons till they come to their senses.' One trigger for Churchill's infuriation was the appointment of Admiral Darlan as Vichy's Foreign Minister. Churchill had never forgiven Darlan for failing to bring the French Fleet over to Britain to continue the war after the fall of France. He wrote again to the Foreign Office: 'We have received nothing but ill-treatment from Vichy. It would have been better to have had Laval, from our point of view, than Darlan, who is a dangerous, bitter, ambitious man, without the odium which attaches to Laval ... An end should be put to the cold-shouldering of General de Gaulle and the Free French move-ment, who are the only people who have done anything for us, and to whom we have made very solemn engagements.' In a fur-ther note to Cadogan he wrote: 'I am sure Darlan is an ambi-tious crook. His exposure and Weygand's weakness will both, as they become apparent, inure to the credit of de Gaulle.' De Gaulle was 'much the best Frenchman now in the arena.' It was a stunning endorsement of the Free French leader. The clouds over their relationship, caused by the Vichy flirtation, seemed to have been cleared and the weather set fair for a long and happy collaboration.

Roosevelt was seeing it all rather differently; indeed the differences in perception, had each fully understood them at the time, were staggering. On 14 January, Robert Murphy, the President's envoy to North Africa had sent a report to Roosevelt on his three-week trip. It was a very remarkable document. Murphy claimed he was later told that the President had based his African policy on it. Weygand, who was no fool, had rolled out an even bigger red carpet for Murphy in Algiers than

Churchill had for Harry Hopkins in London. The doors of five star generals, admirals and all the region's highest-ranking governors were opened to him. Weygand told Murphy that it was high time for America to develop its own independent policy towards France and its Empire. The British Empire, he asserted, correctly as it turned out, could never be the same. Weygand produced as evidence Britain's concession of naval bases to the United States in return for the First World War destroyers. Murphy confessed to being disconcerted when Weygand went on to congratulate the Americans for driving such a hard bargain with the impoverished British.

In Dakar, Murphy met Pierre Boisson, the man who had repelled 'Operation Menace'. Boisson spun the line with which the Vichy authorities intended to catch Murphy, and, by proxy, Roosevelt. At heart, they claimed, they were pro-British and admired their resolution. Despite the dastardly deeds of Mers-el-Kebir and Dakar, they would join them in the fight when the time was right. The only obstacle was de Gaulle and the injurious influence he exerted on his British paymasters. The Vichyites heaped all the blame for Dakar on de Gaulle, not Churchill. They further claimed that Churchill had lost confidence in de Gaulle after Dakar and had approached Weygand to replace him as the leader of French resistance. But Churchill was too impatient. Weygand himself told Murphy: 'There are so many ways in which we could help the British if, for once, they could learn something of subtlety and did not feel that everything must be shouted from the rooftops.' The possibility that Britain, in desperate straits, might need help straightaway and not in some indefinite future was not countenanced.

From the evidence of his report to Roosevelt and the account in his later memoirs, Murphy appears to have swallowed the bait whole. His report began with the unequivocal assertion that: 'General Weygand and his associates are engaged in laying the necessary foundation for substantial independent military action against Germany and Italy. Their program is being formulated with Marshal Pétain's approval.' This was the same Weygand whom Churchill had accused of showing 'not one scrap of nobility or courage'. However Murphy was able to explain away any such suggestion by reporting Weygand's view that, ' he must <u>pretend</u> to stand for the policy of collaboration and use the pretext of the de Gaulle and British action in Africa as a bargaining point with the Germans.'

As for de Gaulle, whom, it should not be forgotten, Vichy had sentenced to death as a rebel, Murphy reported Weygand's certainty that 'eventually the British will withdraw de Gaulle from French Africa as a disturbing factor.' Overall, Murphy had clearly been convinced that Weygand and his Vichy colleagues in North Africa, backed by Pétain, were playing a long game of building up their forces in preparation for an eventual resumption of the war against Germany. Murphy concluded that America should help them: 'The Weygand organisation regard French Africa as France's last trump which must be cautiously and skilfully played. They are all eager for American sympathy and immediate economic co-operation. I believe they merit our interest.'

Murphy's concrete recommendations were that America should immediately send small shipments of 'automotive gasoline, kerosene and gas oil to Dakar and Casablanca.' In North Africa, unlike the French mainland, food was plentiful. Weygand expressed his willingness to provide any guarantees the Americans might require. Over the next few weeks the recommendations of the Murphy report led to the so-called

Murphy/Weygand Accord, under which American 'consuls' would be posted throughout French North Africa to monitor the use of supplies. Murphy's intention was that these 'consuls' would, in effect, be spies working behind the scenes with sympathetic Vichyites to prepare for the day when they rose up against the Nazis. It was a beguiling scenario; and it did not include General de Gaulle.

While Murphy's report was landing on the President's desk, Roosevelt's second envoy, Admiral Leahy, was settling in as the new American ambassador to Vichy. Leahy would turn out to be a more sceptical and realistic observer than Murphy; but he was hampered by one curious blind spot for an American democrat, an apparently cavalier disregard for human rights. In June 1940, as the Germans were about to enter Paris, the United States was besieged with scares about Nazis under the bed throughout the Americas. The Secretary of State for the Interior, Harold Ickes, recorded in his diary that Leahy, who was then the governor of Puerto Rico, was reported to have said that there were several hundred Germans in Puerto Rico and that 'they were suspect as fifth columnists'. On being asked what should be done with them if the war spread across the Atlantic, Leahy had remarked, 'they would simply disappear; no-one would ever hear of them again.' Ickes noted, 'I like Leahy and think that he is an able, strong man, but this streak in an American naval officer who has come out of the soil of Iowa does startle me a little.'

It was not Leahy's job in Vichy to report on the morality of its regime's politics. His mission was to ingratiate himself with the Vichy leaders; he was to use every stick and carrot to steel them against German threats and keep their fleet out of Hitler's hands. Yet he might have performed a more rounded job for the President by warning him in greater detail of the unpleasant and brutal regime with whom he was dealing. In particular Vichy had sprinted out of the starter's block to beat even the Nazis in the Occupied Zone in introducing repressive legislation against Jews. It was as if there were a competition to see who could be the most anti-Semitic. In October 1940, using the standard terms of his pronouncements, 'We, Marshal Pétain, head of the French state, decree . . .' Pétain had spelt out the terms of Vichy's *Statut des Juifs*. Jews were to be excluded from a broad list of professions, ranging from head of state to teaching, journalism, the judiciary, entertainment, and all civil service and elected posts. Several months into his appointment, Leahy did inform Roosevelt that Vichy was assuming a Fascist character, but its anti-Semitism did not seem an important matter for comment. By this time Jews were regularly being rounded up, stripped of all their belongings, and sometimes murdered. Later, in his memoirs, all Leahy managed to recall about anti-Semitism during his sixteen months in Vichy was that, while there was discrimination, 'So far as I know, however, no Jewish houses were searched.'

However Leahy conscientiously performed his task of getting to know the regime's leaders. Immediately on arrival he met the 84-year-old Pétain and remarked that 'he gives every appearance of a remarkable virility and mentality.' The next day he found that, by contrast, 'the Marshal gave every appearance of a tired old man.' By the time he wrote his first assessment for Roosevelt in late January, he had synthesized his view: 'Marshal Pétain is remarkably capable for a man of his age but the burden of work which he has assumed is beyond his physical capacity.' He reported that Admiral Darlan 'is very friendly with me and we "talk shop" easily'; he was also 'incurably anti-British.' A month later, after Darlan's appointment as Vichy's Foreign Minister and heir apparent to Pétain, Leahy talked of the French Admiral's 'psychopathic hatred' for the British Navy. A few days later, Churchill sent Roosevelt his own warning about Darlan, 'Dealing with Darlan is dealing with Germany, for he will not be allowed to agree to anything they know about which does not suit their book.' By the end of March, Leahy wrote to Roosevelt with his conclusion that: 'The only two persons who have impressed me as completely devoted to France without thought of personal advantage are Marshal Pétain and General Weygand.'

A mutually reinforcing picture was beginning to emerge from the two key envoys, Leahy and Murphy. Pétain and Weygand were the two men who carried France's hopes. Murphy was already opposed to de Gaulle, and, during these months in Vichy, Leahy developed his own virulent hostility. It was the siren voice of Pétain that seemed to be guiding him. In his March dispatch Leahy wrote to Roosevelt, 'The Marshal spoke to me yesterday at length about the de Gaulle movement, which he considers a threat to his government by a "group of traitors . . ." Mr Churchill has informed him privately that de Gaulle has been of no assistance to the British cause . . .' This latter allegation was the purest propaganda, and yet it all dripped into the President's calculating mind. At the same time Leahy wrote to the Secretary of State, Cordell Hull, 'I have no doubt whatsoever that the Marshal feels personally very strongly about de Gaulle and that his elimination from the picture would go far in swinging the old soldier more towards the British camp.' This was untrue. But Leahy was forming a view that would remain with him after he returned to Washington in mid 1942 to become Roosevelt's Chief of Staff. Years later in his memoirs, he wrote that, 'de Gaulle thirsted for power . . . his political philosophy appeared to be little different from that of the government of Pétain.'

There are few clues as to precisely how Roosevelt perceived de Gaulle in early 1941. According to Murphy, any confidence he might have had was dispelled by Dakar. A further hint comes from an intriguing entry in the diary of Harold Ickes. A good many prisoners had been escaping from the barbaric French penal colony of Devil's Island where the Vichy French custodial system was in chaos; they were apparently taking refuge in Puerto Rico and Florida. The French wanted the prisoners back but Roosevelt said he would not send them back. It was pointed out to him that many of these convicts were murderers, drug addicts and utterly degenerate. The President then demanded that an attempt be made to send them to join de Gaulle's Free French Army in French Equatorial Africa. He told Hull to raise the idea with de Gaulle. Nothing seems to have come of it and whether the President's eccentric request was designed to help or hinder the Free French leader must remain unclear.

More significantly, in a nation of lobbyists and pressure groups, the Free French had no co-ordinated machine with which to knock on the President's door. Looking around him at the French émigrés in the United States, Roosevelt would only have noticed chaos. Though some had left it in disgust, the Vichyite Embassy remained a coherent political force. But the Free French in America had not yet gelled. Henri de Kerillis, a distinguished journalist and pre-war politician, wrote to de Gaulle in February: 'The little far off cells of the French family are suffering from the terrible disease which wrought such havoc to the body and soul of the central family. Wherever there are twenty Frenchmen they fight between themselves. There are those for de Gaulle and those against him, those for him and against the British, those for the British and against him, those for Pétain, those for Weygand, and those for Laval. There are also the fools, the cowards, and those who are afraid.' And that was the verdict of someone who, at that time, was supporting de Gaulle. It was small wonder if American administrators kept some distance.

De Gaulle understood the problem and in May sent René Pleven, a businessman who had worked with Jean Monnet on the French Purchasing Mission, to America to bang heads together and try to arrange lend-lease supplies for the Free French. The British ambassador, Lord Halifax, tried to press Pleven's case to the State Department but received a brush-off. He reported to London, 'Mr. Hull said that the United States Government would not wish to take any such action at the present time until they knew better how Weygand stood. To quote his own expression, he said that he thought it was better for the United States to walk down one side of the street while we walked on the other.' The British agreed that America should keep its link with Vichy but saw no reason why it should not also show sympathy for the Free French. Hull's insistence that the former should preclude the latter was viewed as absurd in London. However, as Roosevelt's grandson, Curtis Roosevelt, argues from what must have been his grandfather's point of view: 'At the time in 1941, 1942, de Gaulle didn't really amount to anything, didn't have any power, any resources, was completely financed by the British Government. Vichy – and I knew this clearly from dinner table conversations – was a pragmatic decision. FDR would always play the odds politically and he thought that maybe under certain circumstances we can wean Vichy away and get Pétain to see that there's more to throwing his lot in with the Allies.' It seemed a no-lose play. The only problem was that, if de Gaulle came out on top but had been treated with contempt along the way, the play was not quite so guaranteed.

There was already an ambivalence in Roosevelt's position. In May, America announced that it was sending food shipments to Vichy France. The aid was accompanied by seven conditions whose main import was that Vichy would not allow any of its forces or territories to be used by the Nazis. Yet, at precisely this time, Leahy's early optimism in Pétain's resolve was beginning to fade. He wrote in his diary for 16 May, 'It is evident that the Marshal and his Government are in the process of going the full distance in collaborating with Hitler, and by so doing France will probably lose the friendship and assistance of America.' Roosevelt himself wrote to Churchill that he recognized that, 'Vichy is in a German cage.'

Yet Leahy would soldier on for almost another full, fruitless year and it seemed never to occur either to him or his boss that it might be worth cultivating another Frenchman waiting in the wings. Not surprisingly, this upset and mystified the Free French who were inclined to attach part of the blame to the British. A Foreign Office official noted the complaints of de Gaulle's mild-mannered and Anglophile colleague, Maurice Dejean, about the American State Department's lack of understanding. De Jean said the obvious reason was that the British Government 'has been riding two horses for months and never once has our Embassy in Washington shown the slightest enthusiasm for de Gaulle. The American press blamed de Gaulle for Dakar. They were never corrected and never since then have they shown any interest in him.' Americans liked winners; and at this moment de Gaulle did not look like one.

While the Free French were neglected in Washington, the

prospects in London seemed plentiful. Churchill's own play with Vichy was over, even if his Foreign Office could not resist dangling the occasional feeler. He was about to forge ahead into new ventures with de Gaulle. As they set out together, the eventual consequences would have seemed inconceivable.

CHAPTER SIX
HERO TO VILLAIN

At dawn on 9 March 1941, Winston Churchill knocked on the bedroom door of his guest, Charles de Gaulle, who was staying for the weekend at Chequers, the Prime Minister's country retreat. He burst into the room 'literally dancing with joy.' He had just received news that the American Congress had finally passed the lend-lease bill. In Roosevelt's words the United States was set to become the 'arsenal of democracy.' De Gaulle, who, as early as Churchill, had realized that American industrial might would turn the war, shared his delight. Four days later, he departed for his African territories, leaving a note for his wife who was staying behind in London: 'I send all my love to my dearest wife, my friend and my bravest companion, through this tormented life.'

The torment remained the shame of his country's defeat; until its honour was restored de Gaulle could never be at peace. However his star was at least in Churchill's ascendant. Just after he arrived in Brazzaville, Churchill sent a telegram thanking him for the help given by Free French forces in the victorious African campaign against the Italians. But for the 'disaster of Bordeaux', Churchill wrote, 'the whole Mediterranean would now be an Anglo-French lake.' Churchill's original draft had referred to the 'treachery' of Bordeaux, which would have delighted de Gaulle even more. The wary Foreign Office had made the amendment. Churchill concluded with lavish praise: 'You, who have never faltered or failed in serving the common cause, possess the fullest confidence of His Majesty's Government and you embody the hope of millions of Frenchmen and Frenchwomen who do not despair of the future of France or the French Empire.' It was some encomium; the trust seemed total.

Yet something was eating away at de Gaulle. His discontent manifested itself in displays of astonishing rudeness. Spears recorded a stopover in Stanleyville in the Belgian Congo during which a troop of smartly turned out African soldiers presented arms to de Gaulle. He made no sign of acknowledgement. His well-mannered ADC, Geoffrey de Courcel, pointed out to him that the Guard was saluting. De Gaulle rounded on him: "I forbid you to make a remark of that kind to me again. If I did not return the salute of those men, it is that I did not wish to do so. As an old soldier I see everything." A few days later Spears had his first major row with de Gaulle. After some 'quite minor action' by the British Government had annoyed de Gaulle, he announced that he was banning the use by British aircraft of the airport at Fort Lamy in Chad. This was now an important stopover point. After Spears threatened to summon British troops to take it over, De Gaulle relented, but not before his show of pique had exasperated the man who had steadfastly supported him.

The problem was inactivity. De Gaulle was desperate to further Free French ambitions, but he was beginning to feel obstructed by the British. His eyes were on the countries of The Levant, Syria and Lebanon, which had been mandated to France after the First World War and, under French influence and guidance, were to be steered towards independence. In June 1940, the local French Commander had made overtures to the British Commander-in-Chief of the Middle East, General Wavell, to bring his men over to the British. Wavell, like the top British military echelons in London, had thought that the addition of tens of thousands of Frenchmen would only cause him command and supply problems. He brusquely refused the approach and the French Army stayed loyal to Vichy. Wavell had believed it inconceivable that French soldiers of any colour would ever do anything to help the Germans and that Syria would therefore remain safely neutral.

However by April of 1941, despite the victory over the Italians in Eritrea, the Middle East was more unstable than ever. The Germans were preparing their invasion of Crete; Rommel was beginning his advance across the African desert; and Britain was facing a German-backed rebellion in Iraq. The Anglo-Iraqi Treaty of 1930 had given the British the right, if any war broke out, to use Iraq's railways, rivers, ports and airfields for the movement of armed forces. In March, a new pro-German Prime Minister, Rashid Ali, had taken power, forcing the pro-British Regent to flee from Baghdad. British bases were suddenly under threat. Germany had every intention of supporting Ali, but would need to use Vichy's airfields in Syria as a stopover point for Luftwaffe aircraft on the way to Iraq. A lethal prospect was in the offing. With air bases in Syria and Iraq, Germany would be able to strike at the Suez Canal, Britain's lifeline to the Far East.

On 1 April, de Gaulle visited Cairo accompanied by Spears, who shared his view that Syria should be invaded. For both of them it was an intensely frustrating stay. The full threat of Rashid Ali had not yet manifested itself and Wavell, surrounded by his other seas of troubles, refused to indulge in what he saw as an extravagant sideshow against Syria. Spears was pained to find himself in violent disagreement with Wavell, who was an old friend, 'a likeable, one might even say a loveable, man.' By contrast he continued to admire de Gaulle's ceaseless striving: 'Constant drive . . . is certainly provided by de Gaulle whom I have really greatly admired on this trip. He never stops working, always remains perfectly balanced, never loses sight of his objective and has proved himself to be astonishingly shrewd in military matters.'

As yet, Spears was unaware that De Gaulle was operating on an additional agenda that went further than merely securing the Middle East against the Nazis. The region had been a melting pot of Anglo-French imperial rivalries for years. Ever since the First World War the local French had been convinced that the region was riddled with British Arabists with a hostile agenda. Stories even circulated that T.E. Lawrence (of Arabia) was subverting French rule in Syria even though he happened to be far away with his RAF unit in India. De Gaulle was convinced that Britain harboured designs to establish 'leadership' throughout the Middle East. Later he wrote: 'British policy would therefore endeavour, sometimes stealthily and sometimes harshly, to replace France at Damascus and at Beirut.' That remained for the future. At the moment, Wavell would not back an expedition and the Vichy French in Syria had shown no signs of responding to overtures from the Free French, conveyed by de Gaulle's representative in Cairo, General Catroux. Thwarted in Cairo, de Gaulle returned to his central African territories, working up a noxious head of steam against British feebleness. During a visit to Chad he asked Governor Lapie whether he had any British there. Lapie replied that he had. "How many?" asked de Gaulle, "Seventeen," replied Lapie. "That's too many", retorted de Gaulle. Shortly afterwards Lapie received a telegram, instructing him to get rid of them.

On 9 May the first German planes landed in Syria, on their way to help Rashid Ali who had now sent his forces to capture the British air-training base at Habbaniya in the Iraqi desert. The same day de Gaulle received a telegram from Spears, who had stayed behind in Cairo, stating that Wavell would not be able to provide transports for Free French troops to invade Syria for at least a month. The telegram also informed de Gaulle that Wavell, 'although personally glad to see you, sees no necessity for your coming to Cairo now or in the near future.' Churchill was now infuriated by what he saw as Wavell's vacillations. He instructed Wavell that if he could not find enough British troops to go into Syria then he was to find transports for General Catroux and the Free French, who would have to do the best they could on their own. On 11 May, Darlan went to see Hitler at Berchtesgaden and formally granted him use of Vichy bases in Syria. The Vichy commander in Syria, General Dentz, was ordered to attack any British planes in his vicinity with all the means at his disposal. It was at exactly this time that America was announcing its supplies of food shipments to Vichy France.

It was all too much for de Gaulle, unaware of Churchill's latest order to Wavell and stuck in Brazzaville kicking his heels. On 11 May, he poured a torrent of complaints into the understanding ear of Robert Parr, the British Consul General. Parr, the perceptive interpreter of de Gaulle's tortured passion, wrote to London: 'De Gaulle is, I think, extremely tired. Certainly exceedingly depressed. He recalled how his advice had been flouted in France until, just before the Armistice, he was called on when it was already too late. He feels that a similar fate has dogged all his attempts to make Great Britain understand what the Free French movement is. In so many quarters it is considered merely in terms of the number of units it can throw into the battle.

Materially that counts for very little and, if Great Britain attaches so little value to the moral side of the movement that, instead of fostering it by all possible means, she weakens it by complaisance towards Vichy, then he must decide what is his fundamental duty towards France for whom he is trustee.' It was perhaps not surprising that the beleaguered British commanders could not understand de Gaulle's mystical perception of himself as the real soul of his nation, obsessed with retrieving it from its dishonour. But, as Parr reported, de Gaulle still trusted in Churchill. 'He then went on to speak of his feelings of respect and friendship for the Prime Minister who, he said, was indeed one of the men who did realize the moral importance of his movement.'

The next day, 12 May, de Gaulle, having finally run out of patience, ordered Catroux to leave Cairo. There seemed no point in having him there. Prompted by this, Churchill signalled de Gaulle two days later, asking him not to withdraw Catroux. His message said that the War Cabinet in London had decided 'to invite you cordially to go to Cairo if you deem this compatible with the Free French territories.' On the same day, Spears telegraphed de Gaulle to report that transport was being arranged for the Free French in Palestine to cross into Syria and that preparations for a leaflet drop over Syria were underway. De Gaulle immediately replied to Churchill:

Brazzaville, 15 May
From General de Gaulle to Mr Winston Churchill, London.
Thank you.
Catroux remains in Palestine.
I shall go to Cairo soon.
You will win the war.

It was the only message to Churchill that de Gaulle ever wrote by hand.

The Free French hoped that an aversion towards the appearance of German planes on their land combined with an unwillingness to fight fellow Frenchmen might lead the Vichy Army in Syria to lie down before them. The chances of this would be much greater if, as was once dreamed of at Dakar, a huge invasion force displayed itself on the Palestine border with Syria. In fact the reverse happened. A large Vichy force of more than thirty thousand men, well equipped with artillery, planes and armour did the massing on the Syrian side, while the Free French could only muster six thousand infantry, eight guns, ten tanks and two dozen aircraft. Furthermore, on 21 May, Colonel Collet, commander of the Circassian cavalry in Syria and a man whom the Free French knew to be well-disposed towards them, had slipped into Palestine. He asserted that the Vichy forces would fight all invaders. Even sympathetic Vichy officers would defend their positions. As de Gaulle later recalled 'The British would have to join in, and a pitched battle lay ahead.'

Wavell sent to the party the scarce resources he felt he could spare. These comprised one Australian division and two Indian infantry brigades. Later two Australian battalions were added. The antipodean-flavoured force could not be expected to understand the niceties of Anglo-French imperial rivalries. At the head of affairs was General Henry Maitland 'Jumbo' Wilson who would turn out to understand them even less. Wilson was far from the lean, ascetic general exemplified by de Gaulle himself. In his inimitable fashion, Spears described Wilson as 'an enormous, bald man, active for his size, unexpectedly so, like an outsize child's balloon rising into space at the lightest touch.' Wilson had just returned from defeat at Nazi hands in Crete and

Spears for one could never quite comprehend why Churchill seemed to invest such faith in him. The only explanation he could find was that Wilson 'had the good fortune to resemble a benevolent owl, which ever since the days of Pallas Athene has conjured up the concept of wisdom.' Spears presumed that Wilson's countenance must have masked his tactical short-comings, thereby leading him to be classified as 'one of those infallible demigods, with the result that by the end of the war he had floated like a Montgolfier balloon from 10 Downing Street, until finally and surprisingly he landed on high Olympus as a Field-Marshal.'

The days leading up to the invasion saw a further rise in Anglo-Free French tension. Both partners believed that, while Vichy forces were not going to come over, favour could at least be curried with the local Arab population by a firm promise of rapid independence for Syria and Lebanon. On de Gaulle's behalf, Catroux made an appropriate proclamation. But Churchill insisted that this should be accompanied by a British guarantee of the French promise. De Gaulle found this insulting and somehow managed to interpret it as further evidence of secret imperialist ambitions. Two days before the invasion he wrote to Churchill that he would 'proclaim and respect the inde-pendent states of the Levant as long as a treaty is agreed upon which gives rights and special interests to France.' The next day John Colville recorded that 10 Downing Street was beset with 'difficulties connected with the Free French . . . Syria and innu-merable complications related to matters of prestige and *amour propre* . . . de Gaulle is showing himself highly-strung and quar-relsome.' Nevertheless cordial messages were exchanged on the eve of the invasion. Churchill told de Gaulle that 'the loyalty and courage of the Free French save the glory of France.' De Gaulle thanked him from 'the depths of my heart' and said that, whatever happened, the Free French would fight at his side 'as faithful and resolute allies.'

On 8 June, Jumbo Wilson sent his motley band into Syria. As always Churchill had kept Roosevelt informed: 'We enter Syria in some force tomorrow morning in order to prevent further German penetration. Success depends largely upon the attitude of local French troops. De Gaulle's Free French outfit will be prominent but not in the van.' It was a considerably more cautious note than that preceding Dakar. Early reports were confused. Sir Alexander Cadogan noted in his diary of 9 May: 'Can't make out what's happening in Syria. General Wilson's technique – directly an operation begins – is to dry up completely and give no news at all. P.M. very angry at this, as he has to make a statement to House tomorrow. He said "it's damned bad manners."'

There was no good news to give. Vichy forces fought hard and the invader soon found themselves bogged down. Spears and de Gaulle were amazed that General Wilson had failed to plan a flanking operation from Iraq, where Rashid Ali had now been defeated by British forces and the Regent reinstalled. This, they believed, was Syria's soft underbelly and would have encountered no Vichy resistance. Another mystery was why Free French members of the Foreign Legion were not despatched to the ancient Roman site of Palmyra to persuade members of the Legion based there to join them. After all, the Foreign Legion was loyal to itself beyond any thought of national boundaries. And a third tactical oddity was the assignment of all the Royal Air Force fighters and bombers to protect British ships, which were ineffectively bombing the Lebanese shore from the sea. Spears for one argued that if the RAF, famous from its exploits during the Battle of Britain, had supported the ground forces, its appearance overhead might have reduced Vichy's soldiers to gibbering wrecks.

As it was, a nasty battle ensued, with thousands of casualties on both sides. Just over a week into the campaign the Vichy forces captured a British battalion at Kuneitra. De Gaulle thought, no doubt rightly, that he would have done a much better job of command. Spears noted in his diary of 18 June: 'De Gaulle told me later he would never again place his troops under British command. As he says one has impression there is no real command here, Jumbo Wilson looks to W, W says Jumbo's in charge . . . de G says rightly the F.F. have succeeded in all their enterprises – though small.' More distressingly, there were fratricidal atrocities. The commander of the Free French Foreign Legion hailed a Vichy officer in his side-car, suggesting that he and his men might like to join them in fighting the Germans. The Vichy officer shot him dead. De Gaulle wrote later of the Vichy solders fighting spirit: 'At a time when the enemy held Paris under his boot, was attacking in Africa, and was infiltrating into the Levant, this courage shown and these losses born in the fratricidal struggle imposed by Hitler upon leaders who had fallen under his yoke made on me an impression of horrible waste.'

Curiously, after twelve days' fighting, which included their victory at Kuneitra, the Vichyite High Commission of the Levant in Washington put out peace feelers. Yet Vichy's commander on the ground in Syria, General Dentz, fought on for a further three weeks. De Gaulle concluded that Vichy was acting under Nazi orders; 'Operation Barbarossa', the invasion of Russia, began on 22 June and the more sideshows tying up Germany's enemies, the better.

The suggestions of an armistice propelled de Gaulle into

urgent action. Ever suspicious of British designs, he met the British Ambassador to Cairo and spelt out his requirements of any peace agreement. These were not dissimilar to the aims he had sent Churchill before the campaign began but, crucially, de Gaulle insisted that Vichy soldiers must be able to make a genuinely free choice as to whether they wished to switch to the Free French, rather than being repatriated to Vichy. In de Gaulle's view, this meant that Free French officers should have the right to present their case to them. However, de Gaulle then learnt that the Foreign Office had sent a text to the Levant High Commission in Washington, which failed to reflect the position of the Free French. He fired off a note of protest to Eden and then left Cairo for a triumphal entry into Damascus – which had now been captured.

On 10 July, Vichy's General Dentz asked for a cease-fire. Armistice negotiations were set to begin three days later at Acre. Meanwhile de Gaulle had done a flit back to Brazzaville. He suspected that a deal between Dentz and the British was about to be cooked up. He had therefore decided to remove himself to as great a distance as possible so that, even if his representative, General Catroux was present, he himself could deny any association with it. He gave himself further insurance by sending Catroux a warning shot on the day after the cease fire: 'I have reserved for my own decision any matter touching the question of Franco-British relations in the Levant.' He had also left Spears on less than happy terms. Spears recorded that, although de Gaulle had not smashed the ornaments on the mantelpiece at Shepheard's Hotel as on a previous occasion, his remarks were equally destructive. "I do not think I shall ever get on with *les Anglais*", de Gaulle told him, "You are all the same, exclusively concentrated upon your own interests and business, quite insensitive to the requirements of others". He went on to say that he was not interested in England winning the war, only in France's victory. Spears protested that they were the same thing. "Not at all," retorted de Gaulle. Privately Spears agreed that de Gaulle was entitled to be 'furious and discouraged.'

As the armistice negotiations began, Spears's representative in Brazzaville sent the War Office a message that 'De Gaulle has been talking ironically in French circles about "*ces Anglais*" with a shrug'. On 14 July, the terms of the *Acre Convention* were agreed. De Gaulle's most pessimistic fears were justified. Jumbo Wilson had done a deal with General Dentz's deputy, General Verdilhac, cutting out the Free French. Catroux had been present but clearly ineffectual. The armistice failed to provide for any opportunities to turn Vichy soldiers who were to be allowed to return to France, carrying their arms with them. Apparently Catroux himself believed it inappropriate for a French soldier of any hue to appear in public without his rifle or revolver. A secret protocol was added that the Free French were not even to be allowed to get in touch with the Vichy troops.

Spears himself later acknowledged that the terms were 'quite preposterous'. Back in Brazzaville, de Gaulle, still unaware of the full details but 'taking as my basis the naturally sugared indications given by the London radio' publicly repudiated the Acre agreement. He then boarded a plane for Cairo. The War Office received a bleak message from Brazzaville that 'de Gaulle left in an anti British mood . . . Would it not be possible to issue a directive to all British commanders reminding them of De Gaulle's contention that he represents the true France . . . It is most important to avoid further treading on his corns for the time being.' Unfortunately the treading of 'Jumbo' Wilson's rotund frame had already done the damage.

On 20 July, de Gaulle descended upon Egypt. Spears, who had now been appointed British Minister to the Levant, met de Gaulle in the early afternoon. He noted in his diary that de Gaulle 'was very pleasant with me personally (his telegram welcoming my appointment to Syria could not have been nicer) but on the general question of the armistice terms and his relations with us his attitude could scarcely have been worse ... He is very angry and bitter over what he rightly considers the incompatibility of the armistice conditions with the possibility of rallying French troops to his cause. He considers that through stupidity or otherwise we have made this impossible.' In the circumstances, de Gaulle maintained a reasonable courtesy. As it turned out, he was keeping his powder dry for the following day.

Three weeks before, Churchill had appointed Oliver Lyttelton, a cabinet minister and old friend, to be Minister of State in the Middle East. Lyttelton was a gentleman of the old school who had won the Military Cross in the First World War, 'kindly and wise' according to Spears, 'amiable and thoughtful' according to de Gaulle. At 10am on the morning of 22 July Lyttelton found himself facing a smoking Vesuvius. Also present were Spears and de Larminat, now one of de Gaulle's key officers. If Dakar was the first defining point in the relationship between the Allies, this meeting in Cairo was the second.

There are different interpretations of its mood, but on its content there is broad agreement. De Gaulle stated that, while the British and Free French together had achieved a notable strategic threat by barring German infiltration via Vichy into the Levant, the armistice agreement was unacceptable. The authority in Syria and Lebanon was mandated to France and could not pass to England. It belonged to Free France, and Free France alone, to exercise it. In addition, de Gaulle's intention of bringing over as many Vichy soldiers as possible had been thwarted. The Free French could not agree to being kept away from a French source of reinforcements. He concluded his case for the prosecution by stating that the Free French would not allow the common effort to end in the establishing of British authority in Damascus and Beirut.

Lyttelton, according to Spears, was already 'perturbed at the prospect of having to face de Gaulle on so bad a wicket.' He opened the defence by restating that Britain had no interest in Syria and Lebanon other than winning the war. That meant that those countries had to be stabilized; the way to achieve this was to offer the rapid independence that the Free French had promised and the British had guaranteed. As long as the war lasted, the British Military Commander must have overriding powers to preserve public order. Lyttelton said that de Gaulle should trust the British as they shared a common cause. De Gaulle retorted that, while the cause was common, the position was not. It was up to the French to decide the timing of independence, and also to maintain order. Lyttelton disputed this on the grounds that the Anglo-Free French agreements of 1940 recognized the authority of the British High Command. De Gaulle replied that this authority was never intended to cover the governance of French territory. As far as he was concerned the Acre agreement did not bind Free France as he personally had not signed it. Lyttelton asked de Gaulle what he intended to do, whereupon de Gaulle handed him a note saying that at noon in two days time, 24 July, he was ordering General Catroux to exert unilaterally his authority over the whole of Syria and Lebanon, whatever the consequences. Effectively the Free French would no longer consider themselves under British command. Lyttelton refused to accept this ultimatum, pointing out that it would mean the complete rupture of the alliance between the British and the Free French. De Gaulle said he could interpret it however he wished, but that these were his orders and he had no intention of going back on it.

De Gaulle later wrote that he tried to avoid explosions and cased himself in ice. He admitted by the end that he was 'somewhat deeply moved'. The accounts of Spears and Lyttelton suggest that this was a masterly understatement. Spears recorded in his diary: 'De Gaulle was in the worst mood I have ever known him in, he looked frightful and as if he had not slept for a week. He was completely intransigent and often extremely rude. He declared he was not in the least interested that we should win the war, only caring for the position of France ... It was evident that de Larminat was thoroughly scared.' In a telegram to Churchill, Lyttelton wrote that 'de Gaulle had worked himself into a state of bitter hostility to everything English.' Lyttelton described him as 'rude and offensive', concluding that, 'if this is a specimen of how diplomacy has to be conducted I feel glad I did not embrace it as a career'.

The first reaction of the British was that de Gaulle must be prevented from going to Syria until things were settled. Spears suggested that his communications were cut and the machinery to do this was set up. The idea of replacing de Gaulle with Catroux was also discussed. This would be implemented by notifying all Free French that their pay would be made through Catroux. At 6pm a second meeting took place. De Gaulle had undergone a violent mood swing. Spears noted that 'de Gaulle had completely changed, and although difficult was, comparatively speaking, amenable.' De Larminat and a British official, Michael Wright, had been working on him in the meantime but this was also a deliberate de Gaulle negotiating tactic. Soften your enemy with the thunder of artillery, make him quake in his boots at the prospect of seeing you again, then when you turn up all smiles and charm for the second meeting, your enemy will concede everything you want.

On this occasion the tactic worked. Lyttelton conceded France's dominant position in the Levant, while de Gaulle agreed to the dominant rights of the British military command during the emergency of war. De Gaulle openly expressed his fear that the British command might try to use military necessity to cloak political manoeuvres. Lyttelton protested that if de Gaulle's mistrust ran this deep, no understanding would ever be possible. Spears noted, 'This is at the bottom of all our difficulties, de Gaulle's infernal and ineradicable suspicion of us.' Nevertheless, the understanding in the second meeting was codified two days later in a document reinterpreting the *Acre Convention*. Among other things it recognised the pre-eminent position of the Free French command in all questions affecting Vichy troops.

De Gaulle had won the argument but was running the risk of losing important friends, most notably Churchill. Churchill realised that de Gaulle was essentially in the right, but was appalled not only by his behaviour but also by his apparent willingness to put the interests of France before the winning of the war. On receiving Lyttelton's report, Churchill sent a message to one of de Gaulle's colleagues in London, asking: "Is de Gaulle still a General, or has he become a politician?"

John Colville's diary for 24 July notes: 'De Gaulle is behaving abominably in Cairo: quarrelsome and neurotic.' A Foreign Office memorandum acknowledged that there was some excuse for de Gaulle's 'indignation' but that he had 'largely destroyed his case by his intemperate and Anglophobe language.' In Cairo, the new Commander-in-Chief Middle East, General Auchinleck, with whom Churchill had now replaced Wavell, wrote to the War Office: 'I have observed with great regret that General de Gaulle, having found that on so many occasions browbeating methods have succeeded in ensuring his having his way, is developing this method into a regular system. In my view it is essential that when occasion offers General de Gaulle should be made to realise that constant threats, an overbearing manner and spates of ultimatums are not the best means of obtaining what he wants.'

The agreement between Lyttelton and de Gaulle was still only a piece of paper. De Gaulle now hovered like a bird of prey waiting to pounce on any signs that it was not being put into practice. In what was evolving into a personal tragedy, General Spears, who had escaped from France with de Gaulle in June, shared the wound of Dakar, and used all his powers to curtail Churchill's flirtation with Vichy, was now becoming his enemy. In the days following the Lyttelton meeting Spears later wrote that de Gaulle 'appeared much of the time to be little better than a raving lunatic.' On 28 July, his diary records that de Gaulle is now 'absolutely denying us the right to apply military martial law in Syria.' Under the agreement this right was vested in the British commander, General Wilson, but de Gaulle's distrust of 'Jumbo' was now axiomatic. Over the next two days all the rivalries flared up.

The British and Free French had not yet taken over the Jebel ed Druze region in the black, volcanic landscape south of Damascus. The Druze were a fiercely independent people who had long disliked the rule of their French masters. On 28 July, General Wilson ordered British troops to take the area. According to de Gaulle, he was obliged to consult with Catroux before any such order could be given. De Gaulle was then informed that the British had taken over the French head-quarters, the *Maison de France*, in the main Druze city of Soueida, done a deal with Druze chieftains to keep the French out, and replaced the French Tricolour with the Union Jack. On de Gaulle's orders, given in contravention of Wilson's overall command, Catroux sent a Free French column under Colonel Monclar to repossess the *Maison de France*. On arrival, Monclar expressed his intentions to the British commander, Brigadier Dunne. Dunne said that he would fight the Free French if he had to; Monclar refused to withdraw. Before fighting could break out, Dunne was given further orders to withdraw. Monclar moved in to the *Maison de France*, hauled down the Union Jack and replaced it with the Tricolour. Spears was appalled at the British command's weakness. He claimed in his diary that de Gaulle was 'much frightened' and on the 'point of giving way' when the British order to withdraw came. 'The position has thus been incredibly badly handled and de Gaulle will have the impression that once again he has, by holding out, scored over us.'

On the day of the Soueida crisis, as British and Free French troops almost engaged in battle, de Gaulle, who was visiting Damascus, expressed, in public, his undying loyalty to his British allies. He said that France would prevent Syria from being enslaved in co-operation with her brave British allies 'who have come here exclusively for strategic reasons.' He was counting on 'the complete union of England and France' to preserve 'the national liberty and integrity' of Syria and Lebanon. It would become a running theme of the relationships between the Allies at war; public expressions of mutual devotion masking unholy rows behind closed doors. Certainly his speech cut little ice with

Auchinleck who was on a brief visit to London. Colville recorded: 'Auchinleck . . . thinks de Gaulle is mad and consumed with personal ambition, which makes him care little for our fortunes in the war.' Colville could not resist a miniature portrait of the new Commander-in-Chief: 'Auchinleck is an impressive man, but – as one sometimes finds on a racecourse – looks do not always bear great relation to form.' No doubt influenced by Auchinleck's comments, Churchill wrote to Lyttelton: 'I am sorry you are having all this trouble with de Gaulle . . . It might be well if you could let him see the gulf on the edge of which he is disporting himself.' Churchill accompanied this message with a telegram for de Gaulle, suggesting that he return to England as soon as possible 'in order that I may discuss with you personally the difficulties which have arisen.'

De Gaulle had no such intention. Such was his fury with Britain that he now tried to play America against her. On 5 August, he went to see the United States Consul General, Engert, in Beirut and poured out all his problems with the British. De Gaulle told Engert that his relations with the British had reached 'a critical stage' and recounted the full history of his troubled dealings with Lyttelton and British commanders on the ground. Engert replied that he could not possibly enter a discussion of this sort and implored de Gaulle simply to speak frankly with his British allies and iron out the problems. De Gaulle now 'startled' him by replying that 'he had found it quite useless to talk to them and from now on he would insist on Free French rights "even if this should lead to a rupture of relations with the British."' Engert told de Gaulle that he deplored such a statement 'for if you should make it to an indiscreet person you would be playing into the hands of Hitler, which I know is furthest from your thoughts.' The Consul General reported the conversation to Washington, saying that de Gaulle had authorized him to make what use of it he saw fit.

De Gaulle's motives for this injudicious conversation are hard to fathom. Perhaps it was a genuine *cri de coeur*. Maybe he believed that the United States, with all its own suspicions of British imperialism, might row in on his side. But then French imperialism was equally suspected in Washington. Or perhaps de Gaulle's grasp of history drove him to seek help from an American. If Britain was traditionally France's arch rival, the United States, back to the days of the War of Independence and the Napoleonic Wars, was her traditional ally. While there is plenty of evidence that de Gaulle's distrust of Britain preceded the war, there is no reason to believe that he viewed America as anything but a friend. It was the experience of the wartime relationship that would change that.

Whatever his motives, de Gaulle could not have been barking up a more erroneous tree. The most recent dispatch to Washington on 18 July, from Admiral Leahy in Vichy, had oozed contempt for the Free French: 'The radical de Gaullists whom I have met do not seem to have the stability, intelligence and popular standing in their communities that should be necessary to their announced purpose. One of them recently told me that all the Ministers of the Vichy Government are under sentence of death which can be carried out at any time and which will be carried out when it suits the purpose of their organization.' This slightly begged the question as to whom Leahy was talking. His job was to cultivate members of the Vichy Government and he mentions elsewhere in his diary the difficulties in holding conversations with Vichy's opponents because of their potential embarrassment. In fact, by now, Leahy was becoming dejected with his mission, having correctly realized that nothing he did or said would cause Pétain to resist Germany. However he hung on, performing his overriding duty of doing whatever he could to keep the French fleet from Nazi clutches.

De Gaulle was losing friends fast. On the day of his visit to the American Consul General, Auchinleck, back in Cairo, wrote to the War Office: 'It is all too obvious that General de Gaulle looks upon the assertion of French sovereignty in Syria as far more important than taking measures to win the war. General de Gaulle would, should we find ourselves forced to impose military law, do a Samson act and threaten to bring down the Free French movement. He has on previous occasions threatened to do so, believing we would never dare face the reversal of opinion in France he believes his desertion of our cause would bring about. The threat is no doubt serious, but perhaps not serious enough to risk jeopardizing our military position in the Middle East or the Arab world. If de Gaulle ceased to be prepared to act as our ally we should have in mind someone else whom we could recognise as leader of the Free French. It would be a difficult but not an impossible operation.' Different British voices were echoing the suggestion that de Gaulle might need to be got rid of. One Foreign Office official wrote: 'his growing megalomania is making him Fascist minded'. The Spears Mission's representative in Brazzaville, where de Gaulle had just returned, reported 'Fascist tendencies' among the Free French there. De Gaulle himself had been heard to say: 'The Americans would shortly come into the war and it is principally to them that the Free French must look for salvation.' The same telegram also stated: 'The fact that Governor of Chad, Lapie, has turned out to be Homo-sexual is not increasing Free French prestige in Central Africa.' The allegations were flying thick, fast and from every quarter.

There was despair too among de Gaulle's staff. On 9 August, Claud Serreulles wrote in his diary: 'There is no-one amongst us who can say to the General, "The tone that you're using when you address the Prime Minister can only be a disservice to you. Far from working in our favour, such words go against us. The moment can't be far off when the British Government, fed up with all your bad language and threats will hold you to what you say. You're dreaming if you think that on that day you'll be of any importance . . . You have the incredible luck that the Prime Minister has shown you sympathy and consideration. Make use of it and exploit it and don't compromise your personal position or that of the future of the Free French."' Looking back nearly sixty years Claude Serreulles still supports every stand that de Gaulle took, but wishes he could have pressed his case with just a hint of a smile. However he admits that is a pipe dream. At the time de Gaulle was simply 'terrible, dreadful.'

In another of those ironies of coincidence which pepper this unfolding relationship, Churchill, on the very day that Claude Serreulles was recording his infuriation, was having his first meeting with Roosevelt since that brush in 1918. The timing makes any idea that America would save the Free French from the British seem pathetically far-fetched. Harry Hopkins, while visiting London in early July on the way back from his first visit to Moscow, had told Churchill that Roosevelt would like to meet him 'in some lonely bay or other'. On 4 August, Churchill, accompanied by Hopkins, glided out of Scapa Flow into the North Atlantic on Britain's latest battleship *The Prince of Wales*. Hopkins later remarked: 'You'd have thought Winston was being carried up into the heavens to meet God!'

The lend-lease programme was now in full swing and, even if they had only communicated by cable and phone, it was, from

Churchill's point of view, as if he was finally about to see his partner in an arranged marriage. To get on with him was not only a personal desire, but a matter of policy. On 9 August, the *Prince of Wales* arrived at Placentia Bay on the Newfoundland coast. Out of the mist appeared sleek new American destroyers and then Roosevelt's cruiser *Augusta*. Churchill crossed over for lunch. That night Roosevelt sent Margaret Suckley his first impressions: 'He is a tremendously vital person & in many ways is an English Mayor LaGuardia! Don't say I said so! I like him – and lunching alone broke the ice both ways.' LaGuardia, Mayor of New York, was a pint-sized battleship of a man, barrel-chested and a non-stop talker. Roosevelt had his sons Elliott and Franklin Jnr. on board with him and two days later wrote to Margaret: 'We had a delightful little dinner of five H. Hopkins, Elliott, Franklin Jnr., Churchill & myself. We talked about everything except the war! & Churchill said it was the nicest evening he had had!'

The concrete result of this first meeting was the *Atlantic Charter* which, among its other clauses, 'respected the right of all peoples to choose the form of government under which they will live.' Later this would be held against Churchill as an assurance of independence for the nations of the British Empire, a project for which Roosevelt, often to Churchill's irritation, tirelessly campaigned. But, for the moment, the liberal and humanitarian tone of the charter, of which Churchill claimed to have written the first draft, was one way of demonstrating to Roosevelt that he was not a stick-in-the-mud reactionary. It was also a means of attaching the United States even further to the allied cause. Back in Britain, many assumed that it would not be long before America, of its own volition, became a full belligerent. Many other matters were discussed at Placentia Bay; Russia, the threat from Japan, the U-boat war. The problem of France, the Free French and de Gaulle was not on the agenda. Very soon it would be, carrying with it the potential to cause serious division between the President and the Prime Minister.

CHAPTER 7
WINTER STORMS

On 27 August, de Gaulle, back in Brazzaville, gave an interview to an American journalist, George Weller, of the *Chicago Daily News*. It sent a shower of high explosive over the British and American capitals.

De Gaulle's intention was to project the importance of Free France to Americans. On 16 July, he had sent a sensibly argued memorandum to the American Minister in Cairo, offering the United States the use of Free French air bases in French Equatorial Africa. He was anticipating the day when the United States would be forced to enter the war and argued that she would need 'bases progressively closer to the front in order to attack the enemy.' De Gaulle claimed that England could only offer 'limited strategic possibilities' and, somewhat more ethereally, that English and American ideas were different and should not be mixed. The latter sounded like a dig at the British allies who had proved so unsatisfactory in Syria. The former was prophetic; de Gaulle's only mistake was in not realizing that American eyes were trained on the possibilities of Vichy North Africa rather than French Equatorial Africa. His memorandum was forwarded to the State Department which, in its continuing rebuff of the Free French, did not bother to reply.

De Gaulle turned to the *Chicago Daily News* to broadcast his offer. It was hardly a diplomatic way of going about things and attracted the ire of the State Department. It immediately denied that any such offer had been previously made and chalked up another black mark against de Gaulle. Its mood was not lightened when de Gaulle went on to suggest that it was high time the United States broke off relations with Vichy.

The interview now switched to Britain. Weller unwittingly set a trap for de Gaulle by asking: "Why in your opinion does not London finally close the door upon Vichy by recognizing your Government?" Though Churchill still firmly supported the Free French despite all the rows, he had never gone as far as recognizing them as the French Government-in-exile. De Gaulle answered Weller without hesitation: "England is afraid of the French Fleet. What in effect England is carrying on is a war-time deal with Hitler in which Vichy serves as go-between. Vichy serves Hitler by keeping the French people in subjection and selling the French Empire piecemeal to Germany. But do not forget that Vichy also served England by keeping the French Fleet out of Hitler's hands. Britain is exploiting Vichy in the same way as Germany; the only difference is in her purposes. What happens in effect is an exchange of advantages between hostile powers which keeps the Vichy Government alive as long as both Britain and Germany agree it should exist. If Vichy should lend or lose its fleet to the Nazis, Britain would quickly bring suspense about recognition to an end. And if Vichy should cease serving Hitler and dismembering its Empire for his benefit, Germany would herself dismantle Vichy."

As a piece of analysis, it was fascinating and acute, apart from the implication that there was some kind of conscious agreement over Vichy between German and Britain. As a piece of diplomacy, it was breathtakingly tactless. To talk of Hitler's Germany and Churchill's Britain in the same breath was, even in the Gaullist pantheon of insults, spectacular. De Gaulle quickly realized that he had gone too far. He sent a panicky telegram to René Pleven, who was still on his soul-destroying mission of promoting the Free French with the American Government: 'Please stop the publication. If it is too late, please say vehemently that this text does not, I repeat, does not, represent what I said and that there was a misunderstanding in one sentence which will lead to a misinterpretation of my intentions." But his remarks were already rolling on the presses. On reading them, Churchill's reaction was instant and tart. He wrote to Eden: 'If de Gaulle's interview with the American press at Brazzaville is authentic he has clearly gone off his head. This will be a very good riddance and will simplify our further course.' John Colville recorded the atmosphere at 10 Downing Street: 'I was on late duty and most of the time was occupied with de Gaulle, whose attitude is deplorable and whose pronouncements, private and public, are intolerable. The P.M. is sick to death of him.'

Two days later de Gaulle tried again to limit the damage with a further telegram to Pleven: 'I repeat that the interview with Weller must be denied. I simply told Weller as I do to everyone, that Vichy does not represent the real France and that the strategic importance of North Africa is considerable. The rest is a series of Chinese whispers from Leopoldville to Brazzaville. I'm going to get Weller sacked.' In fact there had been a failure of the normal machinery to regulate de Gaulle's more outrageous outbursts. He had a new ADC in Brazzaville, François Coulet, who despite the reservations of de Gaulle's local director of information, allowed the text to go out uncensored. Looking back nearly sixty years, Claude Serreulles, who by now had over a year's experience of de Gaulle's ways, remarks: 'I thought it was a great mistake to let this cable go. We had the bad luck of having just lost one aide to de Gaulle, Courcel, and to have taken on a new one, Coulet, who had no experience of how to behave with de Gaulle, or how to manage him. If Courcel or I had been there, we would have retained the cable until the next day. And if on the next day it was still impossible to convince de Gaulle to withdraw it we would have waited for the next day, but we would never have let this cable go.' Serreulle's contemporaneous note in his diary for 30 August indicates the infuriation in the London office: 'Terribly annoying day for all of us. He made some unpardonable suggestions and said things about England that they'll never forget . . . All in all, a catastrophe.'

In the same diary entry Serreulles noted a further setback: 'De Gaulle learnt today in Brazzaville that Roosevelt refused to make any kind of contact with the Free French.' Serreulles was reporting a considerable disappointment. René Pleven had been in the United States in June, knocking heads together inside the shambolic Free French organization and doing the rounds of American Government departments in his efforts to win a lend-lease agreement. His greatest supporter was the Treasury Secretary, Henry Morgenthau, who found Pleven 'very able and charming.' Pleven told him: 'I want as much treatment or consideration for the Frenchmen who are fighting democracy's battle as you give the traitors who sold out to the Germans.' Morgenthau told Felix Frankfurter, a close friend of Roosevelt: 'It's like a breath of fresh air to talk to that kind of Frenchman.' But, despite Morgenthau's entreaties, the White House door was shut. 'I cannot see Pleven,' Roosevelt wrote to Morgenthau, 'the matter has been taken up before.' It was all very annoying for de Gaulle. From Brazzaville the British Consul General, Robert Parr, had reported that de Gaulle 'has stated his opinion that the United States will win this war, and he is apparently anxious to trim his sails accordingly.'

De Gaulle prepared to travel to London. Churchill had wanted him to return weeks before for a face-to-face meeting after the row with Lyttelton. Now de Gaulle was in hotter water. The diplomats on both sides tried to lower the temperature. Parr, whose enthusiasm for de Gaulle was being strained by all the rows, told the Foreign Office: 'My impression is that, in addition to his physical fatigue, he is finding the moral responsibility and mental strain of his position more and more exhausting. Probably things might improve if he were able to take a rest.' In London, Maurice Dejean, de Gaulle's liaison with the British Government, told a Foreign Office official that 'General de Gaulle had no political experience whatever and was quite like a child in politics' but 'it would be a great pity if General de Gaulle ceased to be head of the movement.' Anthony Eden replied to Churchill's suggestion that de Gaulle was 'off his head' with a suitably soothing and flattering note: 'It may well be we shall find that de Gaulle is crazy: if so, he will have to be dealt with accordingly. If, however, he shows indications of repentance, I hope that you will not underestimate your power to complete the cure. He has a real and deep respect for you which he does not extend to any of our military commanders.' Eden was now de Gaulle's most important supporter in the British Government. He believed that Britain needed a strong France to emerge after the war as the first line of defence in Europe and he was convinced that only de Gaulle was the right leader to achieve this.

Churchill was unimpressed with all the emollience. On 30 August, the day before de Gaulle touched down, he sent a rocket through Whitehall. Instructions were sent that:

1. No-one is to see General de Gaulle.

2. No English authority is to have any contact with him when he arrives.

3. If he asks to see Sir A Cadogan, Sir A Cadogan should not see him.

4. If the occasion demands, it may be conveyed to him that a most serious situation has a risen with which the Prime Minister is dealing in person.

General de Gaulle is to stew in his own juice for a week if necessary.

Senior Foreign Office officials feared that a break was in the offing. One wrote that 'the French people would hardly know what to think if de Gaulle, the only Frenchman of note who's standing up and fighting the Germans, were to be eliminated.' Aware of these trembles, Churchill made clear that, while de Gaulle was to be frozen out, limited contacts with the Free French could be maintained, but 'a chilling and dilatory attitude should be adopted towards all requests made by the Free French.'

On 1 September, Claude Serreulles drew the short straw of meeting de Gaulle at the airport. He recorded their reunion in his diary: 'As usual he stayed as silent as a mouse until he got into his offices in Carlton Gardens. He was completely conscious that the harmful declarations he had made were crashing down around him. He shouted all day about the English . . . He wouldn't stop repeating: "we're going to lose the war with such people . . . They're no good rascals."' The next day de Gaulle met Churchill's personal assistant, Desmond Morton. When Morton questioned him about one particularly obstreperous telegram de Gaulle admitted that he was 'in a violent temper at the time.'

While de Gaulle let it be known that he regretted the newspaper interview, even though he denied saying the words attributed to him, he was unrepentant on his disputes with the British in Syria. He announced that he wished to broadcast to France on the BBC; the response came back that, in accordance with the Prime Minister's instructions, facilities were to be denied him. De Gaulle simply stated that he would withdraw all Free French personnel from the BBC. As the day of his summit meeting with Churchill, set down for 12 September, drew near, the Whitehall airwaves were fizzing. On its eve John Colville noted: 'There is much speculation on the interview which the P.M. is to have with de Gaulle tomorrow. Sparks will fly, but de Gaulle apparently thinks he can appease the P.M. by playing the "Soldier of France", etc. Meanwhile he continues to use very anti-British language in his conversations with others.'

Just before 3pm on the afternoon of 12 September, General de Gaulle approached 10 Downing Street. It is impossible to resist quoting Colville's delectable account of what transpired. 'Churchill informed me that when de Gaulle arrived he would rise and bow slightly but would not shake hands with him . . . No doubt as a supreme mark of disapproval, he announced that he would not speak to him in French, but would converse through an interpreter. "And you," he said, "will be the interpreter". Punctually at 3pm the General arrived. Churchill rose from his chair in the middle of the long Cabinet table, inclined his head slightly and gestured to the selected seat opposite him. De Gaulle seemed quite unabashed. He walked to his chair, sat down, gazed at the Prime Minister and said nothing. "General de Gaulle, I have asked you to come here this afternoon". Churchill stopped and looked fiercely at me. "Mon General", I said, "je vous ai invité de venir cet après-midi". "I did not say

Mon General", interrupted the Prime Minister, "and I did not say I have invited him". Somehow I stumbled, with frequent interruptions, through the next few sentences. Then it was de Gaulle's turn. After the first sentence he turned to me and I interpreted. "Non, non", he interjected, "ce n'est pas du tout le sens de ce que je disais." But it was. Churchill said it was clear to both of them that if I could not do better than that I had better find somebody who could.'

Another interpreter was found and the meeting began with formal hostility, Churchill complaining about de Gaulle's trail of Anglophobia, de Gaulle complaining about the attitude of British officials in Syria. Then the second interpreter too was asked to leave. The two men were left alone. John Colville waited outside, 'An hour slipped away and I began to fear violence. I tried to eavesdrop, but because the Prime Minister alleged that the noise from the Private Secretaries' room interrupted the deliberations of the Cabinet, double doors had recently been installed. I could hear nothing. I walked out into the hall and tried on General de Gaulle's cap, registering surprise at the remarkable smallness of his head. I did my best to concentrate on the papers on my desk. I had decided it was my duty to burst in, perhaps with a bogus message, in case some dire act had been committed. Perhaps they had strangled each other? Just then the bell rang and I went in to find the two of them sitting side by side with amiable expressions on their faces. De Gaulle, no doubt for tactical purposes, was smoking one of the Prime Minister's cigars.'

In the midst of such rediscovered harmony, Churchill did insist on one thing: that de Gaulle should form a French National Committee to avoid the charge that he was authoritarian, an allegation that de Gaulle rejected. Of course, Churchill's intention was to clip de Gaulle's wings. De Gaulle promised to give the 'utmost weight' to this advice. Churchill, always a bad hater and quick to forgive, circulated a note, affirming his faith in his troublesome protégé. Exuding optimism, he concluded that de Gaulle's 'character and personality may yet prove him to be a greater man than recent events have caused some to suppose.'

On day of the Downing Street summit, Admiral Leahy had a long meeting with Pétain and Darlan in Vichy. They renewed all the old Vichy gambits designed to show that de Gaulle lay at the bottom of every trouble. Darlan claimed that, by attacking Pétain personally, the London Gaullist radio was playing into German hands. He suggested that its campaign to incite revolution against the Vichy regime would soon result in a Nazi occupation of all France after which the German Army might proceed on into North Africa with nothing to stop them. This was the purest whimsy; Hitler may sometimes have had such thoughts, but they had nothing to do with Gaullist broadcasts. However, the tone of Leahy's report suggested that he gave it credence. And he faithfully reported Pétain's view that de Gaulle was 'a viper that he had warmed in his bosom'.

In London the snakes were active in the Carlton Gardens' undergrowth. Encouraged by Churchill's insistence that de Gaulle should at least be subdued, Admiral Muselier now attempted a coup against his leadership, suggesting that he should be President of the new London committee, in charge of 'National Defence, Merchant Navy, and Armament.' He suggested that his friend, Professor Labarthe, whose espionage activities for Russia at least meant that he was now working for the Allies, should become head of 'Political Direction and Propaganda.' De Gaulle would be permitted to continue as

President of the Movement worldwide. De Gaulle thought Muselier was unreliable and had previously sacked Labarthe. Determined not to lose control of London, he slapped Muselier down. Muselier retaliated by saying that he was going to secede with the Free French navy and join the British.

Churchill intervened, insisting that the council should be broadly representative; that de Gaulle should be guided by it; and that Muselier should stop being disruptive. Once again Whitehall crackled. Colville wrote: 'A breach between de Gaulle and Muselier threatens to cause a public rift in the movement. De Gaulle is autocratic and right wing; Muselier is a Liberal (and a very loose living one) who wants de Gaulle's powers to be delegated to a Council. The P.M., who is heartily sick of the Free French, ended by handing the whole matter over to the reluctant Eden.' Under such pressure, Muselier gave in and agreed to continue to serve under de Gaulle. De Gaulle went about appointing his committee and told Claude Serreulles that he was 'very grateful to the English for the solid support that they have given him.'

On 26 September, *The Times* published the committee's names. Churchill realized that he had been sold a pup, venting his anger at Eden: 'This is very unpleasant. Our intention was to compel de Gaulle to accept a suitable Council. All we have done is to compel Muselier and Co to submit themselves to de Gaulle. It is evident that our weight in the immediate future must be thrown more heavily against de Gaulle than I had hoped would be necessary. I am renewing my directions that he is on no account to leave the country.' A week later a report reached the Foreign Office from reliable Free French sources that de Gaulle had been saying, 'Since the English have let me down, I turn to the Americans . . . Since the Americans are probably as bad as the English, I turn to the Soviet Union.'

De Gaulle was unrepentant about the hard-line tactics he had been employing since June. Throughout these bitter months, his colleagues in London had constantly worried that their leader was throwing it all away and that their movement would be excommunicated by the British. De Gaulle, standing astride his new committee and with Britain apparently bowing to his every demand, felt vindicated, even triumphant. He told them: "Our grandeur and our force consist uniquely in the intransigence we show in defending the rights of France. We will need that intransigence until we cross the Rhine."

For once, in Free French affairs, a season of calm now passed by. In November 1941, after the prolonged lobby begun by Pleven, the American Government even extended lend-lease to the Free French, but only to help them defend their territories against Nazi incursion. For all his pride, de Gaulle had been willing to ask for it, was happy to accept it and welcomed an American lend-lease official to Equatorial Africa with open arms. The decision also showed that Roosevelt, despite his apparent view of Free France as an infectious disease, was realist enough to see that it had a role to play in the war.

At the same time ugly clouds were forming over Vichy. Pétain and Darlan removed General Weygand from his post as Delegate General in North Africa. It was a crushing blow to Roosevelt's attempt to play the Vichy card. Churchill, whose soldiers were grappling with Rommel in the African desert, wrote to him that it would be 'disastrous if Weygand were to be replaced by some pro-Hun officer' and asked him to 'try your utmost at Vichy to preserve Weygand in his command.' He concluded his message by saying, 'It is now or never with the Vichy French and their last chance of redemption'. Roosevelt replied: 'I am taking steps to bring forcibly before Pétain the disastrous consequences of any action with regard to the authorities in North Africa which would result in aid to Germany.' Roosevelt was sufficiently disillusioned to write: 'We are reviewing our whole policy towards France.'

Leahy was told by Pétain that Weygand had been removed after Hitler had threatened otherwise to occupy the whole of France. If this really was the case, there was a curious irony. The Germans had broken the codes being used by Robert Murphy in his reports to Washington. These telegrams, which constantly exaggerated Weygand's will to resist, may have been the most serious evidence against him in German eyes, in which case Murphy had effectively helped to ditch the man he was rooting for. However, there was no other evidence for Pétain's claim. A more significant reason may have been a calculation by Darlan that Weygand was becoming a potential rival to his own power and had to be removed. After the Nazi invasion of Russia, Darlan, the canniest of Vichy operators, was already foreseeing the day when the fortunes of war might turn and North Africa might become an important power base which he would need for himself. No successor to Weygand was appointed, leaving Algiers in the control of Admiral Fenard, a loyal associate of Darlan.

The sacking of Weygand was driving Roosevelt towards a rethink about Vichy. Then on 7 December he was at war. The 'arsenal of democracy' had kept the Nazis away, only for the Japanese to end the dream that a world war could be won without American soldiers dying. Hitler recklessly declared war on the United States. Both Churchill and de Gaulle understood that the outcome of the war was effectively decided. Churchill later wrote, 'At this very moment I knew the United States was in the war, up to the neck and in to the death. So we had won after all!'

De Gaulle told an aide who brought him the news: 'Well, this war is over. Of course there will be more operations, battles and combats. But the war is over since the outcome is now known. In this industrial war, nothing can resist the might of American industry. From now on, the British will do nothing without Roosevelt's agreement.'

It seemed that the days of cultivating a Nazi puppet like Vichy must be drawing to a close. Yet Churchill himself still wanted the Americans to keep the connection going, writing to Roosevelt on 11 December: 'I see reports that Admiral Leahy is to leave Vichy. Trust your link with Pétain will not be broken meanwhile. We have no other worthwhile connection.' But what worthwhile connection could there be? For months Leahy had known his task was pointless. On 22 December, he wrote to Roosevelt: 'While I entertain for the Marshal a very high personal regard there is little if any reason to believe that he will do anything to help win the war or that he will offer any effective resistance to future German demands that are accompanied with the usual threats of punishment in the event of refusal to agree.' Despite everything, the admiration for Pétain, which seemed to defy all logic, persisted.

Two days later, on Christmas Eve 1941, all the American and British prejudices about de Gaulle, Vichy, and the Free French were suddenly forced together in a teapot typhoon whose epicentre was two tiny islands just off the Newfoundland coast.

St Pierre and Miquelon are not household names, but in French eyes they have symbolic value that goes far beyond their appearance; their 242 square kilometres are all that is left of a French Empire in North America which once stretched from Labrador to Louisiana. Today some six thousand French souls live there. They have their own Prefect, send deputies to the

French Assembly in Paris, and possess an excellent chocolate and wine shop, its produce all sold at French mainland prices. Numerous gendarmes on attachment from France stroll the streets, although there is no apparent crime. However a few years ago the independent-minded locals took against the Prefect and put him out to sea in a boat; now he is better protected. St Pierre even has a new airport to keep France one step ahead should oil be discovered in local waters.

St Pierre's harbour can be a forbidding place. A few miles to the south the cold waters of the Labrador current collide with the warmth of the Gulf Stream, resulting in a veil of fog and a coastline littered with shipwrecks. These days it is quiet, but over one hundred years ago St Pierre was the busiest cod fishing port on the Atlantic seaboard. Then large trawlers and changed fishing techniques savaged the little islands' economy. In the 1920s prohibition recharged the economy. St Pierre, outside the jurisdiction of the United States, became the bootleggers' transit station. Taxes were charged on alcohol exports and Al Capone became the islands biggest taxpayer, honouring them with a personal visit in 1927. But with the lifting of prohibition, the dog days returned. After the fall of France in 1940, the islands, to the displeasure of most of the inhabitants, stayed under Vichy's thumb, part of the deal America had negotiated with the local Vichy commander, Admiral Robert, after the fall of France.

Then, on the morning of Christmas Eve 1941, the people of St Pierre and Miquelon woke up to a surprise. Just after seven o'clock George Farvacque, a young man on his way to work, was told by a friend that that some ships had appeared on the horizon. Mlle. Augusta Lehenuen drew back the curtains in her bedroom and saw them waiting outside the harbour. Was it the

Vichy navy, dispatched by Admiral Robert to keep the islanders in order? Farvacque went down to the quayside and as the flotilla of three corvettes and a submarine drew nearer, he saw the Cross of Lorraine. Eugene Théault joined the gathering crowd and, for the first time, heard the music of the March of Lorraine. Admiral Muselier, who had emerged from the conspiracies of September still in charge of the Free French Navy, leapt ashore and announced that he had come to liberate the islands. 'It was the best Christmas present we ever had', says Farvacque, looking back sixty years. Immediately Muselier and his men captured the island's communications, the local radio transmitter and the Western Union office, and arrested the Governor. Conscious as always of publicity, the Free French had invited a journalist from the *New York Times*, Ira Wolfert, to join them. The gallant action of a few plucky, freedom-loving Frenchmen was about to hit the world.

Muselier cabled Churchill news of his mission: 'I have the honour to inform you that in compliance with order quite recently received from General de Gaulle and request of inhabitants I have proceeded this morning to Island St Pierre and rallied people to Free France and allied cause with enthusiastic reception.' Churchill was staying at the White House in Washington, having rushed there as soon as possible after Pearl Harbour. On the face of it, with America now enmeshed in the war, the spirited *attaque* of the Free French operation might have seemed cause for celebration. But instead the American Secretary of State, Cordell Hull, issued a thundering statement to the press. 'Our preliminary reports show that action taken by three so-called Free French ships at St Pierre & Miquelon was an arbitrary action contrary to agreement of all parties concerned and certainly without knowledge or consent in any sense of the United States Government.'

While his statement was hardly well-judged for garnering sympathy, Hull's irritation was, in the circumstances of the lead up to the Free French action, understandable. De Gaulle had been sizing up St Pierre and Miquelon for months. Back in February Emile Cormier had set out from St Pierre and hitched a ride across the Atlantic to join the Free French in London. Muselier asked him about the mood on the islands; Cormier replied that the local Vichy administrator was highly unpopular. Curiously he had solemnly promulgated Vichy's anti-semitic laws, even though no Jews lived on St Pierre. After Pearl Harbour, de Gaulle thought the time was right for a show of aggression and Muselier happened to be in Canada inspecting three Free French corvettes and the submarine *Surcouf* at port in Halifax, Nova Scotia, only a short voyage from St Pierre. De Gaulle sought British permission for the operation and both Churchill and the Admiralty were enthusiastic. However Churchill insisted that the Americans should be asked whether they had any objections. Roosevelt replied, after consultation with the State Department, that he did indeed strongly object. After Pearl Harbour the United States had reaffirmed its deal with Admiral Robert and Roosevelt had confirmed in a message to Pétain that the agreement of the 1940 *Havana Convention* would continue to be observed.

Roosevelt's objections were passed on to de Gaulle who showed a remarkable and instant compliance and said that he would cancel the operation. But de Gaulle then heard that, at America's request, the Canadian Government was sending monitors to oversee St Pierre's radio transmitter which, it was feared, might be used to give Nazi U-boats the whereabouts of allied shipping. The news that Canada, part of the British Empire, was about to enter St Pierre, part of the French Empire, prompted an instant U-turn. On 18 December, de Gaulle sent the fateful order to Admiral Muselier: 'We know for certain that the Canadians intend to destroy a radio station at St Pierre. Therefore, I order you to carry out rallying of Miquelon Islands with means at your disposal and without saying anything to the foreigners.' The foreigners were, of course, his allies, the British and Americans. Having bowed to Roosevelt's wishes only two days before, it was an extraordinarily rash message which de Gaulle, even in his memoirs, never managed to explain satisfactorily. He lamely stated, 'Perhaps, on my side, I had provoked it in order to stir up the bottom of things, as one throws a stone into a pond.' It was some stone, some pond, and some provocation.

In London de Gaulle was delighted with Muselier's coup and treated Hull's press statement about the 'so-called' Free French with pleasurable disdain. He cabled Muselier: 'Very secret. The storm that recently brewed in the State Department in Washington through the rallying of St Pierre, cannot worry us. The English are totally satisfied. Vichy are furious. The State Department are upset because it comes from the fact that they made an unofficial arrangement with Admiral Robert. We threw a spanner in the works.' Despite Hull's infuriation it seemed at this early stage that the incident might just blow away. The Canadian Prime Minister, Mackenzie King, was also in Washington and Churchill sent a relaxed message back to London: 'I agreed with President that Mackenzie King and Hull should work out a solution and present it to us. Do not think any serious difficulty will arise.' Churchill had more important business. This was his chance to impress American political and public opinion and on Boxing Day he addressed, for the first time, the

American Congress with characteristic pugnacity. "Here we are together facing a group of mighty foes who seek our ruin," he orated, "here we are together defending all that to free men is dear." That night Churchill, while trying to open a stiff bedroom window, felt a pain over his chest and arms and became short of breath. He had suffered a mild heart attack about which his travelling doctor, Charles Moran, decided to tell no one, including his patient.

Despite Churchill's hopes, even the greater concerns of the war could not prevent Hull from maintaining his anger. He summoned the British Ambassador to Washington, Lord Halifax, who mildly suggested that the matter could be dropped, and told him:

'According to you we should ratify the unlawful action of the Free French, taken in absolute violation of their pledges to Great Britain which means that the United States would have to throw over the entire problem of Vichy and French Africa which we've been nursing for a considerable period.' It was a bizarre piece of logic from an irate man who was clearly not in a rational mood. Churchill tried to smooth things over, telling Hull he would apply a headmasterly rebuke to his wayward pupil: 'I am prepared to take de Gaulle by the back of the neck and tell him he has gone too far and bring him to his senses. He has on more than one occasion behaved in a troublesome way.' There was a long historical precedent which helped to explain Hull's stubbornness. For a century and a half the United States had operated a principle of 'No Transfer' which stipulated that no territory in North America should be transferred from one sovereignty to another without its consent. Even if this less than democratic policy was in the back of Hull's mind, such a strict application in these circumstances remained odd.

While Hull was raising the stakes, so too was de Gaulle, cabling Churchill with his contempt for what he saw as the American Government's appeasement: 'I am afraid that this sort of preference shown publicly by the US Government for those guilty of collaboration will make an unfortunate impression on Free French supporters. It does not seem right to me that in war the prize should go to the apostles of dishonour.' Churchill replied that he had pleaded de Gaulle's case 'to our friends in the United States.' However, while admonishing his pupil for his precipitate action, he was still confident that he had managed to smooth things over: 'Your having broken away from agreement about Miquelon and St Pierre raised a storm which might have been serious had I not been on the spot to speak to the President.'

Hull, however, was not to be denied. On 28 December, he remonstrated with Churchill again: 'I pointedly accused de Gaulle of being a marplot acting directly contrary to the expressed wishes of Britain, Canada, and the United States, and I asked the Prime Minister to induce him to withdraw his troops from the St Pierre and Miquelon islands.' Churchill replied that if Hull insisted on such a request it would impair his relations with the Free French. Hull retorted that the presence of the Free French on the islands, without doing anything about it, jeopardised his relations with the Vichy Government. He even brought out the standard line from Leahy in Vichy, reporting Darlan's claim that de Gaulle's action at St Pierre would lead the Axis to occupy French North Africa 'in order that it may be protected against a similar invasion.' Hull passed this on to Roosevelt, warning him that this was just the beginning of 'ominous and serious developments' to come. It was all grossly exaggerated.

Hull was now in the firing line of the American press and

public alike for appeasing the collaborationist Vichy regime. His initial remarks about 'so-called' Free French ships brought hostile letters to the 'so-called' Secretary of State and his personal dignity was at stake. There were particular reasons for Hull's sensitivity. He had been Secretary of State since 1932 and, confining himself to abstruse questions of trade policy, had never had to suffer the brickbats of Roosevelt's 'left-wing' New Dealers. Personal criticism was therefore a novelty for the white-haired, distinguished-looking former judge from Tennessee who was now a rather vain grandee of the Democrat Party. Politically, the onset of war had left him a forlorn figure in Roosevelt's administration. The State Department, and Hull in particular, were always something of a running joke inside Roosevelt's *ménage* and, once it had failed to forestall war, there was nothing much for it to do. But Hull, by stoutly opposing any threat to the Vichy policy was, in the light of the Free French action, able to show that he still counted.

Hull's stubbornness was now compounded by Churchill himself. In a speech on 30 December to the Canadian Parliament in Ottawa he condemned the men of Vichy who 'lay prostrate at the foot of the conqueror' and lavished praise on de Gaulle and his Free French who 'continued to fight on' and 'would not bow their knees.' De Gaulle was delighted, cabling Churchill: 'What you said yesterday about France at the Canadian Parliament has touched the whole French nation. *Du fond de son malheur, la vieille France espère d'abord en la vieille Angleterre.*'

Hull was more dyspeptic than ever, all the more infuriated because Churchill himself had encouraged America to keep its link with Vichy and was now making political capital out of attacking it. Hull wanted to respond publicly, justifying the Vichy policy to his American accusers, but, although the row was unabated a full week after the Free French action, Roosevelt was still inclined to let it all drop. He told Hull that he thought it 'inadvisable to resuscitate this question by making a statement; that the French Admiral has already declined to leave St Pierre-Miquelon; that we cannot afford to send an expedition to bomb him out.' At the New Year's Day lunch with the President, Churchill tried to laugh it all off. He told Roosevelt:

"You're being nice to Vichy, we're being nice to de Gaulle. That's a fair division of labour."

Roosevelt answered: "Leave it to Hull and Halifax."

"Hell, Hull and Halifax," muttered Churchill.

Nevertheless Roosevelt was beginning to indicate that it was perhaps not quite so amusing after all. New Year's Day saw the Declaration of the United Nations of Allies against the Axis. At one stage Roosevelt thought of finding a way to associate the Free French with the Declaration; by the time it was signed they had been excluded. The next day Hull, making sure that Roosevelt was present, protested again to Churchill, saying that his remarks about Vichy and the Free French 'were highly incendiary and had brought far-reaching injury to me and the State Department.' A few days later Halifax reported to the Foreign Office that Hull 'stated at length how aggrieved he felt over the fact that abuse of the meanest kind was being hurled at him and the State Department in connection with this matter and that while he was the victim of these attacks His Majesty's Government stood by silently and "took the benefits".'

Back on St Pierre, Admiral Muselier had organised a plebiscite which resulted in over ninety-five per cent support of the Free French. Local democracy meant little back in Washington where Hull was now drafting an agreement which would keep the islands neutral but under joint British, Canadian and

American control until the end of the war when they would be returned to France. Churchill said he would agree, but only if de Gaulle agreed. The idea that account should be taken of de Gaulle's views was enough to send Hull to the brink. On 11 January, he sent an ultimatum to the President. 'The St Pierre-Miquelon incident strikes at a serious and fundamental phase of this Government's policy in relation to the Western hemisphere. At a time when this country is called upon to put forth its total war effort on two oceans, an outside element has chosen this moment to inject itself into this area, jeopardising the whole structure of inter-American relations.' The implication was that it was time for the President to rally round his Secretary of State; Hull even drafted a letter of resignation.

Roosevelt, whether he liked it or not, was now embroiled. While he did not take Hull seriously, politically he could not afford to lose him. In 1940, Hull had believed that he was Roosevelt's anointed successor and had felt betrayed by Roosevelt's decision to stand again for President, believing it was orchestrated by left-wingers like Harry Hopkins, whom he despised. It was another cause of Hull's wounded pride but he had rallied round and became a powerful force in Roosevelt's re-election campaign. It was time to repay loyalty and, in any case, an embittered resignation from a trusted party servant five weeks after Pearl Harbour would have been a disaster. Roosevelt now leaned on Churchill who cabled his Foreign Secretary in London, Anthony Eden, insisting that Hull's proposed agreement on St Pierre must now be accepted. The President, he wrote, had raised the issue with him as an urgent matter and the Hull agreement was a reasonable compromise. 'This means,' he told Eden, 'that you should tell de Gaulle that this is our settled policy and that he must bow to it.

I cannot believe that he will refuse. If he were to, they are in a mood here to use force – i.e. the battleship *Arkansas* which the President mentioned or starvation without stint.'

In less than a fortnight Roosevelt had moved from a shrug of the shoulders to a threat to take the islands by force. De Gaulle was threatening the most vital plank of Churchill's policy, his relationship with the American President. 'It is intolerable,' he told Eden, ' that the great movement of events should be obstructed, and I shall certainly not intervene to save de Gaulle or other Free French from the consequences.' Unlike the President, who was responsible to no-one but himself, Churchill was only first among equals in the British Cabinet and Eden replied that the Cabinet would feel the greatest reluctance in coercing de Gaulle: 'It would be impossible to justify this to public opinion here.' Churchill retorted: 'If de Gaulle will not settle on these terms, I shall authorise the issue of the amended communiqué, and it will be for the United States to enforce it – which they will certainly do . . . and will not hesitate to use whatever force is necessary. You may tell de Gaulle this from me . . . This business must be settled.'

Eden summoned de Gaulle who, predictably, rejected Hull's agreement. The whole point of St Pierre's liberation was to attach it to the Free French war effort and sitting out the war under Allied control was also an affront to French sovereignty. Eden asked de Gaulle what would happen if American warships moved in to St Pierre. "Our people would have to open fire," replied de Gaulle though, with a twinkle in his eye, he suggested that it would not come to this with the democracies. Eden cabled de Gaulle's refusal to Churchill and on 14 January, three full weeks after the incident, Churchill was forced to confess his deep embarrassment to the President: 'I have encountered very strong and unanimous resistance in the Cabinet. I therefore suggest to you that I have a try, when I get back, to make de Gaulle drop or modify these objectionable reservations, and I was very glad and relieved when you told me that you thought the matter might stand over till I have returned. This is only on a par with all the consideration which you have shown us.'

Back in London Churchill prepared for his showdown with de Gaulle. It was preceded by a note of caution from his Foreign Secretary: 'The trouble is that de Gaulle sees himself in the role of Joan of Arc, liberating his country from Vichy. His war is a private war against Vichy and his co-operation with the Allies is secondary in his mind . . . I continue, however, to be uneasy at the prospect of your threatening to break with him on the issue of the communiqué. The islands have now rallied to him . . . De Gaulle knows very well that he is on strong ground here and that the great majority of people in this country, and no doubt a considerable section of American opinion, support him.' After strong arm-twisting from Churchill, de Gaulle finally agreed that a communiqué, saving Hull's face, could be published. It never actually was. Hull eventually cooled down and St Pierre remained under Free French control. But at their meeting Churchill showed his anger at de Gaulle. The Frenchman had asked him whether the agreement meant that the islands still belonged to France. "I do not know what you mean by France," replied Churchill. "There is the France represented by your comparatively small movement, there is Vichy France, and the France of the unfortunate inhabitants of the occupied territory." De Gaulle protested that Hull's proposals were contrary to his agreement with the British of August 1940. Witheringly, Churchill answered: "That agreement was based on a hope, which has since proved false, that you would be able to rally an impressive number of Frenchmen. As the agreement stands, it is entirely in de Gaulle's favour without corresponding benefit to His Majesty's Government."

De Gaulle's single-mindedness had won out, but he was playing a risky game, ignoring the old diplomatic adage that it is dangerous to play little tricks on great powers. To his supporters and colleagues he had once again proved his strength. On 31 January, Claude Serreulles noted: 'We all know this man has his downsides but his intellectual strength is extraordinary. The General lives alone in his Olympic-like solitude. He thinks alone, he decides alone . . . but he does think and he does decide!' The President and the Prime Minister were less enamoured. As together they planned the future of the war, with France and its empire at the centre of their thoughts, affection for de Gaulle would not be playing a major part in their thinking.

CHAPTER EIGHT
CHURCHILL'S PRISONER

In his history of the war Churchill made light of the St Pierre incident, writing that Hull 'pushed what was little more than a departmental point far beyond its proportions.' Of his own attitude, he baldly stated: 'Strongly urged by our Foreign Office, I supported General de Gaulle and "so-called" Free France.' To use a modern phrase, Churchill was being 'economical with the truth'. He was, in fact, much displeased and his displeasure would multiply as the troubles with de Gaulle rolled on.

The first provocateur was Admiral Muselier, the hero of St Pierre. While his Free French colleagues fêted him on his return to London, the voyage back across the Atlantic had filled the admiral with dark thoughts of rebellion. On 3 March, he announced that he was fed up with de Gaulle's dictatorial tendencies, which, over St. Pierre, had marred his relations with the Americans, and that he was resigning from the French National Committee. De Gaulle instantly sacked him from the command of the Free French Navy and put a new admiral in charge, at which Muselier declared that he was taking the Navy with him to fight alongside the British. The history of the previous autumn was repeating itself.

De Gaulle's opponents in London and, more importantly, the First Lord of the Admiralty, A.V. Alexander, lined up behind Muselier, insisting that he must retain his command. The War Cabinet decided to support Alexander. Eden, who was unhappy with the decision, conveyed it to de Gaulle, pointing out the serious consequences if Muselier were not reinstated. De Gaulle replied that Muselier was an unbalanced drug-taker and, ignoring Eden's warning, put him under house arrest for thirty days, as he was entitled to do under his agreements with the British Government. He was also entitled to ask the British authorities to enforce the arrest and promptly did so. The British went silent and de Gaulle retreated to his house in the country. From there he wrote a secret testament to be read to the French people in the event of the irrevocable break that would result if the War Cabinet continued to support Muselier. In it he cast doubts on the 'genuineness' of the British as allies and quoted Syria and the Muselier affair as two in a series of pressures and abuses which had been heaped upon him by the British. As in the past and as it would be in the future, Eden rescued him, finally winning the argument in full cabinet against Alexander. Muselier stayed sacked and was prevented from contacting anyone in the Free French Navy for thirty days.

It all left a sour taste. One senior Free Frenchman, Pierre Brossolette, remarked to a colleague: "The General must constantly be reminded that our enemy number one is Germany. For if he followed his natural inclination it would be Britain." De Gaulle's temper was further irritated by a bout of malaria, caught during his travels to Africa. This did not stop him wishing to return there for an inspection of his territories, but he was still under a travel ban, first imposed by Churchill after the autumnal rows of the previous year. De Gaulle relied on the British to supply a plane to fly him out of England and the ban was enforced simply by producing an ingenious variety of reasons as to why transport could not be made available. On 10 April, Eden wrote to Churchill asking him to lift the ban, arguing that, with the Muselier affair patched up, 'I doubt whether it would be wise for us to stand in the way of his visiting his own territories.' The note was returned with Churchill's hand-written comment, 'I think it would be most dangerous to let this man begin again his campaign of Anglophobia in which he indulged when last in Central Africa, to which he is now more than ever attracted.' Five days later Churchill's assistant, Desmond Morton, gave him fuller reasons for Eden's request. Churchill simply responded: 'He must not go.'

On 24 April, Morton told Churchill that André Tixier, de Gaulle's representative in Washington, was reported to have said, somewhat disloyally, that de Gaulle "considers himself to have been suppressed by the British and insulted by the Americans. If he gets to Brazzaville in this mood M. Tixier considers that he may attempt any sort of madness." This was grist to Churchill's mill; he noted, 'This is what I have long feared, and explains why I have given directions (some months ago) to prevent de G. leaving in any aeroplane from this country.' Three days later Churchill ordered Morton to check that the 'utmost vigilance' was being exercised to stop de Gaulle escaping. Morton conveyed this to the service chiefs and M.1.5, reporting back to Churchill: 'In each case I have made a special point of the absolute necessity for preventing General de Gaulle getting any notion that we are taking special precautions against his slipping away.'

De Gaulle was Churchill's prisoner. Yet the British Prime Minister neither broke with him nor ceased to admire him. Before Christmas, there were hints that Roosevelt too might at last be feeling twinges of regard for de Gaulle. He had begun to understand the hopelessness of treating with Pétain and granted the Free French lend-lease. But, after Churchill's stay in

A characteristic portrait of General Charles de Gaulle.

Winston Churchill in a typical wartime pose.

Admiral William Leaky and Franklin Roosevelt.

The famous Casablanca conference. Roosevelt, de Gaulle and Churchill are well known, but lesser so is General Giraud, far left.

St Pierre, off Newfoundland, today.

Secretary of State Cordell Hull with Roosevelt, 1941.

De Gaulle in New York with Mayor La Guardia, July 1944.

Generals Giraud and de Gaulle, North Africa 1943.

Roosevelt and his commander of US forces in Europe, General Eisenhower.

'The big three' at the Malta conference, de Gaulle is conspicuous by his absence.

Washington, he had swung firmly back to his Vichy policy. This was not merely a result of St Pierre, though that, reinforced perhaps by late night conversations over the whisky and brandy bottles with Churchill on de Gaulle's histrionics, can only have confirmed his suspicions of the Free French. It was also a result of the two men's strategic discussion on how best to advance the war.

After Pearl Harbour Churchill had headed for Washington with all the speed of an athlete sprinting from the blocks. He was desperate to ensure that Roosevelt would not divert America's strength into the war with the Japanese in the Pacific, but instead preserve the conquest of Germany as his priority. Instead of a frontal assault on the Atlantic beaches of France, which Churchill, ever mindful of the carnage of the First World War trenches, believed would result in appalling casualties, he played to Roosevelt's fondness for his personal Vichy policy by suggesting that Hitler could be attacked through the soft underbelly of North Africa and the Mediterranean. This also had the advantage for Churchill of protecting Britain's imperial interests in the Middle East. Before his arrival in Washington Churchill had written to Roosevelt: 'We ought . . . to try hard to win over French North Africa and now is the moment to use every inducement and form of pressure at our disposal upon the Government of Vichy and the French authorities in North Africa.' Unhelpfully for de Gaulle, Churchill had added: 'Our relationship with General de Gaulle and the Free French Movement will require to be reviewed. Hitherto the United States have entered into no undertakings similar to those compromised in my correspondence with him. Through no particular fault of his own he has not been of any important help to us. Indeed, his Movement has created new antagonisms in French minds.' Churchill was willing to undermine his protégé for the greater prize of aligning Roosevelt to his overall strategy.

A clandestine approach was made to General Weygand, now living in retirement in France after his removal from North Africa. Precisely because of its covert nature, Admiral Leahy was unable to act as intermediary and the third secretary at the American Embassy in Vichy, Douglas McArthur, was entrusted with the mission. He met Weygand at a hotel in Grasse on 20 January and delivered a hand-written note from Roosevelt, which contained his *bona fides* and a large dose of flattery. He then gave the main import by word. McArthur painted in the new developments of the war: German reverses in Russia; British successes in Cyrenaica, which secured the Suez Canal; and the entry of the United States into the war. He then outlined various scenarios of German aggression which might impel America to move into French North Africa. In that eventuality, asked McArthur on Roosevelt's behalf (and Churchill's too, though his name could not be mentioned for obvious reasons), would Weygand consider going to North Africa and, in co-operation with the United States, rally resistance to the Nazis, as there was no-one so well equipped as he?

McArthur was told to make it clear that 'the United States has no desire whatever to replace France in North Africa, nor to see the British or the supporters of General de Gaulle take over the area.' Weygand politely declined even to consider any such possibility and said he must inform Pétain of the conversation, which he duly did. After the failure of McArthur's mission, Leahy noted in his diary: 'I cannot escape a belief that it will become known to others, and that it will be transmitted to the German authorities.' The trail that had begun with Robert Murphy's optimistic assessment of Weygand's fighting spirit a year before had finally petered out with the defeatist of 1940 sneaking to the collaborationist Marshal. In his memoirs, Murphy still managed to view Weygand as a patriotic and gallant old soldier.

Pétain was in no mood to help either. At the end of January, Leahy sounded him out on whether he would accept military aid from the United States if Germany or Italy invaded French North Africa. Roosevelt reported to Churchill that 'the Marshal made the somewhat cryptic reply "If we ask for it"'. Roosevelt's cultivation of Pétain's regime on the French mainland was becoming more futile than ever. In February, Pétain failed to respond to his demand never to give military aid to Hitler. In April, the pro Nazi, Pierre Laval, replaced Darlan as head of Pétain's government, although Darlan remained Commander-in-Chief of all French armed forces and heir apparent to Pétain. Though Leahy was recalled to Washington for 'consultations', Roosevelt continued to maintain the embassy in Vichy.

Churchill believed that Laval's return might offer one last chance for Pétain and Darlan to retrieve themselves. He asked Roosevelt to offer them American and British support even if all they did was carry the French Fleet to Africa to coincide with an unopposed British landing. 'It seems to me that they ought to be offered blessings as well as cursings,' wrote Churchill. Roosevelt replied that it was best first to 'let the situation jell'. But in their hearts everyone knew that all of this was whistling in the wind. Any hopes for the Vichy policy would have to be concentrated on the Vichyites of North Africa. The only question was who, in Weygand's absence, might lead them. Ironically it was Churchill, not an American, who spotted a likely candidate. On 29 April he wrote to Roosevelt: 'I am highly interested in escape of General Giraud and his arrival at Vichy. This man might play a decisive part in bringing about things of which you had hope. Please tell me anything you know.' But Giraud's time was months away. The more immediate concern was the latest problem with another French General closer to home.

May 1942 was a depressing month for Churchill's prisoner, Charles de Gaulle. At 3am on the morning of 5 May 1942, de Gaulle received a telephone call from a press agency informing him that a British squadron was landing on the French island of Madagascar. De Gaulle was shocked: 'Our Allies were occupying a French possession by force without even having consulted with us!' The offence was all the greater since De Gaulle had been writing for six months to the British Chiefs-of-Staff and Churchill himself about the need for such an operation, suggesting that it should be conducted by Free French forces with British naval support.

Churchill had agreed the need for an invasion and, after Pearl Harbour, had become alarmed by stories that the United States was willing to guarantee recognition of the Vichy regime in Madagascar. Diego Suárez, the island's most important harbour situated on its northern tip, was an obvious temptation as a base for Japanese submarines seeking to destroy Allied shipping around the cape of South Africa. Vichy had already rolled over to allow the Japanese into French Indo-China and there was no reason to suppose that it would not do the same in Madagascar. Roosevelt assured Churchill that he would give no guarantees to Vichy on Madagascar and acquiesced in a British invasion.

By the time the expedition force set out from Durban, Churchill had decided there was no place for the Free French. There were strategic problems in ferrying Free French troops anyway and the experience of Dakar and Syria had shown that their presence only reinforced the will of Vichy troops to fight.

But Churchill went one step further and decided that de Gaulle should not even be informed. It was a sorry indication of how far the trust of June 1940, the hopes of Dakar, and even the initial co-operation in Syria had vanished. For the British, the Diego Suárez operation was a triumph at a time when everything else in the war was grim. It was their first large-scale amphibious operation since the disaster of Gallipoli twenty-seven years before, which had been the cause of Churchill's downfall in the First World War. This time, despite fierce initial resistance, the commando landings, supported by bombardment from air and sea, worked like clockwork and Diego Suárez was quickly taken with fewer than four hundred British casualties. The political fall-out would be more severe.

On the day of the landings a communiqué was issued from Washington that 'the United States and Great Britain are in accord that Madagascar will, of course, be restored to France after the war or at any time that the occupation of Madagascar is no longer essential to the common cause of the United Nations.' Rather than seeing any consolation in this, de Gaulle immediately spied an Anglo-American conspiracy. On 11 May, he saw Eden who gave him the customary assurance that Britain had no designs on Madagascar and wanted it to be governed by Frenchmen. This raised an awkward question. Having captured Diego Suárez, Churchill was inclined to seek an accommodation with the local Vichy regime over the rest of the island as long as it guaranteed to keep the Axis powers out, rather than become bogged down in a long jungle campaign over its full nine hundred mile length. Negotiations about this would drag on until September when the continuing obduracy of the Vichy Governor persuaded Churchill that British and South African troops should take all of the island.

After the meeting with Eden, the British Government stated publicly that the Free French would play their due part in the administration of liberated French territory. For de Gaulle, this constituted an important undertaking, but it did not ally his suspicions over Madagascar. He would have been even more upset if he had known that just three days after the Diego Suárez operation, Sumner Welles, the Under Secretary at the State Department and Roosevelt's most trusted foreign affairs adviser, had told the British Ambassador, Lord Halifax: 'It is very clear to me that the Free French movement as represented by General de Gaulle and his associates is rapidly falling to pieces.' Public insult followed. On 30 May, a solemn ceremony took place in Washington to commemorate Memorial Day. At that very time a Free French brigade was putting up a heroic resistance against vastly superior German and Italian forces at Bir-Hakeim in Eastern Libya. Their action prevented the retreating British 8th Army from the threat of encirclement by Rommel's Afrika Korps. However, Vichy diplomats were invited to the Memorial Day ceremony and the Free French excluded. Raoul Aglion, one of de Gaulle's representatives in the United States, later wrote that 'these Vichy officials strutted about ... and were congratulated on the fierce resistance of the Free French at Bir-Hakeim.'

At the end of May Eden once again raised the lifting of de Gaulle's travel ban with Churchill, complaining that he was running out of reasons for refusing him a plane to visit his own territories. He continued: ' I induced him a month ago to postpone his proposed visit to Africa. I fear, however, that a further attempt on my part would merely increase his suspicions of us which are seldom far below the surface, and that we should find him even more difficult to deal with than he normally is. I hope you will agree that for the sake of your future relations with him it would be best to let him go.' Churchill's hand-written comment showed no mercy: 'I cannot agree. There is nothing hostile to England this man may not do once he gets off the chain.' At their next meeting, Eden tried to sell de Gaulle the line that his presence in London, and the advice he could offer his Allies, was far too valuable to permit of his absence at this crucial phase of the war.

De Gaulle knew it was all phoney. His reasons for discontent were multiplying. Britain wanted immediate elections in Syria and Lebanon; de Gaulle wanted to postpone them until the end of the war. Some American top brass had been in London for secret talks; de Gaulle rightly suspected that French North Africa was on the agenda. And he himself remained a captive. He later wrote of June 1942 in London: 'the members of the Government, the Ministries, and the British general staffs enclosed themselves in a thick atmosphere of secrecy, not to say mistrust.' The explosion came on 6 June. De Gaulle sent a 'strictly personal' telegram to his commanders in Africa and the Levant. It was sent in Free French code, but, as usual, it had to go via the Foreign Office, the Free French not having their own telegraph service in London. De Gaulle's tone and content were devastating: 'In agreement with the United States, the British are doing everything possible to dispossess us, as in the Madagascar affair. I am not disposed to remain associated with the Anglo-Saxon powers and I am today sending the British Government a warning to this effect. We must form a united front against all comers and have no relations with the Anglo-Saxons under any circumstances and at whatever cost. We must warn the French people and the whole world by radio of Anglo-Saxon imperialist designs. I have been asked to visit Beirut and Brazzaville, but the

British have prevented it.' So much for the efforts to keep his captivity secret.

Ironically Eden had just persuaded Churchill to grant de Gaulle an interview to discuss Madagascar. It took place four days after de Gaulle sent his furious telegram. When the two men got together, the atmosphere, as had happened before, was suddenly cordial. Churchill took the lead by congratulating de Gaulle on the magnificent conduct of his troops at Bir-Hakeim. They discussed Madagascar and Churchill explained his reasoning for excluding the Free French. De Gaulle pointed out that the appearance of negotiating with local Vichyites muddied the waters; Churchill protested his eternal friendship for France, which he only wanted to see restored in all its glory. De Gaulle reminded him that the Free French were the soul of such a France, as Churchill himself had recognized from the outset. De Gaulle complained of American hostility to him, arguing that the months of treating with people like Weygand only lulled the fighting spirit of Frenchmen. Churchill unconvincingly tried to explain America's hopes for Vichy but expressed his pleasure that France was recovering and regrouping around de Gaulle.

It all went famously well, Churchill assuring de Gaulle as he parted: "I shall not desert you . . . you can rely on me." The following day de Gaulle sent a further telegram to the recipients of the 6 June missive. This time he wrote: 'I had a satisfactory meeting with M. Churchill yesterday. I think that the Prime Minister and the British Government sincerely desire an improvement in our relationship. On the other hand, the US remains sullen.' Unfortunately the next day Churchill received a copy of the 6 June telegram, which had now been deciphered. He noted to Eden: 'So much for General de Gaulle. It is lucky he is not loose at Brazzaville.' There was a similar reaction from de Gaulle's own Commander in the Middle East, General Catroux. The British Commander-in-Chief in the Mediterranean had lunch with Catroux on 14 June and reported to the First Sea Lord: 'Catroux considers De Gaulle is at present so unbalanced that he may abolish or create neutrality of Free French movement and broadcast that Allied declaration and promises can no longer be trusted.'

Yet, on the outside, things were looking up. Bir-Hakeim had been a triumph, widely reported in the British and American press. On 18 June, the second anniversary of *L'Appel,* ten thousand Frenchmen and women crowded into the Albert Hall, and, after a rousing speech from their leader, launched into spirited renderings of *La Marseillaise* and the *Marche Lorraine.* At the end of June, Cordull Hull even issued a statement that the Government of the United States 'recognizes the contribution of General de Gaulle and the work of the French National Committee in keeping alive the spirit of French traditions and institutions' and promised 'all possible military assistance.' America sent two senior officers to London to be its representatives to the French National Committee. One of them, Admiral Harold 'Betty' Stark, a former Chief of Naval Operations, would become one of the most acute observers of de Gaulle's psychology. He was himself a calm and wise old bird, never provocative and always managing a judicious combination of tolerance and toughness. His diary entry of one of their early encounters tells it all: 'When de Gaulle started to get himself worked up I became even more calm and smiled a little broader than usual. I was told after that it had a very quieting effect on him. We all wound up smiling.' At one stage Eden mused to Stark that perhaps he might like to take on British relations with de Gaulle too.

Amidst these swirling currents, a momentous decision on the

future of the war in the West was about to be taken. On 18 June, Churchill arrived in Washington and flew the following morning to Hyde Park, the country seat of the Roosevelt family on the idyllic shore of the Hudson river. The two men were now showing an easy familiarity. Margaret Suckley observed their relationship at lunch on the day Churchill arrived. 'It was a fascinating lunch. One could only watch these two men talking. They were both in fine form, rested and playing on and with each other . . . There seemed to be real friendship and understanding between FDR and Churchill. FDR's manner was easy and intimate – His face humorous, or very serious, according to the subject of conversation, and entirely *natural*. Not a trace of having to guard his words or expressions, just the opposite of his manner at a press conference, when he is an actor on stage – and a player on an instrument, at the same time.' The President took Churchill for a scary drive around the grounds. Without the use of his legs, he relied on arm strength to apply the brakes and suggested that his nervous passenger feel his biceps, which had apparently been admired by a prize-fighter. As the car juddered to halts on various precipices overlooking the river, they continued to talk shop, Churchill believing that any comments on dangerous driving might interrupt the policy flow. The continuing strategic issue at stake was whether to concentrate on a cross-Channel operation to establish a bridgehead on the Cherbourg peninsula or an invasion of French North Africa. Churchill had always wanted the latter, but the American Chiefs-of-Staff, in particular General George Marshal, head of the Army, were lobbying hard for the former. Roosevelt veered towards the North Africa option with its chances of vindicating his Vichy policy but, by the end of the conference, the question remained unresolved.

As the choice hung in the balance, so did the future of de

Gaulle. If the Allies went for a cross-Channel operation he could be vital. In early 1942, Jean Moulin had been parachuted into France as de Gaulle's representative with a mission to unite the resistance inside France under de Gaulle's leadership. Despite the many different underground movements and the political span they covered, Moulin's mission was succeeding. It became clear by mid 1942 that the resistance largely viewed de Gaulle as its figurehead, even if some of its determined individualists were not yet inclined to take orders from him or anyone else. It was also known that in the region of three to four million French people were listening to Free French broadcasts on the BBC. Even if the United States would, for a long while, refuse to acknowledge it, a Gaullist constituency was building inside the mainland. However, if the French North Africa option was chosen, de Gaulle would be perceived by Churchill and Roosevelt as a hindrance. All their experience to date showed that the presence of the Free French would harm the prospects of the Vichy French coming over.

The chronology of what followed shows how this logic was remorselessly played out. On 13 July, the British Government agreed with de Gaulle that the Free French movement would henceforward be known by the name of 'Fighting France', consisting of all French people and territories which joined forces with the Allies in the fight against their common enemies. De Gaulle took this to mean that he would exercise authority over all parts of the French Empire as they joined the war. The next day 'Fighting France' held a Bastille Day parade in London, which was attended by the new Commander of American forces in Europe, General Dwight Eisenhower, who looked on in approval. On 22 July, the American Chiefs-of-Staff, over in London for the decisive summit with the British, agreed that the cross-Channel invasion should be dropped in favour of the French North Africa option, which was now given the code name 'Operation Torch'. The next day de Gaulle arrived with an interpreter for what he thought was a one to one meeting with Marshall to discuss Fighting France's contribution to the Allied war effort. Instead he found Marshall accompanied by Eisenhower, who would soon be named supreme commander of 'Torch', his future deputy, General Mark Clark, and two other American top brass.

The meeting was sticky from beginning to end. Champagne was laid on but de Gaulle did not partake of it. He told Marshall that he was placing at his disposal all Free French forces scattered throughout the world and that these fighters would joyfully welcome the opening of a second front. He asked what Marshall could tell him. Marshall was only able to give him polite nothings. De Gaulle then asked specifically what the plans were for the second front. Once again Marshall was noncommittal. At this point de Gaulle announced that he would not take up any more of Marshall's time, rose stiffly and walked out of the room. Mark Clark later wrote of de Gaulle that none of the Americans 'had been impressed with his diplomacy or personal charm.' But what on earth did they expect? They had just frozen de Gaulle out of the liberation of the French Empire. Five days later de Gaulle received the news that Churchill had no objection to his travelling to Africa and the Levant. The documents do not show whether the timing of the lifting of the travel ban was chance or coincidence. What is certain is that, as the planning for 'Torch' began in London, nobody wanted de Gaulle hanging around. The treatment of him had been cunning and ruthless.

De Gaulle had a friendly farewell meeting with Churchill and it is also true that, whatever the precise motives for the lifting of the travel ban, a succession of conversations during the previous weeks with the sympathetic Eden had softened de Gaulle's suspicions of the British. But now he had only had to sniff the Middle Eastern air for them to be renewed and the history of the previous year to be re-enacted all over again.

Syria and Lebanon had become a cesspool of national rivalries and personal jealousies. There was the running argument between Britain and de Gaulle over the timing of local elections and independence; the constant conflict between the British military need for stability and the Free French insistence on civilian control; the playing of the British and French against each other by local political leaders; and, underlying it all, de Gaulle's paranoia (for which there is no basis in British records) that Britain had long-term designs on establishing its leadership in the Levant. On top of all that, General Spears, the British Minster, and General Catroux, the Free French Governor, disliked each other and their wives were at daggers drawn.

De Gaulle touched down in Cairo on 7 August to find Churchill also there, stopping over on his trip to Moscow to see Stalin, and they had lunch together. The next day de Gaulle saw the British Minster of State, the Australian Richard Casey, who had succeeded Lyttelton. They argued over the need for elections and de Gaulle accused Britain of seeking to oust France from the Levant. It ended in a shouting match. This was unfortunate, as Casey had previously persuaded Churchill to recall his old friend, Spears, to London as an emollient gesture. Hearing of de Gaulle's behaviour, Churchill took his revenge by revoking the decision. That evening he called de Gaulle "insufferable".

Claude Bouchinet Serreulles recorded de Gaulle's foul mood as, after a general swipe at the feebleness of the British army, he launched into an attack on his private gallery of fools: 'His conversation turned to the Americans, "the Americans are no better! My opinion is made up on Roosevelt. He's a very good politician on internal matters. Cordell Hull, Sumner Welles? They're Chautemps (one of the June 1940 defeatists) and Baudouin. Cordell Hull is a stupid and proud old man. These are the men that surround Roosevelt! And then there's Leahy who has found his soulmate in Pétain!" The general came back to the English. This time I was literally trembling. "And these English beaten all over, turned out of the Far East, of India, badly threatened in the East, and yet it's these same English who are trying to kick the French out of Syria!"'

Ironically these same English were sitting on an offer which de Gaulle might appreciate. Discussions with the Vichy Governor of Madagascar had led nowhere and British and South African troops were preparing to take over the whole island. De Gaulle was to be told in confidence of the operation a few hours in advance and asked to have someone ready to take over as Governor-General. But the deal was put aside while the Levant tempest raged. The British were mounting a *quid pro quo*; de Gaulle would only get Madagascar if he played ball in Syria and Lebanon.

He was still showing no indication of doing so. Churchill, on his return from Moscow, again stopped over in Cairo and had lunch with Spears and the chief of the Imperial General Staff, Alan Brooke. Spears recorded Churchill's remark that he still liked de Gaulle for one thing, 'namely that when he came to see him just before the French collapse to ask him to send over all the British planes to France and Winston refused, de Gaulle hung back to tell him that he thought his decision was right.' However, the store of affection and admiration was clearly running dry: 'He said that de Gaulle was completely subservient with him but what was odious was his insufferable rudeness to anyone on a lower level ... Brooke, spitting with rage at de Gaulle, said the greatest public service I could render would be to knock him on the head.' De Gaulle was asked to return to London to discuss his differences with the British face-to-face with Churchill. He refused, saying that he was too busy.

On 3 September, Spears was visited by the acting American Consul who had just received startling news from the State Department in Washington. It had heard that de Gaulle was proposing to take over command in the Middle East in a week's time. Spears noted: 'We have often joked about the possibility of de Gaulle's doing this, but had not really thought he would be so crazy.' De Gaulle's colleagues in London, in particular the long-suffering Maurice Dejean who had responsibility for relations with the British government, were beginning to panic at his antics. Hearing of this, de Gaulle sent a telegram to another member of the French National Committee, René Pleven: 'In today's difficulties, I need to be upheld by the National Committee. I have a feeling that Dejean has once again been intimidated by those troublemakers in the Foreign Office. The solution always comes from firmness. Please keep me informed of Dejean's attitude.' A few days later he followed this with even stronger words: 'The fact in itself that our Allies do not let us know things and do not consult us is unforgivable and gives us the right to react as we can. We must not be troubled or intimidated ... The English have done everything to stop me from coming here. That shows you the kind of atmosphere there is.'

Much of this was seeping back to Washington and, on 11 September, Halifax reported back to London on an interview with Roosevelt: 'President spoke to me this morning about de Gaulle and said that apart from his recent troublesome behaviour he had been greatly disturbed by indications of de Gaulle's picture of himself after the war as head of a Provisional Government in France. He did not like this at all and plainly will not go any further to meet Fighting French at present.' Two days later de Gaulle did a typical public volte-face, extolling his and the Allies' solidarity in a radio broadcast. The next day, still refusing Churchill's request to return to London, he flew to Africa. Spears wrote: 'De Gaulle's sudden departure has taken everyone by surprise, including myself . . . He is no doubt patting himself on the back and telling himself how clever he is in that his policy has undoubtedly paid.' On that flight, Bouchinet Serreulles recorded a vignette which showed the overwhelming love of his nation which was de Gaulle's bedrock: 'We were going from Syria to French Africa in the plane. We saw on the map that we were entering French territory . . . The General suddenly became really enthusiastic and said, "Serreulles, look! We're in French territory!" he cried. His mind was in the clouds and then he suddenly cried, "look Serreulles, the vegetation is starting, what a wonderful country!"'

Finally de Gaulle agreed to return to London to see Churchill. Serreulles warned him against it. "I told him, you shan't be able to leave England again, you will be refused a plane, England will be a jail. But he thought he would be able to go to London for a fortnight or so and then back to Africa." On 25 September, De Gaulle returned to Britain, breezily confident that he would be able to sort things out with Churchill. After all, he had always been able to do so before. Three days later Morton heard from a Free French source that de Gaulle had been going around saying that, "he had only to make a sufficient nuisance of himself and the British give way." Eden sent

Churchill a long note in advance of the meeting, suggesting that: 'Occasion might be taken to deliver a homily on de Gaulle's general behaviour. We are tired of the series of crises into which, on the slightest pretext, he throws Anglo-Free French relations. He gives us more trouble than all the Allied governments in London put together.' Churchill was unlikely to need any prompting to deliver what might amount to rather more than a homily. However Eden registered the one growing guilt at the back of British minds, de Gaulle's exclusion from 'Torch': 'This will mean a crisis between us and de Gaulle.' Cadogan saw only one way to assuage the guilt, telling Eden that '*if* de Gaulle gives us guarantees about Syria we must honour our (implied) promise about Madagascar and let him in *at once.*'

At 5.30pm on the afternoon of Wednesday 13 September, de Gaulle once more arrived punctually at the door of 10 Downing Street. It was just over a year since John Colville had recorded the strange dénouement of the previous confrontation following a de Gaulle sortie into Syria and Lebanon. This time there was no Colville and no convivial smoking of peace cigars. The conversation is recorded in the matter-of-fact tones of a Foreign Office memorandum, which cannot hide that it was blunt and hostile. Eden remarked of de Gaulle's behaviour that he had seen 'nothing so rude since Ribbentrop.' All the old grievances about Syria, Lebanon and Madagascar were aired, exposing an apparently unbridgeable chasm between the two men. De Gaulle said that this very serious situation 'called into question the collaboration between France and England.' The Foreign Office record continues:

'THE PRIME MINISTER corrected General de Gaulle and said between General de Gaulle and England.

GENERAL DE GAULLE asked why we were discussing matters with him if he was not France.

THE PRIME MINSTER explained that all this was written down. General de Gaulle was not France but Fighting France.

GENERAL DE GAULLE maintained that he was acting in the name of France. He was fighting with, but not for England.'

As the meeting degenerated, Churchill said that he had hoped that they could conduct their campaigns together but that de Gaulle, 'not content with fighting Germany, Italy, and Japan, also wanted to fight England and America.' De Gaulle responded that he took this as a joke, but did not regard it as a very good one. As the conversation drew to an end Churchill told de Gaulle that he 'had shown marked hostility to us. Wherever he went there was trouble. The situation was now critical. It made him sad, since he admired the General's personality and record. But he could not regard him as a comrade or a friend.' Churchill concluded that matters must now take their course. General de Gaulle, 'had not shown the slightest desire to assist us, and he himself had been the main obstacle to effective collaboration with Britain and America.' The record ends with de Gaulle's final statement that, 'he would accept the consequences (je tiendrai les conséquences),' at which point he left the room.

It was a dreadful and bruising encounter. De Gaulle had gone to the ultimate in displaying the 'intransigence' he believed necessary to protect 'the rights of France'. Cadogan noted: 'Eden and P.M. had a pitched battle with de Gaulle – quite indecisive, I understand from Desmond Morton. On their instructions I put a stop on all outward telegrams from de Gaulle!' From their own perspectives, both men felt that they had right on their side. Now, for the first time in their relationship, the middle ground had disappeared. De Gaulle understood how far he had gone and, the following day, offered his resignation to the French National Committee if its members felt that he had overstepped the mark. They backed him one hundred per cent and Admiral Auboyneau even threatened to remove the Free French Navy from British command.

It was a mess from which there was no obvious escape. And all the time, behind de Gaulle's back, the planning of 'Torch' rolled on.

CHAPTER NINE
A BUMPY LANDING

At the beginning, the middle and the end of Operation 'Torch' was confusion, nerve, muddle, ingenuity and chance. This was nobody's fault. The shifting sands of North Africa created a fine dust of rivalry, intrigue, and shifting loyalties. Americans and British were working for the first time in a combined operation, with contrary military objectives and an ocean of difference in political perception. At the peak of this unstable mass of activity, partly reflecting and partly moulding the divergences beneath them, sat the Prime Minister and the President.

Planning for 'Torch' began at Norfolk House in St James's Square, London, in early August 1942. Although Eisenhower was not officially appointed overall commander until 14 August, he and his staff rapidly drew up a plan that would cater to both Churchill's and Roosevelt's aspirations. For the British the key was to link 'Torch' with the campaign against Rommel, which was hanging in the balance. While Churchill had been in Washington in June, news of the fall of Tobruk and the capture of 25,000 British prisoners had come through. It was a bleakly shattering moment. Churchill and General Alan Brooke had been standing beside Roosevelt at his desk in the Oval Office when Marshall walked into the room bearing a single piece of pink paper. Brooke never forgot the heartfelt display of sympathy from Roosevelt: 'I cannot remember what the actual words were . . . but there was not one word too much or one word too little.' Marshall immediately set about to see what American equipment could be sent to help the 8th Army, and three hundred Sherman tanks were soon on their way. Brooke felt that that this episode did much to create a bond of friendship between Churchill, himself, Roosevelt and Marshall which endured through the war. If the Prime Minister ever had a single experience with the President that came near to matching his baptism of fire with de Gaulle in June 1940, this was it.

The strategic upshot was a British desire to strike from the west at Rommel's rear to relieve the battered 8th Army which was holding on for grim life to the east. Therefore, 'Torch' made sense if there were landings in Algiers and points east along the coast to Bizerte, the crucial port at Tunisia's northern tip, rapidly followed by a full occupation of Tunisia. The Washington agenda, while seeing that Tunisia was an important objective, gave first priority to the occupation of Morocco and Algeria to ensure that they were immune from Axis attack. Roosevelt and the American Chiefs were particularly fearful that 'Torch' would provoke Spain to enter the war, or at the very least grant right of passage to Hitler to attack Gibraltar and open the gate to North Africa. This made them cautious about pushing too far into the Mediterranean. The British believed that there was no serious risk from Spain. However, the insuperable problem to this combination of objectives rapidly emerged; there were not enough landing craft, aircraft carriers and planes.

Throughout August the planning drifted along without a clear sense of direction from either Roosevelt or Churchill. The latter was away on his trip to Moscow, which included facing de Gaulle's latest antics during his stopovers in Cairo. Churchill arrived back in Britain fired with a new determination to make 'Torch' work, not merely because of Stalin's pressing need for a second front, but also because the carnage of the Dieppe raid of 19 August had proved to everyone, including the American Chiefs, that cross-Channel operations against bristling German shore defences could only be countenanced with hardened troops and overwhelming strength. Therefore 'Torch' had to be big and it had to work. When he returned to London, Churchill would discover to his horror that 'Torch' had gone into reverse.

The cooling off had come from Washington. Marshall, who was advising Roosevelt, had never liked 'Torch' anyway and the President himself was operating as always to a political agenda. Congressional elections were due in November and Roosevelt wanted to see a purely American operation with American troops carried out with no risk of defeat on a scale that would appear sufficient to satisfy Stalin. As Marshall indicated in a cable to Eisenhower, landings at Casablanca in Morocco and Oran in Algeria would suffice: 'The President pictures the landing of some 80,000 men in the two assault convoys and thinks such a number would be necessary to his *political* (my italics) purposes.' Roosevelt did not think that this would provoke the Germans to rush troops into Tunisia or Algiers. As 'Torch' would eventually show, he was as wrong about the threat to Tunisia as he was about the threat from Spain.

Eisenhower and his deputy, General Mark Clark, were the first in London to hear news of Washington's clawback. It put them in an embarrassing position as they were due to dine that night, 25 August, at Downing Street with Churchill who had just flown home. Churchill enthused about the possibilities of 'Torch', telling his American guests that it 'offers the greatest opportunity in the history of England . . . it is the one thing that is going to win the war. President Roosevelt feels the same.'

What Churchill did not know was that the President had just cut the British out of his plans. He could not help noticing a disconsolate look on the American generals' faces, but they were unable to have a frank discussion as Marshall's information was for American eyes only. However Clark suggested that 'Torch' was crying out for someone at the top to make some decisions on all the logistical plans, although he did not tell Churchill that the key strategic decision had already been made. To Clark's amazement Churchill, despite the late hour, immediately summoned the First Sea Lord, Sir Dudley Pound, to discuss how the transport of troops could be speeded up. The evening concluded with a Churchillian battle cry: 'I want troops pouring into the area. I want them to come through the walls, the ceilings – everywhere! The French will go with us if we are going to win, but they can't afford to pick a loser.'

On the next day, 26 August, Churchill cabled Roosevelt that, in order to focus minds, Eisenhower needed to be given a directive establishing a date for the start of 'Torch', when he would attack 'with such troops as are available and at such places he thinks fit.' He stressed the importance of attacking in as many places as possible, with forces cunningly allocated to give the appearance of a huge invasion. Later that day the British Chiefs-of-Staff were told of the reduced American plan. On 27 August, Churchill, having discovered Washington's proposed scale down, sent a further cable starkly expressing his concerns: 'We are all profoundly disconcerted . . . It seems to me that the whole pith of the operation will be lost if we do not take Algiers as well as Oran on the first day.' Given what Roosevelt knew from Robert Murphy and the other 'consuls' in North Africa, the American plan was indeed odd. Vichy resistance was estimated to be strong at Casablanca and Oran, while Algiers was the centre of pro-Allies French conspirators and had good chances of being taken peacefully. Most significant of all, if the landings were confined to Oran and Casablanca, it would be an open invitation for the Germans to swarm into Tunisia and allow the Allies no chance of forestalling them. Churchill concluded with a plea that Eisenhower be allowed to go forward with the plans he has made 'upon which we are all now working day and night.'

There then followed what Eisenhower called the 'transatlantic essay contest', as the President and Prime Minister horse-traded over the nature and extent of 'Torch'. While it was going on, General Clark assembled thirty-seven British and American officers engaged in the planning at Norfolk House and told them, "Some of you men are less confused than others about 'Torch'. Let's get equally confused". There was Plan A, Plan B and so many others that one wit suggested that they start moving on Plan Z. The one clear demand was that the invasion should be made in October and the penny was dropping in Norfolk House that this would be neatly in time for the November Congressional elections. Finally, on 3 September, Roosevelt and Churchill reached a compromise; the main landings would still take place at Casablanca and Oran but these would be accompanied by a smaller landing at Algiers.

Although Britain was supplying forty per cent of the ground troops and the majority of warships, Roosevelt insisted that 'Torch' should appear to be a totally American operation. He wrote to Churchill extolling the benefits that were about to accrue from his Vichy policy and, by implication, devaluing Churchill's alliance with de Gaulle: 'Our latest and best information from North Africa is as follows: American expedition will meet little resistance from the French Army in Africa. On the other hand a British commanded attack in any phase or with de

Gaullist co-operation would meet with determined resistance. I consider it vital that sole responsibility be placed with Americans for relations with French military and civil authorities in Africa.' Roosevelt was determined to see his Vichy policy vindicated and, in one sense, his forecast was accurate. The main opposition would come not from the French Army, but its Navy.

Churchill was more sceptical than Roosevelt that the cultivation of local Vichy commanders by Murphy and his colleagues would guarantee a peaceful entry, believing that the size of the invasion force was a more persuasive weapon than words or deals. However, he had achieved so much of his desired strategy that the concession of American control seemed trifling. While some of his colleagues, particularly Eden, would resent that Britain was supplying such a substantial part of the expedition with no corresponding power of decision, Churchill was content to tell the President: 'In the whole of 'Torch', military and political, I consider myself your Lieutenant asking only to put my viewpoint plainly before you. This is an American enterprise, in which we are your helpmates.'

On the matter of de Gaulle's exclusion from 'Torch' there was unanimity. On 1 September, panic seized Norfolk House. An American colonel, serving as a liaison officer at the Free French headquarters in Carlton Gardens, had caught sight of a telegram sent by de Gaulle from Syria in which he seemed to have gleaned remarkable knowledge of the Allies' plans. De Gaulle told his London colleagues that the Americans were planning a landing in North Africa in conjunction with a British attack on Dakar and 'Vichy . . . had kept the Germans informed of the plan.' De Gaulle claimed, correctly as it turned out, that Pétain would order all French forces to resist and gave a further indication of either acute intelligence or deduction: 'The idea of the Americans at first was to invade Europe this year, then they needed the help of the Free French . . . Now they have resumed their former attitude of stand-offishness towards the Free French.' Churchill heard about the telegram and cabled Roosevelt: 'Free French have got inkling and are leaky. Every day saved is precious.'

Churchill was in no mood to feel friendly at this time towards de Gaulle; these were the days when the clouds of de Gaulle's vituperation were building up over the Levant. In response to Roosevelt's rejection of 'de Gaullist co-operation' Churchill wrote: 'I agree with you that de Gaulle will be an irritant and his movement must be kept out.' Two days later, on 16 September, Roosevelt drafted a reply which was never sent but confirmed his thinking: 'I agree fully and consider it essential that de Gaulle be kept out of the picture and be permitted to have no repeat no information whatever regardless of how irritated and irritating he may become.' Intriguingly Roosevelt added at the end of the same draft telegram: 'What would you think of our asking him to come to Washington about November 10th? He might advertise this unduly but on the other hand it might tend to soften his attitude after a certain event takes place.'

Roosevelt clearly realized that some form of accommodation with de Gaulle would have to be devised, probably requiring his own unique charm and persuasiveness. Though the idea of a visit by de Gaulle continued to be mooted, the date kept slipping. While Roosevelt was taking a less rigid view of de Gaulle, Churchill was also showing flexibility. Earlier in the summer he had chided Eden for his black and white view of Vichy and de Gaulle: 'The position is so anomalous and monstrous,' he wrote, 'that very clear-cut views, such as you are developing, do not altogether cover it. There is much more in British policy towards France than abusing Pétain and backing de Gaulle.' Churchill had moved some way from his own clear-cut views of the spring of 1941 before the Syria debacle.

If de Gaulle was a non-starter, one overriding question for the Allies, now that the military decisions had been taken, was with whom they would deal once they disembarked on French Africa shores? With America in charge, it would have to be an American decision and the picture was incredibly confused.

Roosevelt and Murphy had always hoped that this would be the time when the knight Weygand rose up in shining brass. His sacking had left no obvious, potentially sympathetic leader in North Africa. Morocco, and therefore Casablanca, was out. Murphy had spent much time trying to cultivate its Resident General, Auguste Nogues. However, having made his decision to support Pétain in June 1940, Nogues remained an obdurate Vichyite. When Murphy returned to Africa in October after pre-'Torch' briefings with Roosevelt in Washington and Eisenhower in London, he went to see Nogues again, enticing him with the prospect of half a million men, fully equipped with planes, tanks, guns and ships appearing on the horizon. Nogues replied that he would meet any such force with all the firepower at his disposal. "It is too late for France to participate in this war now", he told Murphy.

Above all Nogues seemed to believe that, if Morocco was dragged into the war, it would be lost to France forever. He was right, but for the wrong reason. Admiral Michelier, commander of the French Navy along the entire coast, also offered no prospects of co-operation and his ships and shore defences would hit the Allies hard. The only chink of light in Casablanca was General Emile-Marie Bethouart, the divisional commander and, coincidentally, a friend of de Gaulle. He bravely committed himself to immobilizing Nogues on the night of the landings but he was a lone and inexperienced conspirator.

Algiers was more fertile ground. Early on Murphy had met a businessman, Jacques Lemaigre Dubreuil, who had moved his peanut processing plant from Dunkirk to West Africa after the armistice, gaining German approval by promising them 25 percent of his proceeds. Lemaigre Dubreuil became a controversial figure in resistance circles. He was very right-wing, a friend of Pierre Laval, and had achieved renown in pre-war France as an anti-tax campaigner. Politically he was much in tune with Pétain but his patriotism directed him to resistance rather than collaboration. By early 1942 Lemaigre Dubreuil and four other important figures in Algiers had formed the so-called Group of Five, which tried furtively to spread the idea of working with the Americans throughout civilian and military circles in Algiers. While these contacts of Murphy were with the senior figures at the top of the conspiracy, America's fledgling covert operations executive, OSS, and the British SOE were creating small units comprising a few hundred young resisters who could lead a *putsch* in the city of Algiers when the time came.

All these contacts carried in their wake seeds of confusion. The British prejudice, largely shared by Eisenhower and his staff, was that the surest means to success was overwhelming force; local intrigue was inherently unreliable. Murphy and, as his telegram to Churchill had indicated, Roosevelt believed that, with the right leader, much of Vichy's Africa command would join the Allies once the Americans showed up. Roosevelt still clung on to the hope that Pétain himself would, at the very least, not order resistance. But who was the leader going to be? For one curious reason, apart from Vichyite venom and Roosevelt's suspicions, it could not be de Gaulle. The Group of Five considered him too much the parliamentarian who would restore the unstable democracy of pre-war France with its ragged mob of Communists and Socialists. Roosevelt, who was developing quite another view of de Gaulle, would have been intrigued by their analysis.

General Henri Giraud's escape from a German prisoner-of-war camp in April of 1942 seemed to provide the answer. Giraud was one of France's top six generals, far superior in rank to de Gaulle. His escape from Königstein, a castle fortress reserved for the most distinguished French prisoners, confirmed his reputation as a man of *élan*, the highest compliment that could be bestowed on a fighting Frenchman. The fact that this had led to his capture during the *Blitzkrieg*, after a dashing but reckless attempt to encircle the Germans in Belgium, did nothing to diminish him. In looks, he was Hollywood central casting's perfect image of the daring French officer: tall, lean, and splendidly moustached. Even de Gaulle respected him and welcomed his reappearance, although he had no intention of conceding to his seniority.

Giraud's escape had brought a thorny problem for Pétain's new head of government, the pro-German Pierre Laval who had just replaced Darlan. The presence of Giraud, whose fighting qualities were well recognized by Hitler, was unhelpful to his attempts to engineer even deeper collaboration with Nazis. Hitler ordered Vichy to return Giraud to captivity and Giraud came under pressure to comply from both Laval and Darlan. Eventually a compromise was reached after Giraud agreed to sign a letter drafted by Laval, pledging his loyalty to Pétain and promising not to disturb his relations with the German Government. The letter was a hostage to fortune; Giraud, who, as his future allies would discover was alarmingly devoid of political *savoir-faire*, seemed blissfully unaware of its potential consequences.

Giraud's escape was noticed by important people outside France. Churchill drew Roosevelt's attention to it. Murphy immediately understood its significance. He had briefly met Giraud in the autumn of 1939 at the Gare du Nord in Paris, where he was watching conscripts boarding trains for the front and was impressed by his energy and optimism in sharp contrast to most of his military colleagues. The Group of Five in Algeria were electrified by the news. Giraud seemed their perfect figure-head; right-wing, not to say reactionary, and a committed anti-Nazi. Lemaigre Dubreuil flew to Lyons and, via intermediaries, was led to Giraud. Giraud gave him a list of a dozen officers in the French African Army who would fight with the Allies, most notably General Charles Mast, who was Chief of Staff of the 19th Corps in Algiers and in a pivotal position in the military command.

On his return to Algiers Lemaigre Dubreuil rushed to see Mast who was initially suspicious and refused to open his door to him. However after Lemaigre Dubreuil had pleaded with him to see his letter of credentials from Giraud, Mast conceded and expressed sympathy for the resisters' aims. Mast also told Murphy that he would do everything he could to help an allied operation. A network of conspirators was now emerging: the Group of Five with Mast in tow; a few thousand men whom the Five claimed were ready to follow their lead; and the five hundred or so young shock troops being trained by O.S.S. and S.O.E.

However, lurking in the shadows was a much bigger fish. Despite his replacement by Pierre Laval, Admiral François Darlan remained the commander of all Vichy French armed forces on land, sea and air. Darlan was infinitely subtle and, above all, an admiral who liked to sail with the wind. After the Nazi invasion of Russia he had detected the first possible change in that wind. Even while he consolidated Vichy's collaboration with Germany, other prospects were churning in the sub-terranean recesses of his finely politicized mind. In August 1941 he told Leahy in Vichy: "When you have 3,000 tanks, 6,000 planes and 500,000 men to bring to Marseilles, let me know. Then we shall welcome you." In November, after he had manoeuvred to remove Weygand from North Africa, he ensured that the title of Delegate-General passed to his place man, Admiral Raymond Fenard, who had been running Weygand's administrative headquarters.

In April 1942, after Darlan had been replaced as head of the Vichy government by Laval, Colonel William Donovan, the founder of O.S.S., suggested to Roosevelt that it might be worth putting out feelers to him: 'Would you think it fantastic, and if not, is it feasible to have someone who is close at hand in Vichy talk with Darlan? His nose must be greatly out of joint at this moment.' Then in May came an indirect approach from Darlan himself. Fenard contacted Murphy and pointed out that Darlan continued to hold the real power as head of all Vichy forces. He passed on the message that Darlan wished America to view the French Empire in Africa as an entity separate from the Vichy regime on the mainland. It would join the struggle against the Nazis, 'but only when the Americans are able to provide the material which will make such action effective.' Darlan's son, Alain, a young naval officer, was also in Algiers and conveyed the same message. Darlan himself, scared of compromising him-self in Nazi eyes should he be detected, never spoke directly to Murphy. He continued to loathe the British.

In mid October Murphy returned to Algiers after his briefings in Washington and London. There were three weeks left to close the conspiratorial ring, but Murphy, who was now charged with an onerous responsibility, had many problems. He was under strict orders to tell no one about the operation until four days before D-Day. Giraud was still in France and believed that he would be Commander-in-Chief of all Allied forces, including American and British, fighting on French soil. And, while Murphy was supposed to be the personal envoy of the President, there was constant difficulty in prising clear and quick directives on what promises he could make to his potential collaborators in such shifting ground.

After his unproductive meeting with Nogues in Rabat on 9 October, Murphy returned to Algiers where, after his two-month absence in Washington and London, he found himself a honey pot to the different conspirators. There was a buzz of action in the air. The build-up of personnel in Gibraltar had not gone unnoticed and the Paris newspapers were reporting that an invasion of North Africa was imminent. Darlan detected the straws in the wind and authorized an intermediary, Colonel Jean Chrétien, to contact Murphy. They met on 12 October. Chrétien hinted that Darlan might be willing to move his base to North Africa and bring the French fleet with him, but only on condition that the Americans arrived in massive force. Darlan knew that any Allied invasion of North Africa would force Hitler into an immediate occupation of all France in order to secure its Mediterranean coast. This was a tantalizing offer and Murphy cabled back to Washington for guidance on how far he could go with Darlan. Darlan would be a huge catch and Murphy thought it vital to encourage him; he also thought that it would be possible to foster a collaboration between Giraud and Darlan.

The next day, while Murphy awaited instructions from Washington, feelers from another big beast of the Vichy African jungle, General Alphonse Juin, came his way. Juin was Commander of all North African Vichy land and air forces and therefore held immense potential to help or hinder the Allies. Murphy, perhaps mistakenly, had not previously attempted to cultivate Juin, and explained to Juin's aide, Major André Dorange, that he had not wished to embarrass Juin by making any contacts which might have left him open to accusations of sympathy with America. Murphy said that he was now officially authorized by the American President to open a dialogue and Dorange indicated that Juin would be interested in receiving him. Dorange opened by stressing that Juin would consider it his duty to resist invasion by any foreign country; Murphy replied that the United States would never set foot on French territory without an invitation. It became a conversation of hints and nuances at the end of which Dorange had understood that America would only deal with the established Vichy authorities in North Africa and Murphy had reason to think that Juin might be sympathetic to the Allies.

While Darlan and Juin nibbled at the bait, Murphy's next meeting was with the Group of Five and Giraud's representative, General Mast. With these committed conspirators he could at last declare that an American invasion was in the offing, although he was unable to give a date and much exaggerated its size. Two of the Five had just returned from a briefing with Giraud in France and, while Giraud would have much preferred a full-scale Allied assault on the South of France, he was willing to go along with an invasion of North Africa. Murphy now broached with Mast his idea of the perfect match; a collaboration between Giraud and Darlan. Mast could not have been more negative. Darlan was an untrustworthy double dealer and he would have nothing to do with him. Furthermore, Mast declared that the French African Army was loyal to Giraud, not Darlan, and the Navy would follow the Army's lead. Murphy cabled back to Washington: 'Mast asserts that Giraud's command will give us entry practically without firing a shot.'

For Murphy, Mast's rejection of Darlan was a disappointment; with 'Torch' only three weeks away and no time left to consolidate the feelers with Darlan and Juin, only one plan was possible. 'Torch' must go ahead on the basis that Giraud's leadership, the Group of Five's networks, and a simultaneous *putsch* by the O.S.S. and S.O.E. trained young resisters would secure Algiers and that its capture would bring the rest of French North and West Africa into line. Murphy sent messages to London and Washington indicating this state of affairs. Only after these had been received did Murphy finally get his reply from Roosevelt's Chief of Staff, Admiral Leahy, on dealing with Darlan. This was vaguely worded, authorizing Murphy to convey to Darlan's envoy Washington's opinion that it shared Darlan's fears of a Nazi move against the unoccupied zone and North Africa and believed that Darlan should resist any such aggression, 'in which case America will provide at once large scale military, material and economic aid in the colonies.' This meant almost nothing. However one significant piece of guidance was implicit; Roosevelt had no objection to dealing with Darlan. Vichy was the French authority that he continued to recognize. It is also the case that at a meeting in mid October attended by Churchill, Eden, the South African leader, General Smuts, and the Chief-of-Staff, Smuts had remarked that Darlan would be a big fish to catch. There is no record of Churchill or Eden dissenting.

At their meeting, Mast had also insisted on his need for a conference with the American commanders to establish the military hierarchy for the joint operation. In what became one of the more ludicrous episodes in the war, General Clark and a handful of officers were dispatched in secret by submarine to Cherchell, seventy-five miles west of Algiers on the Algerian coast. After a night of missed rendezvous and an awkward landing in inflatable craft buffeted by the Mediterranean surf, Clark met Mast at a deserted farmhouse. Mast wanted an assurance that forty-eight hours into the operation Giraud would assume overall command. Clark hedged, saying that this would be done as soon as possible. The meeting could not amount to much more than a fostering of personal relationships as neither Clark nor Murphy were able to tell their new French allies the date of the landings; Mast and the Group of Five still assumed that they were months away. The meeting became famous less for what it achieved than for Clark's later regaling of journalists with all the purportedly funny things that happened. The house was invaded by local police who thought that they had stumbled on a gang of drug smugglers. While Murphy pretended he and the Frenchmen were having a party and acted drunk, Clark and his men hid in the cellar below. A British officer from the submarine could only be stopped from coughing by Clark stuffing a piece of spent chewing gum in his mouth. Finally, Clark lost his underpants on the way back to the submarine when one of the landing boats overturned. But, if Mast and Giraud would prove able to deliver, Cherchell would be worth the risk.

As the final plans were laid, with ten days to go, two last-minute panics intervened. On 28 October, Murphy received permission from Eisenhower to tell one Frenchman, Mast, the date of the landings, the night of 7 and 8 November. Mast got into a terrible flap, accusing the Americans of a lack of trust in their French allies, but, as soon as he cooled down, word was sent to Giraud in France. His reply seemed to spell disaster. The man, whose mere appearance was supposed to bring instant conversion of Vichy forces, announced that he could not possibly leave France until 20 November. Murphy cabled Washington that 'Torch' had to be postponed for two weeks to conform with Giraud's timetable. Otherwise, he wrote, 'I am convinced that the invasion of North Africa without favourable French High Command will be a catastrophe.' As Murphy himself later acknowledged, his was a preposterous request; transports heading for Casablanca from America under General George Patton's command were already crossing the Atlantic. Eisenhower found it 'inconceivable' that Murphy could recommend such a delay and, on Roosevelt's behalf, Leahy gave his request short shrift and conveyed the President's order that 'Torch' would proceed on schedule. Murphy would just have to do the best he could.

Lemaigre Dubreuil was dispatched to see Giraud and was richly upbraided by him. However, Giraud consented to travel to Algiers a day or two before the invasion, persuaded by a letter from Murphy that, 'the Government of the United States has no thought or desire but to put the military command of the region in the hands of the French as soon as possible.' On his own admission, Murphy went rather further in his letter than he was entitled to, but felt that he had no choice, so strongly did everything seem to hinge on Giraud. On the eve of 'Torch', Eisenhower's political advisers decided that Giraud should be brought to Allied Headquarters at Gibraltar rather than Algiers. Giraud insisted that he would only travel on an American submarine, but there were none in the Mediterranean. In another comic turn, a British submarine was given an American flag and an American officer put in technical command so that Giraud could be greeted on board by the right accent.

The second panic was the unexpected arrival in Algiers of Darlan on 5 November, two days before the 'Torch' D-Day. A month before, Darlan had tried to resign from Pétain's cabinet, while retaining his position as Commander-in-Chief. Pétain had refused his resignation, but it was an intriguing indication that Darlan was beginning his journey of disassociation from Nazi collaboration. On 23 October, Darlan began a tour of North African defences, during which Chrétien brought him a message from Murphy that the 500,000 American troops might not be so far away. Darlan still gave no indication that he wished to make personal contact with Murphy and his every public act continued to give the appearance of co-operation with the Germans. He had rushed to Algiers after hearing that his son, Alain, in hospital with polio, was near to death. Whether or not Darlan had ulterior motives, the presence of the Commander-in-Chief of all Vichy forces in Algiers on the night of the invasion was a bolt from the blue.

The scene was set for 'Torch'. While many shades of Frenchmen with varied thoughts of resistance or co-operation and different levels of knowledge waited in Africa, one Frenchman was out in the cold. The terrible things de Gaulle and Churchill had said to each other on 30 September seemed to herald an irreconcilable breach. However, three important factors were unchanged. Firstly, de Gaulle had the full support of the French National Committee. On 2 October, the head of the Free French Navy, Admiral Auboyneau, had even gone so far as to tell Admiral Dickens, the Admiralty's liaison officer with Allied navies, that 'as the British Government had apparently broken off relations with de Gaulle, he must warn me that the

Free French Navy was on the side of de Gaulle and would follow him.' The message was clear; if the British wanted to maintain their alliance with the Free French, they were stuck with de Gaulle. Secondly, there were many people of good will on both sides who were determined not to allow a fracture. Thirdly, Churchill himself, however infuriating he found him, continued to believe that de Gaulle was a great man.

Churchill was also naturally magnanimous. On 23 October, he sent his personal assistant, Desmond Morton, to mend some fences. Morton conveyed Churchill's congratulations on the exploits of the Free French submarine *Juno* and her troops in Egypt; he also reported the Prime Minister's 'intense admiration' for de Gaulle and all that he had accomplished in the previous two and a half years. De Gaulle, in return, asked Morton to give his congratulations to Churchill on the great successes being won by British troops in Egypt. Two days later, de Gaulle arrived for a conversation about Syria with a Foreign Office official, who was expecting the usual fireworks. Instead he found de Gaulle in a softer mood and greatly touched by Churchill's *rapprochement*.

Of course, it was not mere magnanimity. Churchill was beginning to feel thoroughly awkward that Roosevelt had refused to allow him to warn de Gaulle of 'Torch'. Knowing that that something big was in the offing, de Gaulle had sent a long letter to Roosevelt on 26 October trying to explain what he really stood for and to remove some of the Presidential prejudices. It was a potent plea for America to understand the immorality of Vichy and to reappraise its relations with the Free French, who had fought for their nation's liberty from the outset. It also repudiated the idea that de Gaulle wished to impose himself as some sort of dictator on France. The letter received no reply.

While Roosevelt felt no loyalty to de Gaulle, Churchill did. Roosevelt had sent him a draft of a letter he proposed to send Pétain on the day of 'Torch', which began 'My dear old friend' and sent his 'warm regards' and friendship. It was a last-ditch effort to secure some form of co-operation from Pétain and vindicate the Vichy policy. Churchill was appalled by such an expression of affection and understood the damage it would cause Roosevelt if the letter became public. He wrote: 'Will you allow me to say that your proposed message to Pétain seems to me too kind. His stock must be very low now. He has used his reputation to do our cause injuries no lesser man could have done. I beg you to think of the effect on the de Gaullists, to whom we have serious obligations and who have now to go through the great trial of being kept outside.' Roosevelt toned down the letter but he remained as dismissive as ever towards de Gaulle. On 5 November, Churchill asked for permission to tell de Gaulle about 'Torch' on the day before the landings, reminding Roosevelt: 'You will remember that I have exchanged letters with him of a solemn kind in 1940 recognising him as the Leader of Free Frenchmen. I am confident his military honour can be trusted.' Roosevelt was curtly dismissive: 'I consider it inadvisable for you to give de Gaulle any information in regard to 'Torch' until subsequent to a successful landing. <u>Admiral Leahy agrees wholly with the thoughts expressed above.</u>'

Leahy's regard for Pétain and contempt for de Gaulle remained immutable and the hand-written reference shows how much it must have weighed with Roosevelt. The next day, the eve of 'Torch', Churchill wrote back in sorrow: 'I am still sorry about de Gaulle. Of course we control all his telegrams outwards. But we are ready to accept your view.' Reaction in the Foreign Office was less polite. Cadogan noted in his diary: 'Some discussion of the President's silly decision that de Gaulle should be told nothing beforehand ... the President's telegram was rather a testy message and can't be ignored, so there it is.' On this day, the British offered de Gaulle his consolation prize for the imminent rebuff of 'Torch'. The campaign to capture all of Madagascar had just ended and de Gaulle was asked to appoint a Free French Governor General. He was also invited to have lunch with Churchill on 8 November. De Gaulle fully understood that he was being thrown a sop.

While the British indulged in against the clock diplomacy, the 'Torch' Armada neared African shores. In Gibraltar, General Eisenhower was holding his breath. He had always known that 'Torch' was a gamble, an operation that would only succeed by military bluff and political manoeuvring. His American troops were green, seeing combat for the first time; the Vichy Navy and Army outmanned and outgunned them. On the morning of 7 November, he cabled to his Commander-in-Chief, General Marshall: 'Tonight we start ashore. We are standing, of course, on the brink and must take the jump – whether the bottom contains a nice feather bed or a pile of brickbats!' Later that day, Giraud arrived at Gibraltar and immediately began to insist that he, not Eisenhower, should be in command. From the messages he had been receiving, Giraud had justification for this view; but his demands failed to impress Eisenhower who reported to his Chief-of-Staff in London, General Walter Bedell Smith: 'Giraud ... even made a point of his *rank*. Can you beat it? Yet he's supposed to be the high-minded man that is to rally all North Africa behind him and to save France.' While Eisenhower, supported by his table-thumping, tough-talking deputy, Clark, began haggling with Giraud, the young resistance groups in Algiers were receiving last-minute orders for their *putsch*. One group was led by a twenty-one-year-old Jewish medical student, Jose Aboulker. Nearly sixty years later he recalls: 'We were ashamed of Pétain, de Gaulle was our French dignity, Churchill was our hope, but the man we were waiting for was Roosevelt.'

In the small hours of 8 November, 'Torch' began. Aboulker and four hundred young resistance fighters, armed only with old guns, moved into action. With the help of a few sympathetic senior policemen, they took over Algiers police headquarters. The 19th Army Corps headquarters were taken over by another group, led by a young army captain, Alfred Pillafort. A further group took over the Government General, which housed key government offices, the telephone exchange, and the radio station. At the same time Murphy knocked on the door of General Juin and informed him that, as he spoke, a huge force of half a million men were landing on the beaches of North Africa. Murphy was delivering the Allies' bluff; the real number was just over one hundred thousand. Juin said that, if it was up to him, he would be with the Allies; however Darlan, who out-ranked him, was in the city. In that case, said Murphy, we shall bring Darlan here.

Once landed, the American troops were supposed to arrive in Algiers at the crack of dawn and seal the city. 'Our aim was to paralyse the Vichy Army so that the landings could take place more easily and General Giraud was supposed to come over from France,' remembers Aboulker. But a disgruntled Giraud was still haggling in Gibraltar, apparently now waiting to see how it all turned out before he made any agreement. Eisenhower's infuriation rose: 'He wants to be a big shot, a bright and shining light, and the acclaimed saviour of France. But he will not (repeat and underline) take one single step or do any single thing that could possibly be interpreted as inimical to the interest of *any* Frenchman.'

Of more immediate importance was the apparent lack of American troops. The night landings had proved chaotic and their British transports had dropped them further up the coast from Algiers than planned. The American commanding officer, General Ryder, decided that the landings needed to be consolidated before American troops could advance into the city. Meanwhile, a British unit had advanced to take over Algiers airport; ironically this meant that the first troops encountered by the Vichy Army would not even be American.

While one of Murphy's consuls, Kenneth Pendar, was fetching Darlan, a resistance group was surrounding Juin's residence. When Pendar returned with Darlan, they found themselves being checked by a new armed guard, which was part of the *putsch*. Murphy and Juin inside were unaware of the action outside. Once inside, Darlan, who had always nursed the hope that any conspiracy with the Allies would have evolved on his own terms, was bursting with indignation and accused the Americans of a massive blunder. Murphy began the long process of talking him round, repeating that half a million men were landing, the very force that Darlan had always claimed would persuade him to switch sides.

This was the supreme moment of truth for Darlan. If he had now used his undisputed muscle and ordered all Vichy forces in Morocco, Algeria and Tunisia to co-operate with the Allies, there would have been some chance of Allied forces racing into Tunisia and preventing the German army and air force gaining a foothold. Ever slippery, Darlan would not commit himself, waiting to see the strength of the Allied invasion and agreeing only to send a telegram to Pétain which informed him of the landings.

With supine weakness, Darlan wrote that he had told Murphy that 'France had signed an armistice agreement with Germany and that I could only conform to the Marshal's orders to defend our territory.' Pendar and one of the resisters, who were to oversee transmission of the telegram, opened it and decided that it should not be sent.

The following hours of 8 November saw only confusion. The Allies' delayed arrival gave Vichy forces and police time to reverse the *putsch*. They overpowered the resistance guards outside Juin's residence and Murphy now found himself under temporary arrest, which was soon lifted on the orders of Admiral Fenard. During firefights in the city, Captain Pillafort was one of several resistance leaders to be killed. Other resisters were arrested and the rest vanished into the undergrowth. Two British destroyers, *Malcolm* and *Broke*, tried to ram the barrier at Algiers harbour. The *Malcolm* was hit by shore batteries and forced to withdraw, sinking the next day, but the *Broke* forced her way through and landed an American battalion. The battalion was soon surrounded by Vichy forces and surrendered. In what were much the highest casualties in the Algiers operation, fifteen American troops, nine sailors on the *Broke*, and some seventy Vichy soldiers died.

However, as the day progressed, Darlan began to realize that the landings were genuine and, seeing that Vichy resistance was futile, ordered a local ceasefire in Algiers City. He did not attempt to extend the order to Casablanca, where General Bethouart had failed in his coup against Nogues and been arrested, or Oran where the Allies were taking much heavier casualties from the Vichy Navy and shore batteries. Pétain was offering nothing to the Americans. Despite all the flattery of the previous two years, he ordered Vichy forces to fight to the end against the Allies, at the same time inviting the Nazis to go into Tunisia where he ordered the local French commanders to assist them. Algiers was now calm, albeit under an unstable ceasefire. Darlan, having failed in his first moment of truth in the small hours of the morning, had to decide his destiny. His dealings with America's commanders would also land Roosevelt with a defining moral dilemma.

CHAPTER TEN
DEALING WITH DEVILS

At 6am on 8 November, de Gaulle was given the news of 'Torch' by his Chief of Staff, Pierre Billotte. "I hope that the people of Vichy throw them into the sea," was his instant response. He informed Claude Serreulles that, at his lunch with Churchill, he would tell him: "so Roosevelt too wants his Mers-el-Kebir". He soon cooled down. Six decades later, Serreulles recalled that de Gaulle had known for two or three months that the Allies were going to invade Africa, either from the north or west: 'He was absolutely convinced that this would happen and of course it was a great step towards the invasion of the continent and he was compelled to applaud.'

At his Downing Street lunch, carefully arranged so that Churchill could attempt to defuse any anger, de Gaulle behaved immaculately, not even seeking to take advantage of British embarrassment. Churchill set the tone, explaining that while the British had conceded American command of 'Torch', they had no intention of abandoning the Free French now that the horizon was brightening. De Gaulle said that the Germans were sure to attempt an immediate occupation of Tunisia and expressed astonishment that the Allied plan did not make landings at Bizerte a priority. As the British agreed with this, there was little to be said. In his memoirs, General Mark Clark also admitted that this turned out to be a strategic mistake: 'Had we struck out boldly and landed forces far to the east, even in Tunisia . . . we would almost certainly have been successful and would have been spared much of the long, awkward overland transportation that now confronted us.'

The only person now able to ease the Allies' passage into Tunisia was Darlan. On the night of 8 November, despite his treatment over 'Torch', de Gaulle did his bit in a BBC broadcast, appealing to all Frenchmen of North Africa: "leaders, soldiers, sailors, airmen, officials and French *colons* . . . Rise up, help our Allies, join them without reservation. Don't worry about names or formulas – rise up!" As in all his public speeches at times of military crisis, de Gaulle did not let Churchill or Roosevelt down.

On 9 November, Darlan began to haggle. He held most of the cards and the Allies knew it. Algiers was back in the hands of Vichy regulars, and the navy at Oran and Casablanca were fighting hard against the invaders. Giraud was still in Gibraltar where, in the light of Darlan's ceasefire order and apparent willingness to negotiate, he was suddenly something of an embarrassment. On the evening of 8 November, Eisenhower had come to a gentleman's agreement with Giraud which would make him Commander-in-Chief of all French Forces in Africa and supreme civil administrator. Soon afterwards the British Admiral, Andrew Cunningham brought Eisenhower the news about Darlan, the man with real rather than paper power, reminding him that Churchill had said: "Kiss Darlan's stern if you have to, but get the French Navy."

Darlan's opening gambit was to insist that he could do nothing without the permission of Pétain and Laval. As Laval was away from Vichy receiving new instructions from Hitler, this deployment of the French officers' oath of allegiance to the 'Marshal' was a useful delaying tactic while Darlan studied his cards. As events unfolded, it was clear that a personal ambition to become the supreme French leader in the African Empire lay behind Darlan's every move; in order to achieve this and to legitimize his command over forces loyal to Pétain, he needed to obtain a cloak of approval from Vichy. This was going to be difficult as, further to issuing orders to his commanders in Tunisia to collaborate with Nazi troops, Pétain had now sent a senior officer to ensure that these orders were carried out. If there was any justification for Pétain's ever deeper slide into the abyss of collaboration, it was to dissuade Hitler from ordering his troops into the unoccupied zone; but, however much he and Laval might fawn before the Nazis, 'Torch' had made this inevitable.

While Darlan reported the military reality to Vichy and awaited instructions, Clark flew into Algiers to preside over the negotiations. He had been preceded by Giraud who had expected to be greeted with fanfares and guards of honour. Nothing of the sort happened and it was immediately clear that Giraud held no sway whatsoever with the local Vichy commanders. In this respect the preconceived American strategy of banking on Giraud's name, backed by the Group of Five and resistance groups, had proved overwhelmingly erroneous. They had given Giraud the code name 'Kingpin'; now he looked nothing more than a pawn at Darlan's court, and the Five and the young resisters looked on in revulsion as Darlan held the stage.

Clark had only one weapon at his disposal; the threat of bombing Algiers to rubble and imposing Giraud over the head of the Vichyites. As Giraud was disconsolate and lethargic after realizing his powerlessness, Darlan could see that this was a bluff. Crucially, it never occurred to Clark or Murphy, who was assisting and acting as interpreter, that there was anything untoward in trying to reach an agreement with Darlan. Roosevelt's

Vichy policy was all about bringing that regime over to the Allies' side. If it came over in the form of a man who had collaborated with the Nazis, invited them into Vichy bases in Syria to fight the British, and stood by while his sailors killed American troops at Casablanca and Oran, that was all part of the game.

On 10 November, after much table-thumping by Clark and more gentle but coherent persuasion from Juin, who was turning out to be a strong sympathizer of the Allies, Darlan ordered a cease-fire of all Vichy forces in Africa. Juin also persuaded Giraud to accept a military command only, thus clearing a possible way to Murphy's dream ticket of Darlan and Giraud. Darlan's order made little practical difference. Oran had already surrendered and Casablanca was on the point of submission. If Darlan had issued the order on 8 November, he might have saved the three thousand dead or wounded on the French side, a similar number of casualties among the Allies, the sinking of many ships on both sides and the destruction of 135 out the 168 French planes which could otherwise have taken part in the push against Tunisia. On this day, the Allies did at least have cause for a more noble celebration, the 8th Army's victory at El-Alamein, prompting Churchill's famous 'end of the beginning' speech.

Darlan's ceasefire was immediately repudiated by Pétain who urged his forces to fight on and announced the appointment of Nogues to replace Darlan as overall commander. Darlan was in danger of losing his Vichy legitimacy, but he had another card up his sleeve. He was in constant communication by teletype to the Admiralty at Vichy from where his Lieutenant, Admiral Auphan, sent a message which could be taken to mean that Pétain had a secret sympathy for Darlan's action. There never proved to be any proper evidence that Pétain intended any such thing, but Auphan's telegram let Darlan off one hook. On the following day, when the Nazis moved into the unoccupied zone, he was sprung free altogether, arguing that any Vichy order was made under duress. In addition, the Nazi move finally clarified the direction of his own ambition; there was no going back to Vichy.

News of the bartering in Algiers and Darlan's cease-fire order was now reaching Washington and London. In the latter, the spectre of de Gaulle was hanging over the apparently successful military outcome in North Africa. Churchill felt it was time to remind Roosevelt that Frenchmen who had chosen to fight from the beginning, as opposed to Vichy *attentistes*, must not be excluded. 'It is surely of the highest importance to unify in every possible way all Frenchmen who regard Germany as the foe,' he wrote. 'The invasion of unoccupied France by Hitler should give the opportunity for this. You will I am sure realise that his Majesty's Government is under quite definite and solemn obligations to de Gaulle and his movement. We must see they have a fair deal. It seems to me that you and I ought to avoid at all costs the creation of rival French Émigré Governments each favoured by one of us.'

Roosevelt was unimpressed and made clear for the first time one of his underlying premises; all potential French leaders were as bad as each other. He replied: 'In regard to de Gaulle, I have hitherto enjoyed a quiet satisfaction in leaving him in your hands – apparently I have now acquired a similar problem in brother Giraud. I wholly agree that we must prevent rivalry between the French émigré factions and I have no objection to a de Gaulle emissary visiting Kingpin in Algiers. We must remember that there is also a cat fight in progress between Kingpin and Darlan, each claiming full military command of French Forces in North and West Africa. The principal thought to be driven home to all three of these prima donnas is that the situation is today solely in the military field and that any decision by any one of them, or by all of them, is subject to review and approval of Eisenhower.' Roosevelt's final sentence demonstrated a second important premise. There was a war to be fought, America had come in to fight it, and, while her commanders worked out the best way to do it, everyone else could step into line and do what they were told. It was no doubt a commendably pragmatic view but it did not take account of the fact that other people had national self-respect too. For Roosevelt, France had lost all right to such respect by her abject failure in 1940; any attempt by an individual to reassert it ahead of winning the war was premature.

The shenanigans were not quite over in Algiers. On the evening of 11 November, Clark still did not have a deal, which, he was told, would have to await the arrival of Nogues the following day. Fed up, Clark threatened Darlan with the Giraud option. To mollify him, Darlan 'invited' the French Fleet at Toulon to join him and finally phoned the French commanders in Tunisia to request that they assist the Allies. From the Vichy admiral at Toulon he received a one-word reply '*Merde*', a French variant on an old-fashioned Anglo-Saxon insult. On the afternoon of 12 November, Nogues flew in and insisted that, while the cease-fire should be made permanent, French Africa should declare itself neutral. Hearing this, Clark packed all the Frenchmen into one room and told them to come out with an agreed chain of command and a commitment to fight with the Allies.

As the latest news reached London, Cadogan for one was anticipating trouble, noting in his diary: 'A. (Eden) still in bed. Went to see him . . . warning of danger of playing in too much with Darlan. If Darlan would give us fleet and Tunisia, I should

be very grateful – and then throw him down a deep well . . .'
Eden shared his worry and immediately sent a memorandum to
Churchill: 'I think you should make it plain to the President or
Mr. Hull that the inclusion of Darlan in French administration
in North Africa would be most unpopular here, unless he had
delivered the goods in the shape of the French Navy. Nor would
de Gaulle or any of the French Movement be willing to collaborate with Darlan, and all hopes of unifying the French Empire in
the war against the Axis would be frustrated.'

The next day, 13 November, agreement was finally reached.
Darlan would be head of Government in North Africa, Nogues
would stay on as Governor of Morocco, and, in due course,
Giraud would be announced as Supreme Commander. To maintain his cloak of loyalty, Darlan claimed that he was acting 'in
the name of the Marshal'. Four days into 'Torch', it seemed that
Eisenhower and his team could celebrate at last. Even if expecta-
tions had been turned on their head, the President's core policy
of converting Vichy French Africa to the Allied cause with rela-
tively small casualties had been achieved. Militarily there was
only one drawback; Darlan's haggling had caused a vital four
day delay in the advance into Tunisia. However, the chances of
instant success there had already been jeopardized by the com-
promises over the size and locations of the 'Torch' landings, and
the failure to anticipate the speed of German reaction and its
facilitation by Pétain. At a press conference in Algiers, Clark
announced his triumph; the journalists wolfed down the jolly
stories of the pant losing and gum chewing adventures at
Cherchell which had preceded it. There was only one problem;
many people in Britain and America, not to mention the Free
French and its leader, did not warm to the idea of a deal with a
treacherous Nazi collaborator. It was only twenty months before

that Churchill had written to Roosevelt: 'dealing with Darlan is dealing with Germany.'

As reports on the bargaining in Algiers filtered through to London, there was dismay at the Foreign Office. Cadogan noted on 13 November: 'N. Africa hopelessly obscure. Americans are playing with Darlan, Nogues, Giraud and Juin. What a party! On military side, things seem to go all right, but I shan't be happy until we get to Tunis and Bizerte.' Later in the day Cadogan heard that, '*Vichy* had put out, through Darlan and Nogues, announcement that Darlan had taken over in N. Africa and ending with "Vive le Maréchal! Vive la France!" Apparently alleged that this has American endorsement! Where are we? And what is going on? De Gaulle can *never* work with that crowd.'

Eisenhower flew into Algiers on the afternoon of 13 November. More politically aware than Clark, he understood that the Darlan deal would at the very least cause consternation, though he believed that Clark was faced with no alternative and backed him to the hilt. On 14 November, Eisenhower sent a long explanation to the Chiefs-of-Staff which starkly highlighted how the political plans had gone awry: 'Can well understand some bewilderment in London and Washington with the turn that negotiations with French North Africans have taken. The actual state of existing sentiment here does not repeat nor agree even remotely with some of prior calculations.

The name of Marshal Pétain is something to conjure with here ... The civil governors, military leaders and naval commanders will agree on only one man as having an obvious right to assume the Marshal's mantle in North Africa. That man is Darlan.'

As confirmation of the terms of the deal came through,

Cadogan recorded his own opposition but hinted that *realpolitik* was asserting itself: 'A. and P.M. still seem to take this lightly. P.M. has telegraphed to Eisenhower "Anything for the battle. Politics will have to be sorted out later." That's all right, but will they be? We shall do no good till we've killed Darlan. Had to walk home in fog (physical and spiritual).' Cadogan's distress was shared by Eden's private secretary, Oliver Harvey, who had been a counsellor at the Paris Embassy during the fall of France and witnessed the conduct of the future Vichyites like Darlan: 'How can we work with Darlan who is a traitor and who has failed either to deliver the French fleet or even to pacify N. Africa without fighting? Darlan is the slipperiest politician, in the Laval class, and Murphy, the American Civil Adviser, is infatuated with Vichy. Our Cunningham is the biggest old bloody fool off his ship, and the American generals are as simple as lambs.' The next day Harvey wrote: 'Eisenhower confesses that he is at the mercy of Darlan and therefore he is obliged to reach agreement with him ... What a document! What a confession! Appeasement and nothing else. What is this agreement worth? And what harm won't it do us everywhere else? Compromising with Frenchmen who have betrayed us and killed our men, for military necessity. It is Munich reasoning over again.'

Such high emotion was not confined to London. In Washington the Treasury Secretary, Henry Morgenthau, was shocked, describing Darlan's record as 'terrible'. His unease was shared by Felix Frankfurter and a posse of younger staff in the administration, and was conveyed to the War Secretary, Henry Stimson. He recorded that the Assistant Secretary, John McCloy 'came in to see me and told me there was much excitement in the "starry-eyed circles", as Hull calls them, over the deal which Eisenhower made with Darlan. To these ardent young gentlemen, the enormous benefits which that deal brought to us in the immediate laying down of the arms of the French were as nothing compared with the sacrifice in dealing with a member of the Vichy government.' Stimson hauled in Morgenthau and the other malcontents and tried to put the matter into a military perspective: 'Poor Henry Morgenthau was sunk. He was almost for giving up the war which he said had lost all interest for him. So I gave them all a little talk.' The little talk failed to convince Morgenthau who protested that Darlan was 'a most ruthless person who had sold many thousands of people into slavery.' He argued that the working people of America, 'if they once get the idea that we are going to sit back and favour these Fascists . . . are going to say, what's the use of fighting just to put that kind of people back into power? . . . Now for the English – Darlan is known as one of the most violent British-haters. How do you suppose the men and women of England feel about this?'

The British men and women's leader, Churchill, was trying to hold the line of support for American action. He had received a bitter lament from de Gaulle who called the deal 'vile' and 'disgusting', even outweighing the importance of the capitulation of June 1940. America, he declared, had recognized 'a power founded on the betrayal of France and France's Allies, a tyrannical regime inspired by the Nazis.' He said that the deal would cause only anger inside France and pleaded with Churchill to disassociate himself from it. In response to a letter from Admiral Stark, explaining the American government's rationale, de Gaulle was unable to restrain his feelings. 'Admiral', he wrote, 'I understand that the United States is financing traitors as it seems profitable to them, but I believe that this should not be paid with the honour of France.'

It was a savage insult and the wise Stark returned the letter to de Gaulle's office, suggesting that it must have been a mistake and could not have been intended for him; otherwise such words could only lead to an end to co-operation between himself and de Gaulle on Free French matters. Shortly afterwards de Gaulle sent an aide to apologize. Nevertheless he kept the letter in his records and leaked it to the press. Stark declined to be provoked and a few days later de Gaulle sent him a further letter, which was the nearest he could bring himself to an apology. In the midst of the present tragedy, the French, he wrote 'attach particular importance to questions of morals. They may occasionally overemphasize (like he himself) such considerations and express themselves in a manner that may irritate or offend their American friends.' Shortly after the letter arrived, de Gaulle called on Stark who noted the problems of assessing the volatile Frenchman: 'If you had been sitting observing him yesterday you would have thought he was the right man in the right place. The trouble is, you can't tell what he will be tomorrow, or how he will react under a different set of circumstances. I am told that he is, no doubt, an excellent soldier, but for the large aspects as a leader of the French movement I do not think he is the right man.'

On 16 November, de Gaulle lunched with Churchill who did his best to explain the military necessity of the deal; while he understood and shared de Gaulle's feelings, what counted now was chasing the enemy out of Tunisia. De Gaulle replied: 'Imagine the incalculable consequences if France came to the conclusion that for her Allies, liberation meant Darlan. You might perhaps win the war militarily; but you would lose it morally, and there would be only one victor in the end: Stalin.' De Gaulle recalled in his memoirs that after lunch Churchill drew him aside for a private conversation and assured him: 'Yours is the true path, you alone will remain. Do not collide head-on with the Americans. It is useless and you will gain nothing. Have patience and they will come to you, for there is no alternative.' De Gaulle replied that he could not understand how Churchill, who had fought the war from the first day, could allow himself to be towed along by the United States 'whose soldiers have never even seen a German. It is up to you to take over the moral direction of this war.' De Gaulle observed that these words made a profound impression on Churchill. He had, of course, hit the crux of Churchill's dilemma; a residual and emotional loyalty to his first ally which now conflicted with the very core of his war policy, the alliance with Roosevelt.

For de Gaulle, the lunch had two positive results. That evening the BBC was allowed to report de Gaulle and the French National Committee's rejection of the deal. Churchill cabled Roosevelt the next day, moved not just by de Gaulle but also by the strength of opposition among his colleagues and the British press: 'I ought to let you know that very deep currents of feeling are stirred by the arrangements with Darlan . . . We must not overlook the serious political injury which may be done to our cause, not only in France but throughout Europe, by the feeling that we are ready to make terms with the local quislings. Darlan has an odious record. It is he who has inculcated in the French Navy its malignant disposition by promoting his creatures to command. It is but yesterday that French sailors were sent to their death against your line of battle off Casablanca and now, for the sake of power and office, Darlan plays the turncoat.' Roosevelt immediately replied: 'I too have encountered the deep currents of feeling about Darlan. I felt I should act fast so I have just given out a statement at my press conference which I hope you will like and I trust it will be accepted at face value.'

Roosevelt's press statement announced that he had accepted Eisenhower's political arrangements 'for the time being' and that they were 'a temporary expedient' to save lives and time. The word 'temporary' was littered liberally throughout the statement. Roosevelt added that he had requested the liberation of all those imprisoned in North Africa for anti-Nazi acts and the repeal of all Nazi-inspired laws and decrees. Churchill replied: 'Thank you so much for your statement about Darlan. This puts it all right for us.'

Two days later Roosevelt described to Churchill a typically folksy piece of guidance he had given American journalists: 'I told the press yesterday in confidence an old orthodox church proverb used in the Balkans that appears applicable to our present Darlan-de Gaulle problem. "My children, it is permitted you in time of grave danger to walk with the devil until you have crossed the bridge." Roosevelt's Chief-of-Staff, William Leahy, was strongly opposed to the 'temporary expedient' statement; it was one of the very few times he disagreed with the President. Darlan's record was of no account to Leahy, who disliked de Gaulle and the British anyway. He noted in his diary: 'If this stupid failure (i.e. to support Darlan without qualification) by America and Britain succeeds in alienating Admiral Darlan, it may cost us the lives of thousands of our soldiers and it may add serious obstacles to the progress of our Expeditionary Force towards Tunis, and beyond whereever that may be.' The Allied lives Darlan himself had already cost by delaying his cease-fire order were apparently of no account.

While the ever-subtle Roosevelt distanced himself in public from Darlan, he was doing the opposite in private. On his behalf, Murphy invited Darlan to fly his polio-stricken son, Alain, at American expense, to the polio rehabilitation centre at Warms Springs, Georgia, which Roosevelt himself had set up in the 1920s. Darlan immediately responded with his gratitude for the 'generous offer' which 'deeply moved me'. No doubt it was a humanitarian gesture but Roosevelt would not have offered such charity to such a man purely out of the generosity of his heart.

As Churchill and Roosevelt reached their accommodation over Darlan, something curious evolved in their attitudes towards de Gaulle. De Gaulle was visibly the victim; the Free French had been trampled on and a deal made with a man who was, second only to Pétain, their worst enemy. However, as so often happens, victims begin to grate. What should have brought sympathy for de Gaulle and the Free French now began to produce the reverse. The full text of the deal, which consolidated Darlan's power in anything but 'temporary' terms, had now come through to London and Churchill was facing an avalanche of criticism, not least from Eden. Eden wanted to amend the terms but Churchill refused to make any recommendations ahead of the Americans and was now turning his annoyance against de Gaulle. Eden noted on 20 November: 'Winston very active on telephone after tea ... One of our telephone talks lasted over half an hour. I cannot get W. to see the damage Darlan may do to the Allied cause if we don't watch it. He can make rings, diplomatically, round Eisenhower. At a moment of the shouting match W. said "Well, Darlan is not as bad as de Gaulle anyway".' The next day, Eden threw Churchill's own argument back in his face: 'Our appeal to the French people, whose resistance has been steadily stiffening, is now stultified. In Europe as a whole the "filthy race of quislings" as you once so aptly called them, will take heart since they now have reason to think that if only they happen to be in authority when the forces of the United Nations arrive, they will be treated as being the government of the country.' It was all very annoying for the Prime Minister, but America came first and tongues had to be bitten.

De Gaulle requested permission to broadcast his opposition to the Vichy 'lords' in North Africa and issue an appeal for 'a single struggle for a unified country.' Churchill vetoed the broadcast but then decided that, as 'Torch' was under American command, he was obliged to refer the request to Roosevelt. This he did in the most unctuous terms: 'De Gaulle was told that as the operations were under the United States Command I felt bound to take your opinion before agreeing to anything which might be detrimental to them. If your view was that broadcasts of this kind were undesirable at the moment, being your ardent and active Lieutenant I should bow to your decision without demur.' The broadcast did not go ahead but de Gaulle's head-quarters at Brazzaville gushed with invective against the Vichyites. Giraud's letter of loyalty and support for collaboration with Germany had now been published by Pétain and was being used mercilessly against him.

The Free French cause was faring no better in Washington, partly because they were inclined to be their own worst enemies. In the run-up to 'Torch', Roosevelt had made provisional plans to invite de Gaulle to Washington, once the landings were over. He had steadfastly refused any face-to-face encounter before-hand, afraid that it might have an adverse impact on the Vichy policy. On 20 November, two of de Gaulle's senior officials, Adrien Tixier, a blunt-spoken trade unionist who had become his front man in America, and André Philip, a lawyer and former socialist depute, finally arrived at the White House for

Roosevelt's first ever meeting with Free Frenchmen. It was a tribute to the President's single-mindedness that he had kept the door closed for so long to a movement that was lionized by much of the American public and press.

It was a thoroughly unfortunate affair. The meeting had been arranged for an earlier date but Philip had arrived late. Despite such rude and counter-productive behaviour Roosevelt had agreed to find another time. However, Philip was whipped into a frenzy by the Darlan deal and harangued the President, all the while puffing pipe smoke into his face. He had been specifically warned not to do this in the light of the disabled President's state of health. Tixier recalled that Philip screamed and almost threatened the President. After enduring such a monologue, Roosevelt gave back as good as he had got, warning the two Frenchman that he would deal with anyone as long is it helped to win the war. Jean Cremieux Brilhac, who was working in the London office, well remembers Philip's return from America: 'André Philip did not report that he arrived too late for the meeting and that he was smoking. But he was very angry with Roosevelt, whom he had greatly admired; he thought that he would convince him to become a Gaullist. He was scandalized by Roosevelt's cynicism and what angered him more than anything was when he said that if Laval were to give him Paris, he would support him. I believe that this had a great influence on de Gaulle who said to one colleague "Roosevelt is a false witness."'

Interpretation of Roosevelt's actions would occupy many minds over the next two years but, for the moment, he was a man with a public relations problem as the Darlan deal continued to backfire domestically. Despite his reckless letter to Pétain, Giraud was at least the epitome of a French cavalier. But something would have to be done about de Gaulle. The meeting with

Philip and Tixier had made Roosevelt more certain than ever that he needed to exert his famous charm on him in a face-to-face meeting. However the American Chiefs-of-Staff, among whom Leahy was an influential voice, advised that such a meeting might have a seriously adverse effect on the military campaign in North Africa. Perverse though such an idea was, it caused Roosevelt to postpone it until the New Year.

Events were about to interrupt any smooth countdown to a diplomatic *entente*. On 27 November, the Vichy French Fleet at Toulon scuttled itself to stop its ships falling into Nazi hands. To that extent the French Navy kept its promise of June 1940, but the Allies had hoped Darlan would be able to bring it over to their side. Despite his failure, Darlan was allowed to consolidate his power, maintaining the full apparatus of the Vichy regime including its anti-Semitic laws. An American correspondent in Algiers heard the despair of the resistance fighters who had risked their lives on the night of 'Torch'. "It is almost impossible to see Mr Murphy", one told him, "He shuns us like a case of contagious disease." Another said: "The army brass hats and the people of the Prefecture whom we arrested hate us because we know what cowards they are."

Churchill shared these concerns. On 9 December, he wrote to Roosevelt that Fascist organizations were victimizing 'our former French sympathizers some of whom have not yet been released from prison . . . Well-known German sympathizers who had been ousted have been reinstated. Not only have our enemies been thus encouraged but our friends have been correspondingly confused and cast down.' Churchill reported that French soldiers had even been punished for desertion because they had tried to support Allied forces during the 'Torch' landings. A week later Roosevelt replied, saying that he was dealing with these problems, but he rubbished most of the allegations: 'There will always be disturbing reports from discontented elements. In French North Africa these include Axis sympathizers, disappointed office seekers, and the de Gaulle element.'

To lump the Free French with 'Axis sympathizers' was a stark indication of Roosevelt's thinking. Even though Leahy with his own prejudices drafted many of Roosevelt's messages, there is no reason to suppose that he was not reflecting his master's voice. However, Darlan's continuing repression caused Roosevelt and Churchill to agree that Eisenhower needed a political adviser who could persuade Darlan to impart a more respectable gloss to his regime. Roosevelt's choice of Robert Murphy for the job produced howls of anguish at the Foreign Office. Harvey noted: 'Murphy, we hear, has been appointed US Civil Representative in N Africa. This is a bad appointment for us; Murphy is the nigger in the woodpile over Darlan and Vichy.' Churchill persuaded Roosevelt that there should also be a British political adviser and suggested Harold Macmillan, who was a firm Francophile with an honourable record of opposing appeasement in the 1930s and also, like Churchill, had an American mother. After arguments over Macmillan's precise status and the timing of his arrival, Roosevelt eventually accepted his appointment.

Helped by their limited political horizon, the American commanders had grown to like Darlan because he delivered. In early December he helped Eisenhower to persuade Pierre Boisson, the Governor of Dakar who had beaten off the British and Free French in 1940, to join the Allies. Dakar's strategic value had always been apparent to Roosevelt and its conversion was perceived in Washington as an immense coup; Leahy wrote: 'This is a major diplomatic victory by General Eisenhower and Mr.

Murphy.' In London the Boisson deal was viewed more cynically, Cadogan noting: 'Every sort of flap about Eisenhower's "negotiations with Boisson". These generally take the form of the Vichy French telling the Americans what they want, and the Americans giving it to them with both hands regardless of our interest or feelings.' On 8 December, after a dinner at the Savoy with de Gaulle, Cadogan recorded the prevailing sentiments in the Foreign Office and Carlton Gardens: 'De Gaulle's one remedy is "Get rid of Darlan". My answer is "Yes; but how?" No answer.'

The answer had been in the offing as long ago as 18 November, just ten days after 'Torch'. Philippe Raguenau was one of the young resisters who had taken part in the Algiers *putsch*. To him and his friends the take-over by Darlan was unbearable. "It was then", he recalls, "that I decided independently, I wasn't influenced by anybody, to settle this issue before going on to Tunisia and fighting against the Germans. I spoke with three of my comrades, who shared the same corner of the barn, and said "we can't carry on fighting when we know there is a traitor to France behind us." So I asked them if they agreed that Darlan had to be executed before we left, and they said "Yes". So I took four pieces of straw from the barn and said whoever draws the shortest straw would be the one to kill Darlan. I at first thought it was me, but Bonnier said "No, Philippe, it's me". He lined his piece of straw next to mine and in fact it was he who had drawn the shortest straw. I said "OK, we will leave for Tunisia and you are to stay behind and do what's necessary."

On Christmas Eve 1942, Fernand Bonnier de la Chapelle calmly walked into Darlan's quarters and shot him five times. He died shortly afterwards in hospital. Ever since, the Darlan assassination has provoked many conspiracy theories. Raguenau's group had been in contact with one of the original Algiers Group of Five, Henri d'Astier de la Vigérie, who had always wanted a royalist coup. Henri's brother, the Gaullist General François d'Astier de la Vigérie, had just visited Algiers on a mission from de Gaulle to try to establish a relationship with Giraud and gave his brother a large sum in dollars to support Gaullists in Algiers; some of it was found on the assassin. There have also been rumours that British Intelligence was involved, because SOE agents had trained Raguenau's group before the *putsch* and afterwards they were billeted with the British. However it seems simpler to believe Raguenau whose recollection is crystal clear. "Of course we recognized de Gaulle as our leader, but we were used to taking responsibility. We were free, independent and determined."

The Darlan assassination provoked very different reactions in the White House and Whitehall. Harvey wrote: 'Darlan is dead! A sigh of relief and satisfaction will run through the country and the European nations at the removal of this horrible quisling who fought us and denounced us while we were fighting alone and finally who fought even the Americans until they capitulated to his terms.' Roosevelt called the assassination "murder of the first degree" which Harvey considered the only 'false note', marring what should have been a universal celebration. By contrast Leahy recorded: 'Darlan, in spite of his fanatical dislike for everything English, was in my opinion, and I knew him well, an invaluable asset to the Allied Cause in Africa. The British will probably make an effort to force General de Gaulle into his place as leader of the French. Such an effort will fall and will be harmful to the Allied Cause.' Harvey offered a prophetic insight: 'Darlan, though dead, hasn't yet finished his deadly work. He will leave a nasty hangover on Anglo-American relations.'

Bonnier de la Chapelle was executed the next day, after a summary court-martial on the orders of General Bergeret, a Darlan loyalist, who had responsibility for the security of his offices. The Vichyites feared that the assassination was the prelude to a Gaullist uprising, but more sensible people hoped that it might at last pave the way for de Gaulle, who had always said that Darlan was the only obstacle, to join the French leadership in Algiers. However Roosevelt insisted that Giraud should succeed Darlan without further ado and any immediate hope of reconciliation was swiftly crushed.

De Gaulle wrote to Giraud, urging an immediate meeting: 'The assassination at Algiers is an indication and warning; an indication of the exasperation into which the tragedy of France has thrown the mind and soul of Frenchmen; a warning of the consequences of every kind which necessarily result from the absence of a national authority in the midst of the greatest national crisis of our history.' Giraud, who most probably consulted Murphy, was unmoved and rejected de Gaulle's overture, claiming: 'Owing to the deep emotion aroused . . . in North Africa by the recent assassination, the atmosphere is at present unfavourable to a meeting between us.' Churchill wrote to Roosevelt that he strongly favoured a meeting between de Gaulle and Giraud as soon as possible, 'before rivalries crystallize.' He included the customary dig at de Gaulle: 'We are putting hard pressure on de Gaulle to shut his Brazzaville mouth . . .' On New Year's Day, Roosevelt replied: 'Why doesn't de Gaulle go to war? Why doesn't he start North by West half West from Brazzaville? It would take him a long time to get to the Oasis of Somewhere. A happy New Year to you and yours.'

The prospects for one happy, united French family seemed distant. But, beyond the jokes, Roosevelt still knew that there would have to be some accommodation with de Gaulle, as long as he could be kept subservient. The attempt was about to be made at Casablanca, in circumstances that would produce a bizarre combination of high farce and bitterness.

CHAPTER ELEVEN
CASABLANCA CAPER

On New Year's Day 1943, in the same cable in which he had suggested that de Gaulle take a running jump from Brazzaville, Roosevelt laid down the basic article of faith which would govern his dealings with the French until the war's end. In previous messages and conversations he had given hints of his attitude, but now the set of his mind was crystal clear and he conveyed it both to Churchill and his military commanders. 'We have a military occupation in North Africa. We must not let any of our French friends forget this for a moment,' he wrote. 'By the same token I don't want any of them to think that we are going to recognize anyone or any committee or group as representing the French Government or the French Empire. The people of France will settle their own affairs after we have won this war. Until then we can deal with local Frenchmen on a local basis wherever our armies occupy former French territory. And if these local officials won't play ball we will have to replace them.'

Over the next year and a half Roosevelt's unyielding pursuit of this policy would bring great conflict, not just with de Gaulle, but also with his own military commanders in the field and the British Government. Churchill would be caught in the middle, torn by opposing loyalties but ultimately determined that, at all costs, a rift with the President had to be avoided. Roosevelt's conduct would provoke many questions about this most elusive of politicians. Was his behaviour that of a cynic or an idealist; an autocrat or a democrat; a man driven by personal animus or genuine considerations of a higher policy?

The appointment of Giraud to replace Darlan had at least removed the most sulphurous trace of the Vichy policy. But Giraud was still presiding over a regime of Vichyites, most notably Nogues in Morocco and Boisson in Dakar. They were now joined by a third, Marcel Peyrouton, a former Minister of the Interior under Pétain, who had ended up as Vichy's Ambassador to Argentina. Darlan had wanted to bring Peyrouton to North Africa as Governor-General of Algeria and, on Murphy's recommendation, Hull had approved the appointment, apparently without Roosevelt's knowledge. Sumner Welles, Roosevelt's trusted adviser at the State Department, had objected but been overruled by Hull who was engaged in a long personal feud with him. Peyrouton's resurgence could not have been better designed to inflame Free French feelings; he was the man who had signed de Gaulle's death warrant in 1940.

Further provocation came from Giraud, who continued to refuse de Gaulle's requests for a meeting, telling him that he would have to wait until the end of January at the earliest. Fed up, de Gaulle resorted to his standard tactic of using the press to blow the lid off the dustbin of obfuscation. Despite a plea from Cadogan to restrain himself, he issued a statement that the continued exclusion of the Free French meant that France was being 'deprived, at the crucial moment, of the trump card which the unity of her vast Empire would constitute.' He then lamented 'the stupefaction of the French people, overwhelmed in its misery.' He made public his offer to meet Giraud and asserted that France's situation allowed no delay in their coming together.

The implicit criticism of America, Giraud's puppeteer, was

clear. Cadogan prophetically noted: 'De Gaulle . . . got his statement in the press. By that, he's probably done for himself. Got
off to A. (Eden) a draft of a frank telegram to Washington trying
to dispel their baleful suspicions about our relations with de
Gaulle. But nothing will cure them.' It did not take long for the
petty-minded and irascible Hull to overreact, complaining to
the British Embassy in Washington that British leaders were
shouting their approval of de Gaulle's statement, which was
aimed at 'arousing bitterness against the United States Government'. Hull warned that this propaganda from London 'would
create inevitably a serious friction between Great Britain and the
United States.' Eden calmly pointed out that no British leader
had shouted approval and wondered whether the Secretary of
State was referring to newspaper leaders.

As usual, the press and public gave de Gaulle overwhelming
support. Amid the pleasing reverberations of his press statement,
his new ADC, Leon Teyssot, recorded: 'The General is optimistic
about events, he told me that the Americans are getting themselves tangled up in North Africa and that one day they would
call on him to sort out the situation.' However, the call came
sooner and less desirably than de Gaulle had been anticipating.

On 9 January, Roosevelt set off from Washington for Africa.
After a brief inspection of Dakar, the strategic base that had
always interested him, his ultimate destination was Casablanca
where he, Churchill, and the British and American Chiefs-of-
Staff were to hold a highly secret conference to plan the Allies'
drive to victory. It was a gruelling journey and Margaret Suckley
worried about how the President would manage: 'I think F. has
mixed feelings about this trip. He is somewhat excited about it –
The adventure of it – seeing all he will see, etc. On the other
hand it is a long trip, with definite risks – But one *can't* and

mustn't think of that. He is going because he feels he must go; to plan for the future, to really *see* the situation in N. Africa – He will see Giraud, Eisenhower etc. Winston Churchill first and foremost, of course.' De Gaulle was not on the agenda.

Despite Margaret's worries, the journey invigorated Roosevelt. Harry Hopkins accompanied him on the first leg as his flying boat left American shores: 'he acted like a sixteen year old boy, for he has done no flying since he was President.' When he arrived in Casablanca five days later, Murphy noticed that, away from the cares of Washington, Roosevelt seemed like an excited child on a school treat. Eisenhower, who put in a brief appearance at Casablanca before returning to Algiers to oversee the faltering campaign in Tunisia, found Roosevelt light-hearted. He also noted his pessimism about the future of France and doubts as to whether she could ever recover her power and prestige.

Churchill and Roosevelt settled in for what would turn out to be an eight-day stay. Their surroundings were comfortable. A luxurious hotel in the affluent suburb of Anfa, previously used by members of the German Armistice Commission, had been requisitioned for the conference along with a number of elegant villas. Churchill cabled home: 'Conditions most agreeable. I wish I could say the same of the problems.' Roosevelt wrote to Margaret Suckley saying that he had been driven under armed guard 'in a car with soaped windows to this delightful villa belonging to a Madame Bessan whose army husband is a prisoner in France – She and her child were ejected as were the other cottage owners and sent to the hotel in town.'

Security was tight as plenty of local agents working for the Germans were left in town. It was still only two months since the hard fought battle in Casablanca harbour. Harry Hopkins's son,

Robert, an army signal corps photographer, had been ordered to proceed to Casablanca without being given any reason. He recalls that: "As we drove through the city the security was incredible, there were barbed wire entanglements everywhere, there were sentries marching in pairs with guard dogs, there were aeroplanes circling overhead, it was just incredible, and this was a thousand miles from where the action was." As Hopkins arrived at the Anfa Hotel, he recognized a familiar face, a Secret Service man from the White House: 'We had a conversation and I heard this deep laughter from the other side of the room and it was the President and he had set this whole thing up and arranged for me to come back.' It was something of a family gathering all round as Roosevelt had also invited his sons, John and Eliot, an American Air Force pilot. Eliot too recorded the jollity, writing that after dinner with Churchill on the first night, which ended well after midnight, 'Father was tired, but still in a talkative mood, excited after his trip, expansive, and happy to see me again. I sat with him while he got into bed, and afterwards kept him up for the time it takes to smoke two or three cigarettes.'

Of course, so many important people had not gathered at Casablanca to spend their time smoothing the internecine quarrels of recalcitrant Frenchmen; there was a war to be planned. But, somehow, as so often seemed to happen, the matter of France hijacked the attention of the President and the Prime Minister. As soon as he arrived, Roosevelt was struck by the press clamour over de Gaulle. With resignation, he cabled back to Hull in Washington: 'It had been my hope that we could avoid political discussions at this time, but I found on arrival that American and British newspapers had made such a mountain out of rather a small hill that I should not return to

Washington without having achieved settlement of this matter.'

Roosevelt set out to apply all his mastery of political fixing to the intractable French allies. In private, a certain frivolity prevailed as he told Churchill: "We'll call Giraud the bridegroom, and I'll produce him from Algiers, and you get the bride, de Gaulle, down from London, and we'll have a shotgun wedding." Churchill told his private detective: "We have to marry these two somehow!" According to Eliot Roosevelt, his father thought that Churchill was playing a game with de Gaulle, preparing a dramatic last minute entrance: "I have a strong sneaking suspicion" – and he accented those words – "that our friend de Gaulle hasn't come to Africa yet because our friend Winston hasn't chosen to bid him come yet. I am more than partially sure that de Gaulle will do just about anything, at this point, that the Prime Minister and the Foreign Office ask him to do." If only, Churchill might have thought.

Back in London, de Gaulle, like the rest of the world had no idea that Casablanca was taking place. In fact, he was becoming fed up with Africa and focusing his future hopes on the support he had established within the resistance in mainland France. Teyssot, who seems to have been remarkably bold with his boss recorded: 'He said to me, "North Africa is nothing." I replied, "But it's the most important part of the Empire, that isn't 'nothing.'" The general's reply was: "What do you want me to do about it if Giraud doesn't want to join me, he's an imbecile and I don't have time to deal with imbeciles." "It sometimes happens that we just have to, General."' Then on 17 January, de Gaulle was given a most surprising telegram sent by Churchill from somewhere in Africa: 'I should be glad if you would come to join me here by first available plane which we shall provide, as it is in my power to bring about a meeting between you and General

Giraud under conditions of complete secrecy and with the best prospects.'

De Gaulle was summoned to the Foreign Office where Cadogan recorded his predictable response: 'De Gaulle arrived at 12 and A. and I saw him. He is a species of mule: he refuses to go, and nothing A. or I could say would move him.' De Gaulle had no intention of being railroaded by foreigners into a meeting on French soil on what he considered to be a purely internal French matter. Eden and Cadogan asked him to take time to think about it. De Gaulle returned to the Foreign Office at 5pm to confirm his refusal, at the same time sending a further message to Giraud that he would be willing to meet him at any time, anywhere on French territory. Disconsolately, Cadogan noted: 'He wouldn't budge, so we had no alternative but to inform P.M. This, I should think, is the end of the Free French movement. Roosevelt will say to P.M. "Look at your friend: this is how he behaves." And Winston will have to agree with him – and shed de Gaulle. A *great* pity. But in point of fact, would de Gaulle, being what he is, *ever* collaborate with *anyone*?' With delicious language de Gaulle drafted his telegram of refusal to be forwarded to Churchill by the Foreign Office: 'I value most highly the sentiments which inspire your message and thank you very heartily for them. Allow me, to say, however, that the atmosphere of an exalted Allied forum around the Giraud-de Gaulle conversations as well as the suddenness with which those conversations have been proposed to me do not seem to me the best for an effective agreement.'

On the same day Giraud was being presented at Anfa for inspection by the President. Eliot Roosevelt recorded the sales pitch which Murphy had given the President two days before: 'Suave, smooth Robert Murphy came in for a few minutes around five o'clock. Murphy was anxious to fill Father in on Giraud, how competent he would be as an administrator, how ideal a choice he was for the Americans to back.' On 17 January, Giraud flew in from Algiers. Despite the initial fracas on the eve of 'Torch', Eisenhower had become impressed by Giraud's fighting qualities and the loyalty he had come to command over the Vichy French soldiers. His political qualities were more suspect. Churchill had already come to the view that he was suited only to military command and Harold Macmillan, the British Minister to Eisenhower, would later write of a meeting with Giraud: 'He is a most difficult man to talk to, because he is really nice and also so stately and stupid.' As another observer put it, Giraud's 'noble brow has never been furrowed by the effort of thought.'

The opinion that mattered was Roosevelt's. Giraud arrived with his sponsor, Murphy, and General Clark; according to Eliot Roosevelt, he showed no interest in political problems, all that mattered was the winning of the war and the rearming of the French Army and Navy. Churchill pointed out that the delay in repealing Vichy's anti-Semitic laws was 'one of the main causes of de Gaulle's pique – or at least one of the alleged causes. Giraud swept these questions aside. He was single-minded.' Eliot recorded that the meeting 'was a vast disappointment to Father. And as soon as Giraud and the others were out of the room, Father showed by expression and gesture what he thought. "I'm afraid we're leaning on a very slender reed", he said. He threw up his hands, and laughed shortly. "This is the man that Bob Murphy said the French would rally around! He's a dud as an administrator, he'll be a dud as a leader."'

Giraud's failure to impress increased the pressure on Churchill to produce de Gaulle, but the frantic messages between London and Casablanca, as de Gaulle continued to dig in his heels, were about to assume a comic opera flavour. Late on 17 January, de Gaulle's telegram of refusal had been accompanied by a despairing message from Eden: 'Despite long argument have been unable to persuade General de Gaulle to go out to join you.' Roosevelt, who was evidently beginning to enjoy his Allies' embarrassment, cabled back to Eden: 'I have got the bridegroom, where is the bride?'

The next day, Churchill upped the ante, repeating his request to de Gaulle and informing him: 'I am authorized to say that the invitation to you to come here was from the President of the United States of America as well as from me.' He then issued a stern warning: 'The fact that you have refused to come to the meeting proposed will, in my opinion, be almost universally censured. My attempt to bridge the difficulties which have existed between your movement and the United States will definitely have failed. I should certainly not be able to renew my exertions in this direction while you remain the Leader of the above movement.' He accompanied this with a note to Eden: 'The man must be mad to jeopardize the whole future of the relations of his movement with the United States. If in his fantasy of egotism he rejects the chance now offered, I shall feel that his removal from the Headship of the Free French Movement is essential to the further support of this movement by H.M.G. I think that, for his own sake, you should knock him about pretty hard.'

Now loving every moment, Roosevelt cabled to Hull: 'We delivered our bridegroom, General Giraud, who was most co-operative on the impending marriage, and I am sure was ready to go through with it on our terms. However our friends could not produce the bride, the temperamental lady de Gaulle. She has got quite snooty about the whole idea and does not want to see either of us, and is showing no intention of getting into bed with Giraud.' It was all very funny but, in the years ahead, when Roosevelt's disrespect became public knowledge, his jibes would leave a less amusing after-taste.

The next day, Roosevelt was still telling Eliot that he thought it was all a British game: '"The next two or three days will tell the story," Father said, now quite cheerfully. "This is Tuesday? I'll take a small bet Winston tells us no later than Friday that he thinks he'll be able to get de Gaulle to come down after all."' In London, Eden was desperately trying to get de Gaulle to come to the Foreign Office, but de Gaulle had decided to go walkabout. He instructed Teyssot to stall: 'At 10am, Eden made it clear that he wanted to see the General about his departure to Algiers. I replied that the General was at the Comité National and could only meet him at 1pm.'

De Gaulle then decided that he was too busy and cancelled the meeting altogether. A Foreign Office official suggested a later time of 6pm. De Gaulle told Teyssot: "I will not go and see him." The tactful Eden sent a further message: 'I am sorry you have found it impossible to call on me today to receive the Prime Minister's message. However, I send it to you now, as time may be short, with the expression of my earnest hope that you will give it the most careful and dispassionate consideration.' But de Gaulle had gone to ground and Eden could only report back to Churchill: 'General de Gaulle, fearing no doubt a dusty answer, has found pretext for not seeing me.'

Churchill was now showing a hint of desperation. He cabled London: 'MOST IMMEDIATE. I must really have an answer about Joan of Arc as things will have moved on.' Roosevelt could not resist sharing the joke with Margaret Suckley: 'De Gaulle has declined a second invitation – says he will not be "duressed" by WSC and especially by the American President – Today I asked WSC who paid de Gaulle's salary – WSC beamed – good idea – no come – no pay!' With no word from London, Churchill sent a second telegram to Eden: 'We have been waiting all day for a further reply from de Gaulle or for some explanation by you. If de Gaulle does not come the President will make an arrangement very favourable for General Giraud which I shall not easily be able to resist. Giraud has made an excellent impression on everyone here, military and political alike.' The compliment to Giraud was something of an exaggeration, but Churchill accurately described the risk that de Gaulle was running.

20 January was make or break day. Eden cabled to Churchill: 'Am doing my utmost. I am having final interview with General de Gaulle in two hours, and will telegraph immediately after it.' By now de Gaulle was also coming under pressure from his own side. In the confines of the private office, Teyssot plucked up his courage: 'I asked him to forgive me for speaking frankly but I thought that he did not realise the strength of the Americans, that he had no right to refuse this invitation in the name of France, even in the displeasing circumstances.' More significantly, the French National Committee believed that de Gaulle had to swallow his dignity. Etienne Burin de Roziers, then a junior member of de Gaulle's staff recalls: 'So de Gaulle did end up going. What is interesting is that this man, who was from the outset portrayed as a kind of dictator, had to, whether he liked it or not, obey the decision of the National Committee.'

De Gaulle finally relented, sending a judiciously worded cable to Churchill: 'President Roosevelt and you are asking me presently to take part, without warning, in discussions of which I know neither the programme nor the conditions, and during which I will be led to discuss matters concerning the whole future of the French Empire and of France itself. I recognize however, despite these questions of form, grave though they may be, that the general situation of the war and the position in which France is temporarily placed cannot allow me to refuse to the meet the President of the United States and his Britannic Majesty's Prime Minister. I therefore agree to join in your meeting.' Relief flooded the Foreign Office. 'De Gaulle came to see A. and me at 5pm. He now agrees to go! But if his plane can't get off tonight, he will have missed the bus!' wrote Cadogan. De Gaulle decided there was no need to rush and took ample time to organize his departure. Eventually, after a stopover in Gibraltar, he touched down at Casablanca on the morning of 22 January. He was greeted by the American General, Wilbur, but there was no fanfare, no guard of honour and just a few American sentries on the periphery. De Gaulle later wrote that, before getting in their car, Wilbur 'dipped a rag in the mud and smeared all the window, These precautions were taken in order to conceal the presence of General de Gaulle and his colleagues in Morocco.'

Lunch with Giraud followed. De Gaulle, burning with resentment that he was effectively an American captive on French soil, protested at the circumstances of their meeting when he had made so many previous suggestions that they should come together. However, they unwound over a cordial lunch and, at de Gaulle's request, Giraud told the story of his escape from Königstein which was indeed dramatic; despite a leg wound which had never fully healed, he had slid down a 150 foot rope to make his getaway from the fortress prison. According to Burin de Roziers, after Giraud had recounted his tale several times over, "de Gaulle then said, "well now explain to me how you managed to be captured", which did not please him very much!" A French lunch could not paper over the differences between the French Generals. Giraud said that he had no time for politics and simply wanted to fight the war; he wished to carry on working with the former Vichy leaders whom he considered effective administrators. De Gaulle responded with blistering tirades against Darlan, Peyrouton and Boisson.

De Gaulle's next encounter was with Churchill who was well prepared for a blunt talk. That morning Harry Hopkins had visited him at breakfast and noted that, to his astonishment, 'I found Churchill in his customary pink robe, and having, of all things, a bottle of wine for breakfast. I asked him what he meant by that and he told me that he had a profound distaste for skimmed milk, and no deep rooted prejudice about wine, and that he had reconciled the conflict in favour of the latter. He commended it to me and said he had lived to be 68 years old and was in the best of health, and had found that the advice of doctors, throughout his life, was usually wrong.' In the late afternoon de Gaulle was summoned to see Churchill at his villa, no doubt further fortified by lunch.

De Gaulle complained that he would never have come if he had known that he was going to be surrounded by American bayonets on French territory; Churchill retorted that they were in an occupied country. After these preliminary snarls, the atmosphere calmed and Churchill laid out the plan he had agreed with Roosevelt for French unity; Giraud and de Gaulle would be joint Presidents of a Governing Committee with equal status except that Giraud would have supreme military command. The former Vichyites would also sit on the committee as, Churchill said, "The Americans have now accepted them and want them to be trusted." De Gaulle retorted that even Churchill himself could not take such a solution seriously. If it had to come to this, "Fighting France would not play their game; if it must disappear, it preferred to do so honourably."

Churchill's doctor, Sir Charles Moran, described Churchill's reaction to the meeting, which said everything about his conflicting emotions: 'When at last they emerged from the little sitting-room in our villa, the Prime Minister stood in the hall watching the Frenchman stalk down the garden path with his head in the air. Winston turned to us with a whimsical smile: "His country has given up fighting, he himself is a refugee, and if we turn him down he is finished. Well, just look at him! Look at him!" he repeated. "He might be Stalin with two hundred divisions behind his words. I was pretty rough with him. I made it quite plain that if he could not be more helpful we were done with him."

"How," I asked, "did he like that?" "Oh," the Prime Minister replied, "he hardly seemed interested. My advances and my threats met with no response." Churchill's admiration for France was indestructible. "France without an Army is not France", he said, "de Gaulle is the spirit of that Army," and then he sadly added, "perhaps the last survivor of a warrior race."'

Churchill and Roosevelt were living in another world if they seriously believed that de Gaulle, with all his pride and intransigence, would meekly lie down with Boisson, who had bested him at Dakar, and Peyrouton, who had signed his death sentence at Vichy. Nevertheless they continued their attempt and that evening de Gaulle met Roosevelt for the first time. Though de Gaulle was unaware of it, the meeting took place in strange circumstances. Halfway through Hopkins, ever present at Roosevelt's side, noticed that 'the whole of the Secret Service detail was behind the curtain and above the gallery in the living room and at all doors leading into the room and I glimpsed a Tommy Gun in the hands of one.' Hopkins left the meeting and found all the Secret Servicemen armed to the teeth with a dozen Tommy Guns: 'They told me they could not take any chances on anything happening to the President. None of this hokus pokus had gone on when Giraud saw the President.' Hopkins thought the Secret Servicemen were 'unbelievably funny' and concluded that they had 'put on this little act on their own', but it was a remarkable indication of how far the smearing of de Gaulle had gone.

De Gaulle would later describe Roosevelt as 'this artist, this seducer', and, at this first meeting, de Gaulle fell for the seduction. Stiff and austere when he arrived, he was soon melted by the President's charm, even if Roosevelt was outlining precisely the same proposal as Churchill a few hours before. Roosevelt later told Felix Frankfurter that he had asked de Gaulle why he could not simply take the field of battle as a military commander. De Gaulle replied that he was no longer a military man but, like Joan of Arc, had become the emblem of national liberation: 'I am the Joan of Arc of today.' In saying this, de Gaulle hoped to convey his concept of the mystique and genius of France; the comparison with Joan of Arc came not from personal vanity, but from a passionate patriotism.

Later, in the very first page of his war memoirs de Gaulle wrote: 'The emotional side of me tends to imagine France, like the princess in the fairy stories or the Madonna in the frescoes, as dedicated to an exalted and exceptional destiny.' He believed that Providence had created France 'for complete successes or for exemplary misfortunes.' To fulfil her genius France would always need a strong national figurehead to respect. At this time, de Gaulle had come to believe that Pétain represented her debasement and he her honour. However he also believed Napoleon to have been the warning that her leader could never be a dictator. It was a combination of ideas with which the pragmatic President was unlikely to sympathize, or even bother to understand.

Tragically, de Gaulle believed that Roosevelt did comprehend. After this first meeting he told an aide: "You see, I have met a great statesman today. I think we got along and understood each other well." The next day, de Gaulle and Giraud met again; Giraud argued that he should be Commander-in-Chief, assisted by two delegates, one for North Africa, the other, de Gaulle, for the territories occupied by the Free French. De Gaulle rejected this out of hand and told Giraud that he should forsake his collaboration with the Vichyites and join the Free French. He could have the post of Commander-in-Chief, while de Gaulle would be the Civil Chief. In other words, said de Gaulle: "you will be Foch to my Clémenceau."

On being told of this remark, Roosevelt found it a matter of huge amusement. He began to tell a de Gaulle joke: 'One day he says he's Joan of Arc, the next day he says he's Clémenceau. I told him, "you've got to decide which one you want to be".' The 'joke' achieved widespread circulation, eventually finding its way into the newspapers. It was all thoroughly offensive to de Gaulle and by the time he came to write his memoirs, his perception of the meeting had dramatically changed: 'Beneath his patrician mask of courtesy, Roosevelt regarded me without benevolence.' It would soon become clear that this assessment made more than a decade later was the correct one. Yet, despite all the trouble de Gaulle caused him, Churchill did empathize. He told Moran, with tears in his eyes: 'England's grievous offence in de Gaulle's eyes is that she has helped France. He cannot bear to think that she needed help. He will not relax his vigilance in guarding her honour for a single instant.'

As 24 January dawned, the final day of the Casablanca conference, there was still no sign of agreement between the two French Generals. Discussions between Churchill and Roosevelt, with Hopkins, Macmillan and Murphy present, had continued into the small hours. Murphy laid his cards on the table, saying that it was useless to continue negotiating with de Gaulle and it would be best to break with him. Roosevelt agreed; earlier, he had told Hopkins that he was ready to destroy de Gaulle before public opinion in the United States. Macmillan, with the important support of Hopkins, argued that there should be another attempt at fusion.

In the morning, a declaration of the Allies' proposal for a 'representative' French committee under joint control was drafted. Giraud agreed to sign it but de Gaulle still refused, maintaining his veto on the presence of Vichyites. Churchill now had a furious encounter with de Gaulle. 'My meeting with Mr. Churchill was characterized, on his part, by extreme acrimony,' de Gaulle wrote. 'Of all our encounters during the war, this was the most ungracious.' Churchill was overheard to say in inimitable Franglais, "Si vous m'obstaclerez, je vous liquiderai!" Through the morning he continued to threaten, "Mon General, il ne faut pas obstacler la guerre," in the full hearing of the Americans. De Gaulle assumed that he was trying to impress them.

Finally, de Gaulle went to see Roosevelt who received him in a 'kind and sorrowful' tone. The President asked him at least to offer the public a joint declaration, which would confirm the drama of the two French leaders' secret meeting. De Gaulle promised him a communiqué 'even though it cannot be yours.' Journalists and newsreel cameras were now gathering to record the appearance together of Churchill and Roosevelt, and to spring the news of Casablanca onto an unsuspecting world. Roosevelt asked de Gaulle if he would agree to appear with Giraud before the cameras and even shake his hand. Robert Hopkins, who was one of the photographers, recalls what happened next: 'I didn't see de Gaulle until he sat down in a chair – they'd brought out two more chairs – and then the President asked Giraud and de Gaulle to shake hands to show that they had reached an agreement. De Gaulle obviously didn't want to shake hands and the President insisted and it was just a brusque shake of the hands, just one shake, and Sammy Shulman, who was a White House photographer said "Mr. President, I didn't get the picture." And so the President made them shake hands again and de Gaulle was obviously very irritated at this, but he went through with it.'

De Gaulle and Giraud issued a blunt declaration: 'We have met. We have talked. We have registered our entire agreement on the end to be achieved, which is the liberation of France and the triumph of human liberties by the total defeat of the enemy. This end will be attained by the union in the war of all Frenchmen fighting side by side with all their Allies.' As the parties dispersed, there was one last turn in the tragicomedy. The plane in which de Gaulle had travelled out to London was unserviceable. He was offered an American replacement but declared that he would not travel in a United States aircraft because American pilots had no idea of navigation, and he had no desire to be landed in France. The following day, the British plane was repaired and de Gaulle departed for London. He told a Foreign Office official travelling with him that Churchill had used "des paroles épouvantables." More importantly he believed that North Africa had become a perpetuation of the Vichy Fascist regime, in which Giraud would be ensnared more firmly every day.

There was one positive development. It had been agreed that General Catroux should travel to Algiers as de Gaulle's representative and start negotiations with Giraud to try to find an agreement which the over hasty pressure applied by Roosevelt, Churchill and their acolytes had failed to bring. However, Casablanca had fostered two illusions. Firstly, Roosevelt thought that the show of unity that he had forced on Giraud and de Gaulle had achieved a genuine success in knocking the two French Generals' heads together. On 5 February his optimism was conveyed in a message to Churchill: 'I take it that your bride and my bridegroom have not yet started throwing the crockery. I trust the marriage will be consummated.' For Roosevelt it was confirmation that his particular brand of personal diplomacy, conducted through envoys who bypassed government departments and reported straight to him, was the best way to conduct international affairs.

For some of his cabinet members, like the Secretary for War, Henry Stimson, these methods could be infuriating. Just after Casablanca Stimson wanted to send the Assistant War Secretary, John McCloy, to Africa to liaise with Eisenhower. Roosevelt told him that there would be nothing for McCloy to do: 'He says he did settle all the matters that were troubling Eisenhower when he was over there.' Roosevelt added that Murphy, who had from the beginning been instructed to bypass the State Department, was handling affairs on his behalf. Stimson recorded: 'This was a truly Rooseveltian position. I told him frankly over the telephone that it was bad administration and asked him what a Cabinet was for and what Departments were for except to have reports considered in that way, but I have small hopes of reforming him. The fault is Rooseveltian and deeply ingrained.' It all added up to a simple fact; this was the President's game and he intended to play all the cards.

The second illusion was that, with the jokes and contempt still concealed behind closed doors, de Gaulle continued to think that he had made headway with the President. Travelling back from Casablanca, Teyssot noted de Gaulle's interpretation of their meeting: "The General got the impression from his conversation with Roosevelt that the President did not want to create two French rivals for his own American political goals. It was a successful personal encounter." Two days later de Gaulle remarked, "The President has discovered the Fighting French." On 14 February, de Gaulle wrote to Hull: 'I would be grateful if you would transmit to the President of the United States an expression of the great pleasure I have had in making a first contact with him. His sentiments of ardent sympathy towards France could not fail to deeply touch a Frenchman.' No doubt his message was partly a matter of diplomacy but he clearly believed that he had shifted Roosevelt towards himself and away from Giraud and his team of Vichyites. If de Gaulle could have heard what Roosevelt was saying about him in the confines of the White House, he would have been devastated.

Curtis Roosevelt, the President's grandson and then a teenager, moved back with his family to live in the White House in early 1943. Before he arrived, he held the popular view of de Gaulle: "When we lived in Seattle, I think I was very much in line with the general American public, who looked upon de Gaulle as a heroic figure waving the Free French flag, resistance to the Germans, a romantic figure, a valiant figure, a courageous figure." At the privacy of the White House dinner table, where, like well-behaved children, Curtis and his sister were expected to be seen but not heard, his illusions were quickly shattered by his grandfather: "I was shocked to hear the dinner table conversation. It was disparaging of de Gaulle, suddenly I was hearing about a different de Gaulle, a difficult de Gaulle, an impossible de Gaulle, a pretentious de Gaulle, a de Gaulle who didn't know his place which, in those days, was a serious condemnation. It was not only the words, it was the expression on his face, the raised eyebrows, the expression of exasperation. 'Who does this man think he is? Who does he represent? Well, he doesn't represent anybody.'" Roosevelt's contempt was further displayed in telling the joke about Joan of Arc and Clémenceau. The observant young Curtis noticed that, "while FDR might make jokes about his political opponents, he was not disrespectful, because they had power. But when it got to de Gaulle he could not see what de Gaulle's negotiating position was at all."

At this moment there was an irony in the triangular relationship. At a press conference on 9 February, in which he called for 'a union of France's empire for the liberation of France', de Gaulle showed warmth towards Roosevelt as 'the man who has the highest aims in this war.' However, still smarting at his treatment by Churchill at Casablanca, he coldly stated: 'I don't think it would have served any useful purpose to tell him things he ought to know by now.' Yet, while Roosevelt privately despised him and sought to undermine him, Churchill, despite his fury after the embarrassment of Casablanca, continued privately to give him a helping hand.

After Casablanca, Churchill's anger had surfaced in the standard way, with mutterings that he was going to break with de Gaulle, deflected as always by Eden and indeed by King George VI, who warned Churchill not to be too hasty with de Gaulle. The King told Churchill that he could 'well understand de Gaulle's attitude, and that of our own people here, who do not like the idea of making friends of those Frenchmen who have collaborated with the Germans.' In addition Churchill maintained his customary ploy of keeping de Gaulle prisoner in London, the Foreign Office being forced to convey as tactfully as possible the Prime Minister's continuing refusal to accede to de Gaulle's request for a plane to visit Africa and Syria.

However, behind the scenes, Churchill worked to undo some of the damage of Casablanca. Murphy had drawn up two memoranda which, contrary to the President's espoused aims of unity and the agreements reached on all sides at Casablanca, provided 'for a supply of arms and aircraft to Giraud on a lavish scale from American sources, the other recognizing him to all intents as the sole authority for French affairs not only in North Africa but everywhere else.' The scheming Murphy had obtained Roosevelt's signature to these, thus confirming either the President's deceitfulness or, more probably, his slapdash attitude to paperwork. Murphy also claimed that the memoranda had been approved by Churchill who, in fact, knew nothing of them. Back at the Foreign Office Harvey noted: 'Sharp work by Murphy!' Over the coming weeks, Churchill, whose attitude to paperwork was more punctilious by far than Roosevelt's, worked patiently and quietly to amend the documents and maintain the rights of the Free French. Meanwhile, de Gaulle was unaware of either the memoranda or Churchill's intervention on his behalf.

The early months of 1943 progressed in strange, uncertain ways, a gathering of the forces whose outcome seemed impossible to foretell as possibilities of confrontation or rapprochement hung together in the air. Militarily, the Allies, delayed by the flaws in the 'Torch' plan and Darlan's prevarications, were stuck in the winter mud of Tunisia. A campaign, which it was hoped would be over in weeks, if not days, had stretched into months. Two sorts of Frenchmen, Giraud's ex-Vichy units and de

Gaulle's Free French, fought separately alongside the Americans and British. Over the coming weeks more and more of the former Vichy forces would vote with their feet, crossing over to de Gaulle's command, much to the annoyance of the Americans. One incident, which took place on American shores, highlighted this inexorable drift.

On 15 February, the French battleship *Richelieu* had put in for repairs at New York harbour to the damage sustained when she had been torpedoed nearly three years earlier by a British submarine in a follow-up operation to Mers-el-Kebir. She had then limped into Dakar harbour from where, with her guns still working, she had helped to fight off the Anglo-British assault of September 1940. Only after the Darlan deal had the *Richelieu's* officers switched sides to the Allies, but portraits of Pétain still decorated the ship and her officers remained imbued with the Vichy ethos. On arrival in New York, the ship's crew was fêted in the streets, but three hundred and fifty of them decided to join the Free French and left their ship. At this time New York housed two rival French recruiting offices, one working for Giraud, the other for de Gaulle.

Giraud was furious at what he claimed was the sailors' desertion and requested help from the American Government. Under orders from the US Navy Secretary and the Department of Justice, twelve of the sailors were arrested and imprisoned in Ellis Island, to await trial for desertion or deportation. This violated an agreement of 1941 between the American Government and the French National Committee in London, which allowed Free French crews passing through the United States to be granted automatic residency permits like other Allied nations' crews. Much of the American press rallied to the sailors' cause. In a wounding editorial, the *New York Herald Tribune* argued that the sailors were entitled to reject the ideology of Vichy and concluded: 'it seems that, in certain circles in Washington, the feeling is that General de Gaulle deserves to be punished for having been stubbornly right all along.' A prominent civil rights lawyer was hired to represent the sailors and, on 2 April, the New York Supreme Court ruled that they should be set free and allowed to set sail for London and join the Free French Navy.

While these early signs of the will of ordinary Frenchmen appeared, the man whom they looked up to as their leader was bristling with hostility at the British and Americans, with the one exception of his most dangerous opponent, Roosevelt himself. De Gaulle, correctly as it seems, had come to believe that he must sustain his position independently of his Allies, whom he could only mistrust. In his private conversations with Teyssot, he laid out all sorts of inimical scenarios, for example: 'Now the game is clear, there is no longer any possibility of an alliance with the Anglo-saxons (Britain and America). We can see the next war panning out; Europe against America. We'll be reconciliated with the Fritzes.' De Gaulle talked of playing the Russian card: 'We'll be a very strong alliance, the Russians will uphold their relations with Japan. Now I want to go to Russia to arrange it all.' And, while he privately painted such subversive pictures of a new world order, his rival Frenchman would be consigned to the dustbin: 'Giraud is a damned idiot who doesn't understand anything.'

Teyssot was a faithful recorder of de Gaulle's table talk and, while there is no reason to doubt his accuracy, de Gaulle was merely sounding off behind closed doors. However on 15 February, a sensational memorandum was sent by the Special Branch in London to the Foreign Office. It reported an extraordinary speech which de Gaulle was alleged to have given to ten members of the Fighting French Parachute Corps, shortly after he returned from Casablanca.

According to the Special Branch informant de Gaulle had said: "I have now become a political man and as a politician I am frequently obliged to say the exact opposite of what I actually think or feel; thus when speaking on the BBC, I pretend to be a good friend of Britain in order to create a good impression abroad and keep going the resistance in France. You all remember how, when you joined me, you were told by my Secret Service that England was no friend of ours and that England, like Germany, is our hereditary enemy. This you must always keep in mind. Russia will undoubtedly win the war in the field, so I am obliged to keep on good terms with that country. I am not a communist myself, however, but it is a question of diplomacy. When I am in power in France after the war, I shall ask Russia for time to re-organise without her intervention. Russia will agree to this as she needs a strong France to balance the power in Europe. I shall then have accomplished what Hitler failed to do – become master of Europe. When I am in power, you will all be remembered and rewarded with money and power. But, remember, money is not important. Power and, above all, honour, are the most important things to have."

Many of the sentiments accorded with the private views de Gaulle had been expressing to Teyssot but, if he really uttered the words "master of Europe", and meant them, his Allies would have had every reason to keep their distance. The report was sent straight to Eden who made inquires of the Commissioner of Police. The Commissioner sent an Inspector Canning to see Eden and explain the report's origin. Eden noted that: 'he did not give me details of his source; he had got the report third hand from one of those present at the meeting. He agreed that we were probably dealing with a number of double-crossers and intriguers.' The phrasing of Eden's note suggests that he put those last words into Inspector Canning's mouth; ever de Gaulle's protector, he dismissed the report. A Foreign Office memorandum recorded that Eden was 'not inclined to attach very much importance to it.' Eden's course was perhaps wise but, in combination with the other evidence, there is an authentic ring to de Gaulle's words.

Whatever de Gaulle said privately and however authoritarian his character, his public statements and actions suggested a firm commitment to democracy. As he told Admiral Stark on 15 February, the same day the Special Branch report was sent to the Foreign Office, his criticism of America was based on his view that the State Department was favouring the establishment of 'Conservative (or Fascist) groups' in all European countries. In particular, he believed that the Americans failed to understand that Giraud was a reactionary, who was being influenced by people with Fascist tendencies. When these remarks were reported back to Washington, they simply increased the hostility to de Gaulle. What he still failed to realize was that Roosevelt did not care which Frenchmen he dealt with, as long as he could keep them under his thumb and they were helping to win the war. This policy continued to be in conflict with the British who wanted a strong, unified French authority.

The role of Eden and the Foreign Office in shielding de Gaulle from Churchill's anger was becoming ever more important and would soon become vital in defending him against Roosevelt too. It showed Eden at his most brilliantly diplomatic, the perfect foil to the roller-coaster emotions of Churchill. At a dinner in February, while everything hung in the air, de Gaulle asked Eden: "And now, what is going to happen?" Eden responded in masterly fashion: "And now, you and General Giraud are going to win the war, helped partly by England and the United States."

While Eden sought to mollify de Gaulle, with Churchill he was engaged in an extraordinary tussle, whose full extent can only now be revealed from hitherto undisclosed Cabinet Office documents. In February de Gaulle requested permission from the British Government to tour Africa, although he did not intend to include Algiers because of the ongoing tension with Giraud. He was already under a travel ban imposed by Churchill, but on 24 February Eden notified the Prime Minister that de Gaulle had repeated his request for travel facilities and wished to leave the country by 8 March. The next day Churchill replied with a hand written note: 'I presume if is quite clearly settled he is not to be allowed to go and that force if necessary will be used to restrain him.' This is the first written reference recording Churchill's willingness to employ force against de Gaulle.

On the same day, Spears sent a telegram from Beirut, reporting a rumour that de Gaulle would shortly be visiting Cairo and pleading that he should not be allowed to set foot in the Levant States. Churchill noted, once again by hand, on Spears's telegram: 'I presume there is no failure in the arrangements to prevent de Gaulle leaving the country, and that force will be used to stop him if necessary.' On 27 February Churchill gave Eden a detailed explanation of his reasoning. It was not simply that, 'once out of our power he (de Gaulle) can go where he likes and he will certainly go where he can do the most mischief.' It was also Churchill's abiding fear of offending Roosevelt: 'I think the United States would take it as an unfriendly act if we let this man loose in the world at the present time.' He instructed Eden: 'I beg you on no account to allow our relations with the United States to be spoiled through our supposed patronage of the man who is also our bitter foe and whose accession to power in France would be a British disaster of first magnitude.' These were savage words, particularly to a Foreign Secretary who believed that de Gaulle was the one French leader capable of restoring the strong France which Britain would so badly need after

the war ended. Churchill concluded his note by saying that de Gaulle 'should not be given any access to the BBC except after scrutiny.' On the same day Churchill was notified that his instructions on using force to stop de Gaulle travelling had gone to the 'Foreign Ministry, Admiralty, Air Ministry and M.I.5. . . . In addition all civil airports have been warned.'

On 3 March the War Cabinet officially rejected de Gaulle's request for travel facilities; he was to be informed that, in view of the unsettled relations between him and Giraud, it was preferable that his trip should be deferred. It was agreed that special security measures should be put in place and preparations be made to brief the press should de Gaulle protest publicly. When the decision was conveyed to de Gaulle, Teyssot noted: 'The reaction was violent! The General ordered all the dinners to be cancelled where any English were invited, the visit to the King for 31 March, Madame de Gaulle's visit to the Queen etc . . .' The Conservative MP, Harold Nicholson, recorded a dinner with Charles Peake, the Foreign Office official who had the thankless task of liaising with de Gaulle: 'Charles tells me about the latest de Gaulle row. De Gaulle had decided to go to Syria and Charles had been instructed to say no. "Alors", he had said, "je suis prisonnier." He retired to Hampstead. Winston had telephoned Charles saying "I hold you responsible that the Monster of Hampstead does not escape."

Nicholson did not realize the extent of the security apparatus which the British government was now erecting around de Gaulle; nor, of course, did the man himself. It is intriguing to speculate how de Gaulle would have reacted if he had. On 10 March, a week after the War Cabinet decision, Eden summed up for the Prime Minister the full extent of the measures now being taken. His memorandum makes astonishing reading. Firstly, he wrote, 'M.I.5. have (i) warned their representatives at all ports and airports, (ii) established a check on the telephone in the General's private residence.' In other words de Gaulle was being bugged by British intelligence, something that some have suspected, but has never, until now, been proved. In addition the 'First Sea Lord has warned all Commanders-in-Chief' and the 'Air Ministry have issued a similar warning to (i) an organisation called "44 Group" which controls all outgoing service aircraft, (ii) the British Overseas Airways Corporation, which controls all outgoing non-service aircraft.'

Finally, recorded Eden, he had explained the position to the United States Chargé d'Affairs in order to make sure that de Gaulle was given no facilities to leave the country by the Americans. The only thing missing was a tail on de Gaulle. Eden wrote that 'M.I.5. have not established a watch over the General, on the grounds that this is extremely difficult to do unobtrusively, particularly for any length of time, and they presume that we would not wish the General to know that a check was being kept on his movements.' M.I.5.'s presumption was entirely accurate. Yet, despite all this, in Washington, Roosevelt's anti-British and anti-Gaullist chief of staff, Admiral Leahy, remained

convinced that his British 'allies' were out to use de Gaulle to stitch up the United States. On 31 March he noted: 'It is certain that Monsieur de Gaulle is interfering with our war effort and that no action to stop his interference is taken by the British government by which he is financed.'

Meanwhile, the negotiations between Giraud and de Gaulle lumbered on, conducted through Catroux in Algiers, with Macmillan and Murphy looking on. On 2 April, Churchill had cooled down sufficiently to meet de Gaulle. De Gaulle complained that, as he was his prisoner, no doubt he would soon be sending him to the Isle of Man. Churchill responded that, for such a distinguished person, only the Tower of London would be good enough. Churchill still wanted de Gaulle to agree to the proposal drawn up at Casablanca; de Gaulle still insisted that he would not work with the unholy Vichy trinity of Peyrouton, Nogues and Boisson. A plane had been put on standby to fly de Gaulle to Algiers but at the last minute it was cancelled. De Gaulle was told that the military situation in Tunisia required a postponement in his trip, but he detected Churchill's hand at work. De Gaulle cabled to Catroux: 'The British Government, out of goodness, or badness, is joining with the American Government. It goes without saying that certain people there have worked so that the door would be closed for me.' At the same time Churchill told a cabinet colleague that, for all his undeniable qualities, de Gaulle was "a great fool and very anti-British."

Towards the end of April there were signs of movement. De Gaulle told Eden that he would be willing to share political authority with Giraud as opposed to the Clémenceau-Foch arrangement he had suggested at Casablanca, if that was what Giraud wanted. He would also work with some of his ex-Vichy collaborators, but not all. In Algiers, Peyrouton, realizing that the writing was on the wall, told Catroux that he would resign as Governor-General of Algeria on de Gaulle's arrival and serve in the Army. In addition to the crossovers by Vichy forces to de Gaulle, there were also mass popular demonstrations for him in Algiers. On 30 April, de Gaulle again met Churchill, who suggested that it was time for him to go to Africa and stake his claim, as the Americans were backing Giraud more than ever. But de Gaulle still believed that Giraud was prevaricating and the ground was insufficiently prepared. Cadogan recorded that de Gaulle put on his "celebrated mule act."

In Algiers, they waited. Harold Macmillan, who had grown rather fond of Giraud, still knew little of the real de Gaulle, noting on 3 May: 'He is really a most difficult man. My General is boring and old-fashioned, but at least a gentleman.' The next day, with no news from de Gaulle in London, Macmillan was beginning to feel impatient: 'He is a difficult kind of horse. He either starts down the course before the gate has been raised, or he won't start at all until the other horses are halfway round.' Simultaneously, de Gaulle set the cat among the pigeons with a highly provocative speech, in which, although he did not mention the Americans by name, he condemned the entire history of what had happened in North Africa since the 'Torch' landings. He also accused Giraud, and by implication the Americans, of stalling, declaring that 'there must be an end to delays'. Also on 4 May, Churchill set sail for Washington on the *Queen Mary* for another conference with Roosevelt.

De Gaulle's speech provoked a difficult meeting the following day in Algiers. Macmillan returned to pre-nuptial metaphors to catch the mood of the cliffhanger developing between Giraud and de Gaulle: 'She loves me, she loves me not. She loves me, she loves me not. She loves me, she loves me not. She loves . . . me . . . she . . . loves . . . me . . . not! Oh dear! Today has been a bad day, and definitely by the end of it, one General does not love the other!' Catroux was becoming fed up with his boss in London; he complained that de Gaulle's speech had put him into an impossible negotiating position and talked of throwing in the towel.

A meeting was called of Catroux, Giraud, Macmillan, Murphy and Jean Monnet who had been asked by the Americans to act as Giraud's political adviser. Macmillan warned his colleagues that they could not call off negotiations simply because one side had made an offensive remark about the other. In Britain, he explained, that was recognized procedure in the lead up to forming a coalition government. 'This chaff didn't go awfully well. It shocked Murphy (who of course didn't particularly want the union to come off anyway) but amused Monnet . . . If you fear de Gaulle, I said, and want to call the whole thing off, you must break on a question of principle.' But when it came to principles, de Gaulle was on strong ground and remained in London sitting on them, biding his time for events in Algiers to turn in his favour. While the arm's length haggling ground on, the action was about to shift to Washington as the *Queen Mary* approached the American coast and the Prime Minister and President's relationship with de Gaulle headed for a climactic showdown.

CHAPTER TWELVE
THE PRESIDENT'S FURY

For the fortnight of 12 May to 25 May, Churchill was closeted with Roosevelt for the third Washington conference, code-named 'Trident'. As always, the agenda was the future direction of the war which continued to reveal the running division between Churchill's desire to concentrate on the 'soft underbelly' of Europe, Italy and the Balkans, as against the American Chiefs of Staff wish to throw everything at a cross-Channel invasion. Both sides had reason for satisfaction; what became known as Operation 'Overlord' was agreed for 1944. This meant that the second front was still a year away, so the Americans agreed with Churchill's suggestion that the long-drawn out victory in Tunisia and the landings planned in Sicily should be followed by an invasion of Sicily and Italy. One other vital matter was also discussed, the latest developments in the construction of the atomic bomb. Yet, with all these momentous decisions at stake, the problem of the French, as at Washington after Pearl Harbour and as at Casablanca, became the most passionate bone of contention.

De Gaulle's speech of 4 May was perfectly designed to goad Roosevelt, and Churchill found himself besieged by a constant stream of taunts about the man whom the Americans despite all his venom, still saw as his protégé. Eventually he could stand it no more and sent a devastating cable to London. It began: 'I must now warn you very solemnly of a very stern situation developing here about de Gaulle. Hardly a day passes that the President does not mention it to me. Although this is done in a most friendly and often jocular manner, I am sure that he feels very strongly indeed upon it and I see real danger developing if matters are not gripped.' Churchill went on to say that there was hardly a day when he was not handed at least one accusing document about de Gaulle and he attached a sample of them with his cable.

One of them was a memorandum which Roosevelt himself had drawn up on 8 May, after de Gaulle's speech, and hand-delivered to Churchill shortly after his arrival. It gave full vent to all the President's frustration and anger with de Gaulle. 'I am sorry,' he wrote, 'but it seems to me the conduct of the BRIDE continues to be more and more aggravated. His course and atti-tude is well nigh intolerable.' Roosevelt accused de Gaulle of taking his 'vicious propaganda staff down to Algiers to stir up strife between the various elements.' In terms of character, de Gaulle might be 'an honest fellow' but he had 'the Messianic complex.' Roosevelt continued with his own analysis of de Gaulle's position: 'He has the idea that the people of France itself are strongly behind him personally. This I doubt. I think that the people of France are behind the Free French Movement; that they do not know de Gaulle and that their loyalty is to the fine objectives of the movement when it was started and to the larger phase of it which looks to the restoration of France. If they only knew what you and I know about de Gaulle himself, they would continue to be for the movement but not for its present leader in London. That is why I become more and more disturbed by the continued machinations of de Gaulle.' Roosevelt then proposed his solution to the French problem. There should be an entirely new French Committee whose membership would be subject to Roosevelt's and Churchill's approval. It should be advisory only and not allowed to act in any way as a provisional government. Giraud would be made Commander-in-Chief of the French Army and Navy. As for de Gaulle, Roosevelt suggested that Churchill might 'like to make him Governor of Madagascar!'

Some of the other documents Churchill sent to London were extraordinary. One was an American Secret Service report, emanating from J. Edgar Hoover, claiming that 'inducements had been offered to the sailors of the *Richelieu* to desert to the Free French. Roosevelt implied to Churchill that this was being done with British money supplied to de Gaulle, which, given Britain's financial relations with the United States made it 'in a certain sense almost American money.' The allegation by Hoover, whom history would judge to be a paranoid and prejudiced liar, was quite untrue; Free French wages were lower than those offered by the Vichy Navy.

Another document supplied by Roosevelt was a memo from the State Department linking de Gaulle to Communism. It stated: 'De Gaulle has permitted to come under his umbrella all the most radical elements in France. Communists in France, probably the most highly organized political group there today, have announced their insistence that de Gaulle be their leader.' Of course, in the eyes of the State Department, de Gaulle could not win. Normally, despite his impeccable record of anti-Nazism, he was accused of being a Fascist. However, grasping for any stick with which to beat him, the taunt of Communist sympathies, acceptable in Roosevelt's friend, Stalin, was another useful smear.

In fact, the State Department and Roosevelt were trying to avoid an unpalatable truth. Just after Churchill arrived in

Washington, de Gaulle's delegate to the resistance inside main-land France, Jean Moulin, had sent a message from occupied Paris announcing the creation of a National Council of Resis-tance, comprising all political groups. The message called for negotiations towards unity between all fighting Frenchmen and insisted: 'The people of France will never agree to General de Gaulle being subordinate to General Giraud, and demand the installation of a provisional government in Algiers under the Presidency of General de Gaulle, with General Giraud as Military Chief. General de Gaulle will remain the sole leader of French Resistance whatever the outcome of negotiations.'

The message enormously strengthened de Gaulle who had realized for many months that his support to the resistance was the one weapon which nothing that the British or Americans did or said could destroy. Indeed, the more fiercely he asserted his independence, the more likely were the resistance groups to see him as their leader. De Gaulle's preoccupation with the resis-tance was witnessed at this exact time by Jose Aboulker, who had gone to London to report on the latest situation in Algiers. 'He didn't listen to a word I said. He was obsessed with these papers on his desk, behind which he paced up and down, smok-ing constantly. He said "Max wrote this" or "Max wrote that"; Max was his delegate, Jean Moulin. Two or three times during this long meeting he sat down in his large armchair behind his desk, lit another cigarette, and explained to me that these were the latest telegrams from France that he had had decoded. De Gaulle was very emotional, he wasn't interested in what was happening in Algiers. He could think only of the resistance movement in France.'

Washington was well aware of the strength of feeling towards de Gaulle in the resistance. In March, Moulin, who had returned briefly to London before the mission to France which would end in his capture, torture and terrible death at the hands of the Gestapo, had been taken by one of de Gaulle's staff to see Admiral Stark. Stark had sent a detailed memorandum reporting Moulin's assertion that all the resistance organizations in France accepted de Gaulle's direction and leadership and that 'Gaullism' had become synonymous with resistance to Germany. However, in the mounting White House hysteria against de Gaulle in May, Roosevelt grasped instead at the straw of a second-hand report from London that the declaration by the Resistance had all been cooked up by one of de Gaulle's officials. While Washington searched for evidence to denigrate de Gaulle, Giraud in Algiers understood the significance of the declaration. On 17 May, he finally conceded that he would have to share power with de Gaulle and officially invited him to fly to Algiers and join him. There may also have been a tragic, psychological factor in Giraud's concession. Two days before, he had heard that his daughter, who was married to an officer serving in his forces, and all her children had been taken by the Nazis from their home in Tunis to captivity in Germany. Macmillan recorded that 'the poor old man was terribly cut up about it.' Such a blow cannot have increased his appetite for a political dogfight with de Gaulle.

Giraud's invitation was not yet known to Churchill, who concluded his diatribe with a set of further allegations against de Gaulle. The most disgraceful was that of cowardice. Churchill wrote: 'He has never fought since he left France and took pains to have his wife brought out safely beforehand.' The latter was simply untrue. When de Gaulle left France in June 1940, he made arrangements for his wife and children to follow him but had no guarantee that they would be able to. And, given his record in the First World War and his courage in going into exile to carry on the struggle, the innuendo that he had funked the fight was shabby indeed. Churchill also claimed: 'The President has even suggested to me that Giraud may be in danger of assassination at the hands of de Gaullists.' Churchill did at least have the grace to admit that the President had not supplied evidence for this. Of course, there was none. Churchill concluded his cable by stressing that, when it came to a choice between the President and de Gaulle, there could only ever be one outcome: 'I ask my colleagues to consider urgently whether we should not now eliminate de Gaulle as a political force ... When we consider the absolutely vital interest which we have in preserving good relations with the United States, it seems to me most questionable that we should allow this marplot and mischief-maker to continue the harm he is doing.'

However much Roosevelt, supported by Churchill, insisted that their campaign against de Gaulle arose out of policy rather than personality, these documents had the feel of a personal vendetta. It was perfectly understandable. De Gaulle was an exceedingly difficult man, proud, haughty, abrupt, at times insufferable, and prone to tantrums. However, although he was by nature authoritarian, he was not a totalitarian. At the root of the trouble was his refusal to submit to his Allies' demands and his willingness to criticize them in public. As far as Roosevelt and Churchill were concerned, de Gaulle's country had been defeated, he was being financed by Britain and America, and he should simply toe their line. Churchill's mood was noted by Roosevelt's Vice-President, Henry Wallace, at a lunch at the British Embassy on the day after he had sent his cable to London: "Churchill spoke very contemptuously of the vanity, pettiness and discourtesy of de Gaulle, saying that he raised him from a pup but that he still barked a bit."

In London, Churchill's cable and the accompanying documents caused shudders. An astonished Cadogan noted: 'Attlee told Cabinet of telegrams that are coming in from Winston about de Gaulle. Former (under American pressure) wants to execute latter. But is this the moment, when de Gaulle and Giraud *may* be getting together?' On 23 May, the War Cabinet met to agree its reply to Churchill's proposal to break with de Gaulle, Eden recording: 'Everyone against and very brave about it in his absence.'

Eden drafted a telegram, responding point by point to the most outlandish of the allegations forwarded by Churchill. While he agreed that de Gaulle's conduct and Free French propaganda had created difficulties for everyone, he comprehensively rebutted every one of them. Above all, Eden argued, with Giraud's invitation to de Gaulle to join him in Algiers, there was now at last some chance of unity within French ranks. To remove de Gaulle would make him a martyr and create far more trouble than to keep him. Eden concluded with a telling blow against Roosevelt's envoy in Algiers, Robert Murphy. 'We suspect that Murphy is becoming impressed by the evidence of rising Gaullism in North Africa which must be reaching him and that he prefers to ascribe this to Gaullist propaganda rather than admit that he was as wrong about Gaullist strength in North Africa as he was about anti-British feeling there. The fact is that Giraud's retention of unpopular men and Murphy's continued reluctance to insist on their removal have helped de Gaulle very considerably in North Africa.'

The proposed meeting between de Gaulle and Giraud was news to Churchill and he replied that any action on de Gaulle should await its results. He said that he would inform Roosevelt of this, but added: 'I have no intention of marring my relations with the President by arguing in the sense of your various telegrams . . . I have given you my warning of the dangers to Anglo-American unity inherent in your championship of de Gaulle.' Not for the first time de Gaulle had threatened to spoil Churchill's party with Roosevelt. The 'Trident' conference had agreed the invasion of Italy, a vital part of Churchill's strategy, and he reminded Eden that this was all because of the personal support of Roosevelt. He concluded bitterly with a reiteration of the rage he had shown during the arguments over the travel ban: 'We are receiving indispensable help, and I should be very sorry to become responsible for breaking up this harmony for the sake of a Frenchman who is a bitter foe of Britain and may well bring civil war on France.' These words were written just sixteen days short of the third anniversary of Churchill's first meeting with de Gaulle in the very different circumstances of June 1940.

And yet all this loyalty being shown by Churchill to Roosevelt was not being reciprocated. At this very moment Roosevelt was secretly and behind Churchill's back, trying to arrange a one-to-one meeting with Stalin at the Bering Straits, believing that he could get along better with the Russian leader if Churchill were out of the way. When Churchill got wind of it, he was deeply wounded. Roosevelt tried to lie his way out, denying to Churchill that he had even proposed the idea. Apart from the breach of trust, it was an indication that the equal partnership in decision-making which Churchill had managed to preserve until Casablanca was beginning to slip away.

On 27 May, de Gaulle prepared to leave Britain for Africa. He wrote to Churchill: 'I am more than ever optimistic about our common victory and convinced more than ever that you will personally be the man of glory as you have also been the man of the worst moments.' He thanked Eden for the wonderful way in which the 'British people' had treated the Free French. Eden perfectly understood the innuendo. De Gaulle later wrote that Eden 'good-humouredly asked, "Do you know that you have caused us more difficulties than all our other European Allies put together?" "I don't doubt it," I replied, smiling in my turn, "France is a great power."'

On 30 May, de Gaulle landed at Boufarik airport in Algiers. Though a small guard presented arms and a band played the *Marseillaise*, Boufarik had been deliberately chosen instead of the main Algiers airport, Maison Blanche, to keep de Gaulle as far as possible out of public view. His route to the Summer Palace, where he was due to thrash out the final details of a new French Committee with Giraud, avoided the city of Algiers altogether. Murphy, in particular, was always fearful of a Gaullist putsch. However, that afternoon de Gaulle was allowed out to place a Cross of Lorraine at the foot of the monument to the dead in the Place de la Poste. At short notice, his supporters had spread the word of his arrival and thousands turned out to acclaim him. Although, as yet, the Administration, the Army and all press and communications were under the control of Giraud and the Allies, de Gaulle was confident that he had seized the moment and could drive a hard bargain.

The heart of the matter was the division between the civil leadership and the military command. Roosevelt had not deviated from his view that the American and British alliance was with the French military command which had to be subservient to Eisenhower; political matters were on indefinite hold until the war was won. De Gaulle was equally determined to create a new French Committee which would become the provisional Government of France with himself at his head. However, he had become cannier and knew that this could not be achieved in one stroke.

The three days from 31 May to 2 June were tense and excited. The talks began at the Lycée Fromentin, where the new Committee would sit. Giraud was accompanied by Monnet and General Georges, an old friend of Churchill, on whose inclusion he had insisted. De Gaulle was accompanied by Catroux, André Philip, a bête noire of Roosevelt after the meeting in Washington, and René Massigli, a calm and experienced French diplomat who had joined de Gaulle the previous autumn. Giraud insisted on the supremacy of the military leadership; de Gaulle retorted that he had come to Algiers to create an effective political force. There was a temporary stalemate, although five out of the seven were veering towards de Gaulle, only Georges offering full support to Giraud. In typical fashion de Gaulle held a press conference, publicizing the dispute and his own claims. Later that day Peyrouton officially offered his resignation in separate letters to de Gaulle and Giraud as Governor-General of Algeria; de Gaulle quickly accepted it before giving Giraud a chance to intervene.

News of Peyrouton's decision rippled through the city. At the end of the campaign in Tunisia in May, a victory parade had been held in Algiers, with Eisenhower and Giraud taking the salute. De Gaulle's commanders, de Larminat and LeClerc, had deliberately marched the Gaullist units in separate file from Giraud's forces. Afterwards, Giraud, with Eisenhower's agreement, had sent them out of Algiers to bivouac around Tripoli. But now, thousands of volunteers began to pour out of Algiers and headed for Tripoli to join them. On 2 June, Giraud responded with a letter accusing de Gaulle of driving men from their posts and seeking to establish a dictatorship. A decree was issued banning all public meetings in Algiers and military and police units moved in to take over key points. That night de Gaulle, protected only by a small guard of ten men supplied by de Larminat, told Giraud that his actions would cause an immediate break unless agreement was reached the following day. On 3 June, Giraud backed off and agreed the formation of a new French Committee of National Liberation (FCNL), with him and de Gaulle as its joint heads and the remaining five involved in the negotiations as founding members. They agreed that, with Peyrouton now out of the way, Nogues and Boisson would in due course be relieved of their posts in Morocco and Dakar. For de Gaulle the dual leadership was merely a temporary fix.

When de Gaulle landed in Algiers, he had found an unexpected surprise; Churchill was there too. He had flown straight from Washington, partly to discuss the forthcoming invasion of Sicily with Eisenhower, partly because he could not resist being a spectator at the impending drama of de Gaulle's arrival. He carried with him all the Gaullophobia whipped up by his Washington visit, and at a dinner with Macmillan and Murphy he launched into an attack on de Gaulle. Giraud had been invited by Roosevelt to visit Washington in June, but Churchill told Murphy that this would be unwise, as de Gaulle was fully capable of a putsch during Giraud's absence. All of this was faithfully reported back by Murphy.

Churchill summoned Eden to join him in Algiers, cabling Roosevelt on the day of de Gaulle's landing: 'The bride arrives here noon today. I though Anthony would make a better best man than I. I am therefore reserving for myself the part of heavy father.' Five months after Casablanca, the condescending marriage jokes were back in favour. After news of de Gaulle's press conference had reached Washington, Roosevelt replied: 'The bride evidently forgets that there is still a war in progress.

Over here we receive only the bride's publicity. What is the matter with our British-American information services? Best of luck in getting rid of our mutual headache.' However, Churchill was now able to convey the pleasing news: 'I have now learned officially from Macmillan that the bride and bridegroom have at last physically embraced. I am entertaining the new Committee at luncheon today, but I will not attempt to mar the domestic bliss by any intrusions of my own.'

The next day Churchill informed Roosevelt that 'everybody seemed most friendly' at the luncheon and gave an encouraging analysis: 'If de Gaulle should prove violent or unreasonable, he will be in a minority of 5 to 2 and possibly completely isolated. The committee is therefore a body with collective authority with which in my opinion we can safely work.' Quite how he came to such an optimistic analysis of the Committee's ability to isolate de Gaulle is hard to see. Perhaps he was relying on his old friend, General Georges; more likely he was trying to soft-soap Roosevelt. De Gaulle recalled a rather different assessment by Churchill. He had suggested that his presence at this particular time was somewhat strange. According to de Gaulle, Churchill replied that, while he was in no way attempting to meddle in French affairs, the military situation compelled him to keep track of events in such an essential zone of communications: 'We should have had to take steps if too brutal a shock had occurred – if, for example, you had devoured Giraud in one mouthful.' Churchill was unaware that, the day before, the Committee had decided to appoint eight further members, de Gaulle and Giraud proposing four each. De Gaulle later wrote: 'These choices were subsequently to make my position secure.'

For four days there was the appearance of harmony. Eisenhower lunched with the Committee on 7 June, cabling

Churchill's Chief-of-Staff, General Ismay: 'All went well. I am extremely hopeful that everything is going to work out satisfactorily.' That afternoon Macmillan saw de Gaulle, finding him 'very friendly and in quite good spirits . . . The Americans are beginning to realise that although de Gaulle is often very tiresome, he is much the most intelligent of the French personalities. He is at least realistic and has a modern mind.'

On 8 June the dam broke. The Committee, still seven as the new members had not yet arrived, met to discuss the critical question of military command. Georges suggested that Giraud should be Commander-in-Chief of all French forces, while also remaining co-President of the Committee but staying independent of it in military matters. To de Gaulle, the whole point was that military command should be brought under political control. He proposed that Giraud could remain Commander-in-Chief but, in due course, would return to the field and cease to play a political role. It was essentially the same idea he had suggested at Casablanca: Giraud as Foch, de Gaulle as Clémenceau. The majority rejected Giraud, and Giraud and Georges refused to back de Gaulle. It was stalemate.

Macmillan saw de Gaulle the next day. He recorded: 'Things are still very difficult here . . . The personal relations between Giraud and de Gaulle are not good. They are men of such a completely different type that it could hardly be otherwise. Giraud is an old-fashioned, but charming colonel, who would grace the Turf Club. De Gaulle is a modern minded, ambitious, conceited but clever politician, who makes no pretensions to good manners and has a delight in violent and abusive attacks on individuals, particularly if they are of an older generation. Then . . . he simply cannot understand why they take offence.' The happy spirit of just two days before had vanished.

De Gaulle now deployed the ultimate psychological weapon. He resigned from the joint Presidency and from the Committee itself, shutting himself away 'shrouded in sorrow, letting it be known to the ministers, officials and generals who came to see me that I was preparing to leave for Brazzaville.' He also wrote in his memoirs that it was a 'calculated outburst', the calculation being that his withdrawal would ignite such a level of support among the French people and soldiers of Africa, and its potential consequences would appear so grave, that that the clamour for his leadership would become irresistible.

Giraud came to see Macmillan on the morning of 10 June, bearing de Gaulle's letter of resignation. Macmillan cabled to the Foreign Office: 'De Gaulle's action was unexpected as all was calm again yesterday evening. I urged that the letter be merely acknowledged and that the Committee not be called until tomorrow to allow time for careful consideration of the new problem.' Macmillan reported that he and Murphy had informed Eisenhower and the three of them all felt that a rupture should be avoided 'at a moment when the benefit of union will certainly be jeopardised and great complications may follow for us all.' Macmillan's decision not to precipitate the crisis was approved by Churchill who told him: 'You are quite right to play for time and let de Gaulle have every chance to come to his senses and realize the forces around him. We play fair with him if he plays fair with us and with France.'

Roosevelt's reaction to de Gaulle's resignation was quite different from Churchill's. He welcomed it, telling Eisenhower: 'In the nature of things this de Gaulle situation was bound to come to a head sooner or later. It may well be better to let him resign now than to have an even more difficult situation a month from now.' Leahy salivated at the prospect: 'There is unfortunately no report of the acceptance of the resignation. General de Gaulle is following exactly the policy I expected him to take in order to elevate himself and his followers to the highest offices. He will be a definite drag on our war effort until he is completely eliminated from the problem. His elimination may be difficult because of past and prospective future support provided by the British Government.'

While Macmillan's telegram of 10 June tried to calm things down, Murphy had simultaneously sent an inflammatory message to Roosevelt that Giraud was intending to resign if he was outvoted in the Committee on the question of the military command. Most significantly, Murphy reported Giraud's claim that de Gaulle 'also demanded the command of French forces not actively engaged in operations which is contrary to what he has told Eisenhower, Macmillan and me with respect to his intentions.' This deeply troubled Roosevelt, as de Gaulle's demand would include the port of Dakar, in his view the strategic base most vital to America. He had already heard the rumour that the French Committee intended to remove Boisson from Dakar; sharing none of the debris of September 1940, Roosevelt had come to the view that Boisson was the most competent French administrator in Africa.

Roosevelt now made Boisson's retention a trial of strength in what was escalating into a personal duel with de Gaulle. His opening salvo was a cable to Churchill on 10 June, provoked by Murphy's message: 'I think this whole matter of de Gaulle domination of Dakar is too serious for me to remain quiescent. Neither you nor I know just where de Gaulle will end up. Therefore I find it impossible to consider any de Gaulle domination of French West Africa.' Roosevelt said that he could not feel happy unless Giraud retained complete control of the French

African Army: 'Control by de Gaulle would create a definitely uneasy feeling about the safety of the rear of the British and American positions, the line of supply and the adequacy of British and American forces left for the protection of the rear.' He copied this message to Eisenhower, thereby directly intervening in his Commander-in-Chief's theatre of operations. 'I trust you will agree with this,' he wrote, 'it is inconceivable to me that in view of the uncertainty of de Gaulle's future attitude, French West Africa should come under his domination.'

Churchill conveyed Roosevelt's message to Eden, who could foresee the looming crisis: 'American hatred is keen and maybe they want Dakar too. But de Gaulle has done much to shake all confidence in him.' Eden's implication was that Roosevelt wanted Dakar as a post-war American base. This was true to the extent that Roosevelt wanted Dakar to become an American-supervised police station in any future settlement to protect the world against further wars. Though Churchill had no reason to love Boisson, he wrote to Macmillan that he was going to back Roosevelt, come what may, and, if that meant ditching de Gaulle, so be it: 'We have agreed to support the President in refusing to allow Boisson to be removed.' In the same message, Churchill raised the stakes on de Gaulle's resignation: 'You may also make it clear to de Gaulle that if he resigns from the Committee and thus mars the unity of Frenchmen, he will not be allowed to return to this country and I shall make public statements both to Great Britain and to France explaining why he has completely forfeited the confidence and goodwill of His Majesty's Government.' Roosevelt had now forced Churchill into a more extreme position than his original response.

Roosevelt sent Eisenhower a message to give to de Gaulle about Boisson. Though it was to be couched in polite terms,

Roosevelt was insisting on a guarantee that the French Committee would retain Boisson in his post. Roosevelt also told Eisenhower that, if such a guarantee were not forthcoming, 'I should have to consider sending several regiments to Dakar and also naval vessels if there were any signs that de Gaulle was proposing to take things over in French West Africa.' On the evening of 11 June, Murphy delivered the message to de Gaulle on Eisenhower's behalf. The next morning Eisenhower reported back to Roosevelt that 'Murphy found de Gaulle in a most amiable state of mind. De Gaulle spent half hour pleading for better understanding by the United States of himself and his movement. Boisson's retention in a place of authority he said is totally unacceptable. His replacement, he declared, could not possibly affect the security of our operations.' Murphy suggested to de Gaulle that this would presumably be a matter for the French Committee, to which de Gaulle agreed but added that 'he could not continue as a member of a committee which would accept such interference in French affairs by a foreign power.'

Also on 12 June, Churchill decided that it was time to do something about all the favourable press coverage of de Gaulle, which had excited Roosevelt's ire. He sent a circular to British newspapers, expressing his concern at the apparent bias in favour of de Gaulle. He told them that de Gaulle had left 'a trail of Anglophobia behind him' and undoubtedly had 'Fascist and dictatorial tendencies.' Churchill expressed his hope that de Gaulle would settle down to 'loyal teamwork' but in the meantime he asked that British newspapers should 'preserve an attitude of coolness and impartiality in these French quarrels.' The following day, Churchill's sentiments were faithfully reported in an article in *The Observer*. A message was also sent from the Ministry of Information to British embassies around the world, warning them that de Gaulle, with his 'autocratic temperament', did not enjoy the unqualified support of His Majesty's Government. De Gaulle was fully aware of the forces ranged against him. On 14 June he wrote to his wife: 'You have no idea of the atmosphere of lies, false news etc that our good Allies and their friends over here have tried to drown me in.' The letter was signed 'from your poor husband.'

On the afternoon of 14 June, Macmillan had a revealing encounter with de Gaulle. After a lunch party, de Gaulle asked him how he was going to spend the afternoon. Macmillan replied that he was hoping to drive out to Tripasa and bathe. De Gaulle asked if he could accompany him and they spent over three hours together. At the end of the day, Macmillan reflected on 'this strange, attractive and yet impossible character. We talked on every conceivable subject – politics, religion, philosophy, the classics, history (ancient and modern) and so on. It is very difficult to know how to handle him. I do my best, and I know that he likes me and appreciated having somebody whom he trusts and with whom he can talk freely. I think I have persuaded him to stay in the Committee for the present and give the thing a chance. But I'm afraid he will always be impossible to work with. He is by nature an autocrat. Just like Louis XIV or Napoleon. He thinks in his heart that he should command and all others should obey him. It is not exactly 'Fascist' (an overworked word), it is authoritarian.' During their walk they were recognized by local people and a small crowd gathered in the village, cheering wildly and clamouring for de Gaulle to make a speech. Macmillan wrote: 'This is very bad for him!' It was indeed the problem; de Gaulle's stand since 1940 and his unwavering devotion to the cause of France had made him a hero in its people's eyes.

In his continuing game of bluff with Giraud, de Gaulle now decided to return to the French Committee. The newcomers had arrived in Algiers and de Gaulle was confident of a solid majority among the fourteen members. It was only on 16 June that the Americans and the British discovered that the Committee had been expanded. Murphy reported to Roosevelt that the new membership 'insures supremacy to de Gaulle.' For Roosevelt, it was the last straw. On 17 June, he sent Churchill the message that he hoped would seal de Gaulle's fate. It began: 'I am fed up with de Gaulle and the secret Personal and Political machinations of that Committee in the last few days indicates that there is no possibility of our working with de Gaulle. If these were peace times it wouldn't make so much difference but I am absolutely convinced that he has been and is now injuring our war effort and that he is a very dangerous threat to us. I agree with you that he likes neither the British nor the Americans and that he would double-cross both of us at the first opportunity. I agree with you that the time has arrived when we must break with him. It is an intolerable situation . . . We must divorce ourselves from de Gaulle because, first, he has proven to be un-reliable, uncooperative, and disloyal to both our Governments.'

Roosevelt wanted to make the break and he wanted Churchill to make it with him: 'Above all I am anxious that the break be made on a basis and for reasons which are identical in both our Governments. There are plenty of emotional and dissident people throughout the world who will try to separate England and the United States in this matter and we must stand shoulder to shoulder, identically and simultaneously through this miserable mess.' Roosevelt called for the creation of a new committee solely composed of 'Frenchmen who really wanted to fight the war' and, until that time, he wanted Macmillan and

Eisenhower to ensure that any further meetings of the existing committee were deferred. On the same day he also cabled Eisenhower: 'I want to state for your exclusive information that at this time we will not permit de Gaulle to direct himself or to control through partisans on any committee, the African French army, either in the field of supplies, training, or operations.'

Roosevelt's problem was that he could not make the break without the British. To gain Churchill's support was not enough; he would also need Churchill to persuade the Cabinet. In Whitehall, the general reaction was that the President had taken leave of his senses. On 18 June, Cadogan noted: 'Roosevelt has lost his patience (and his head) about de Gaulle, and is asking for the latter's head on a charger. P.M. of course disposed to agree with him. But of course it's most unwise. I don't know what case there was against St. John the Baptist, but public opinion was less formed – and less formidable in those days.' Eden recorded that Roosevelt's telegram 'seemed pretty hysterical to me and Winston didn't really try to defend it. We shall be hard put to it to keep in step with Americans, or rather pull them into step with us, over the French business, and not commit some folly which will give de Gaulle a martyr's crown or control of the French Army or both.' He described Roosevelt's mood as that of a man 'who persists in error. It has all that special brand of obstinacy, like Hitler at Stalingrad.'

Churchill now found himself pitched into the greatest crisis so far of this tangled, triangular relationship. He decided to stall, but in the most tactful way possible. On 18 June he sent two telegrams to Roosevelt. In the first he gave his unequivocal backing for the order to Eisenhower to keep de Gaulle away from military control. However, he also said that he was not in favour of breaking up the French Committee; he would rather that

Eisenhower, Murphy and Macmillan work towards restraining de Gaulle's power of command within the structure of the Committee. In this case, it would be the Committee that would be at fault if it placed itself 'in definite opposition to the two rescuing Powers'. If de Gaulle resigned because the Committee would not back him, he would 'put himself in the wrong with public opinion'. In his second message, Churchill gently told Roosevelt that his colleagues had questioned the suggestion that Churchill agreed that the time was right to break with de Gaulle. He reminded the President that this harked back to the exchanges during the Washington conference, which had been superseded by the news of Giraud's invitation to de Gaulle to join him in Algiers.

Thwarted for the moment by Churchill and his cabinet, Roosevelt now returned to the tussle over Boisson, which he summoned up as a reserve *casus belli* with de Gaulle. He cabled Eisenhower in his own handwriting: 'I want it distinctly understood that under no circumstances will we approve the removal of BOISSON from Dakar or any changes in his command unless they are approved by you.'

Eisenhower was in a thoroughly awkward position. He thought that Roosevelt was beginning to behave ridiculously and cabled Marshall: 'The Boisson question seems to be acquiring a significance far out of proportion to its real importance to us. It is not repeat not control by Boisson in French West Africa that is so important to us here but control by a competent, liberal, cooperative official who is entirely acceptable to us.' Eisenhower wisely pointed out that if the Americans insisted on intervening in what was essentially a civil government matter, it would give de Gaulle every chance to whip up local French rage at foreign interference. He also suggested that Murphy was over-egging things: 'It is my opinion that Murphy's telegram to the President gave a more gloomy picture than was justified by the facts. I am not repeat not particularly apprehensive.'

Macmillan recorded that Eisenhower asked him, as a friend, for some private advice on how to reply to the President. Macmillan told him, 'I thought we might interpret these instructions in our own way. Finally he sent a very sensible reply to the President, which he dictated in front of us. He asked me to suggest amendments, and I made a few'. Eisenhower's message was a model of sense, tact, and calmness: 'I assure you Mr President that I am fully alive to the potentialities of the situation and that I will not repeat not accept any solution proposed by the local French which will jeopardise the success of the vitally important military operations scheduled soon to begin.' He offered a further reassurance that 'the local French difficulties in reaching workable agreements have been magnified in certain reports.' Einsenhower was pointing the finger at Murphy but to mention by name such a favoured envoy would hardly be tactful.

The White House was far from satisfied with such blandishments. Leahy noted on 19 June: 'It appears to me that Eisenhower is following a dangerous appeasement policy in his relations with the de Gaullists in Africa.' Eisenhower was now so fed up with Presidential encroachments on his patch, that he pleaded with Marshall: 'I hope you will say to the President that I beg of him to avoid any action that could increase our local difficulties after HUSKY (the codename for the invasion of Sicily) is at least a week old.' But Roosevelt was not finished. On 22 June, he repeated his orders to Eisenhower: 'In my opinion the retention of BOISSON is not solely a question of civil administration but it is a matter of high military importance to us. It is expected that you will succeed in accomplishing the purposes of this Government in the area under your control.' Eisenhower had no choice but to cable back that he would obey orders: 'Instructions with regard to the retention of Boisson and control of the French Army in Africa are clearly understood and will be carried out.' It also seemed increasingly absurd to Eisenhower that he should have to rely so heavily on Giraud when, as he told Marshall, it was felt throughout the region that he was 're-actionary, old fashioned, and cannot be persuaded to modernise the forces already organised. It must be admitted that he moves with ponderous slowness. He has no repeat no political acumen whatsoever.' But it was what the President wanted.

De Gaulle had now made a small concession. Eisenhower and Macmillan had knocked French heads together and extracted an agreement that French forces would be split into two commands. Giraud would retain North and West Africa, while de Gaulle kept French Equatorial Africa and Syria. For de Gaulle it was simply another interim stage. His consolation was that Giraud had now been inveigled by Monnet into signing a decree which stated that the military commanders came under the control of the Committee. Although Monnet had been asked by Roosevelt to act as Giraud's adviser, he was coming to the view that de Gaulle was the obvious leader for France.

Eisenhower believed that this agreement accorded with Roosevelt's instructions and he and Macmillan both pleaded that the solution should be accepted by both London and Washington. Eisenhower reported to Marshall: 'Under the terms of this decree de Gaulle cannot obtain control over the military forces in North and West Africa.' Macmillan told Churchill that any attempt to upset the agreement 'will land us into very deep water indeed and may well compromise our future military plans. You may be assured that this is General Eisenhower's personal view.'

That evening Macmillan sent Churchill an extraordinary cable marked 'MOST SECRET AND PERSONAL' and intended for the Prime Minister's eyes only. It began: 'For your private information which should of course be kept very secret, Generals Eisenhower and Bedell-Smith (Eisenhower's Chief-of-Staff) are getting more and more concerned about the President's autocratic instructions.' Macmillan went on to say that the two American commanders felt that they must be allowed a certain latitude to exercise their command. Most subversively, they believed, according to Macmillan, that 'the President is inclined to use military security, where there is no real danger, for political purposes.' Macmillan was aware of the dangerous step he was taking in reporting their views: 'Of course these remarks would gravely prejudice the officers concerned if they became known and are only expressed to me as a trusted friend.'

Churchill was horrified by Macmillan's telegram. The next day he sharply replied: 'Strictly personal and secret. I am shocked to hear that Generals Eisenhower and Bedell-Smith should have communicated to you their differences from their own President and Commander-in-Chief. You may be sure I shall not allow this to become known. Be careful yourself however to give no encouragement to such moods, remembering that the President and I act together in this war and that very great advantages come to our country and to the common cause from our association.' As the stand-off over Boisson, which was the main cause of the breach, continued, Churchill added: 'the dismissal of Boisson would mark a signal victory for the de Gaulle faction and would be bitterly resented by the President and the

State Department, even if they allowed it to take place, which I very much doubt.'

Churchill and Roosevelt were both sceptical about the agreement within the French Committee. Churchill told Roosevelt that he doubted whether it would work or last. Roosevelt replied: 'I agree with you about the so-called agreement of the French Committee in Algiers. I still have my fingers crossed.' However, after Eisenhower's and Macmillan's pleas, they decided not to intervene further and, while Giraud retained his forces, de Gaulle, having achieved the supremacy of the political committee over the military command, was well on the way to winning the game. Suddenly, the Boisson crisis also disappeared, Boisson resolving it himself by resigning on 24 June. As before with Peyrouton, de Gaulle quickly accepted the resignation before Giraud had time to react. Eisenhower told Roosevelt that Boisson had fallen on his sword because of 'popular agitation against him in West Africa. It was stated about a week ago that he had a most embarrassing time when he passed through a hostile crowd of civilians.' It all went to show that, even though the President was the most powerful man in the world, it was difficult to buck the will of the people.

Though it was not yet apparent to the world beyond or perhaps to Roosevelt himself, it was clear to de Gaulle that he was winning his duel with Roosevelt and was now unstoppable. With the Committee now up and running, the next question was whether, and in what manner, Britain and America would recognize it. Roosevelt remained resolutely opposed to any form of political recognition and Churchill, to the despair of the Foreign Office, had no intention of hurrying him. In public the Allies continued to fête Giraud as the most important Frenchman and in July he flew to Washington to be sold to the American public as France's leader. Margaret Suckley noticed how pleasant Roosevelt found the company of this French General, as opposed to the monster of Hampstead: 'The general is tall and fine looking – a real gentleman of the old school. As usual, the rest of us listen most of the time. General Giraud is charming, talks easily. The President talks easily in French to him; even tells him a joke in French. The President says he does not know how to deal with de Gaulle, who is out for himself, and wants to be the next ruler of France – in whatever capacity may be expedient when the time comes.'

American newspapers took the opportunity of criticizing de Gaulle, stoked up by Churchill's June press briefing and a whispering campaign by the State Department which circulated some of the stories Roosevelt had passed on to Churchill in May. The British Embassy reported that an article describing de Gaulle as 'a dangerous near-Fascist against whom drastic steps may have to be taken' was inspired by Hull personally. The Embassy report continued: 'The only natural deduction from this campaign is that State Department are out to break up the Committee of National Liberation and get rid of de Gaulle. This seems all the more regrettable when . . . the tension is rapidly declining.'

The attacks were discussed with mounting concern by the War Cabinet in London, but Churchill himself viewed them robustly. He told the Washington Embassy not to worry, adding: 'I have had long experience of the character and conduct of de Gaulle and it would be an ill day for France, and afterwards detrimental to England, if he gained the mastery. Holding this conviction, I must stand with the President, who is our greatest friend, even when I do not entirely share his view on methods.' In any case the smear campaign did not matter. While

Giraud was away, de Gaulle secured his hold over the people of French Africa, finding acclamation wherever he travelled. On 3 July, after a rapturous crowd wildly applauded a speech by him, Macmillan noted: 'I begin to feel that there is not much disunion in the French ranks at bottom. I fear terribly that they may, in spite of all our efforts, be the cause of disunity in ours.' Eleven days later, on Bastille Day, even Robert Murphy was impressed, complimenting de Gaulle on the number of people who had turned out to hear him. "Those are the ten percent Gaullists you reckoned on in Algiers," de Gaulle replied.

In his cable to the Washington Embassy during Giraud's visit, Churchill had poured balm on the wounds caused by the press criticism of de Gaulle by saying that he would soon attempt to ease Roosevelt into some form of recognition of the FCNL. On 21 July, he applied some tactfully phrased pressure: 'I am under considerable pressure from the Foreign Office, from my Cabinet Colleagues, and also from the force of circumstances to "Recognise" the National Committee of Liberation in Algiers. What does recognition mean? One can recognise a man as an emperor or as a grocer. Recognition is meaningless without a defining formula.' The British had already suggested a formula that fell well short of recognizing the Committee as a provisional government, but Roosevelt held back. Churchill said that he would soon have to move forward for the sake of Anglo-French interests but continued to worry about upsetting the President: 'If I do, Russia will certainly recognise, and I fear lest this might be embarrassing to you.' For the sake of mutual harmony, he concluded with the standard insult to de Gaulle: 'I am no more enamoured of him than you are, but I would rather have him on the Committee than strutting about as a combination of Joan of Arc and Clémenceau.' Despite Churchill's gentle entreaties, Roosevelt continued to reject the use of the word 'recognition'; he considered that it would be construed as recognizing the Committee as a government-in-waiting and preferred the less cogent word 'acceptance'. Churchill still had no wish to rush him. Nine days later, he told Eden: 'Indeed I think that a certain delay is salutary. It must be remembered that de Gaulle has been bitterly attacking American policy, that he has gained many successes against the wish of the President, the most notable being the overthrow of Boisson. All this will cost him and the Committee dear. It is often easier to offend potentates than to placate them. For this I consider time and proofs of goodwill are needed.'

Recognition was finally settled in late August at the Quebec conference, code named 'Quadrant', where, as usual, the great matters of the war were rudely interrupted by emotional arguments about France. Nearly two years after St Pierre, Hull was still smarting at all the abuse which had been hurled at him and insisted on giving Eden a long-winded justification of all the benefits brought by the Vichy policy. Roosevelt insisted that he would not provide de Gaulle with 'a white horse on which he could ride into France.' Finally the two governments issued different statements but agreed to recognize the FCNL in those territories that recognized its authority. While Britain accepted it as the body qualified to conduct the French war effort, the United States insisted that this should be viewed on a case-by-case basis. Specifically, America stated that its statement did not constitute recognition of a government of France.

Both Roosevelt and Churchill hoped that de Gaulle would find himself reined in by the Committee and subjected to its collective authority. De Gaulle had different plans. He intended to be seen as the undisputed leader of the provisional government of France. Roosevelt's determination to thwart his ambition would lead to an extraordinary crisis on the eve of the most important Allied operation of the Second World War.

CHAPTER THIRTEEN
D-DAY CRISIS

It did not take long for de Gaulle to 'devour' Giraud, although the lamb helped to lead himself to the slaughter. Giraud had never fully understood the consequences of the agreement he had signed in June; as was his wont, he had probably not bothered to read it. The fact remained that, although he was joint President of the FCNL, he was obliged to report to the Committee in his separate role of Commander-in-Chief of French forces in North and West Africa. Having no interest in politics and being entirely devoid of political acumen, he tended to carry on his military activities alongside the Americans without even paying lip service to the Committee. This was precisely the limited military alliance Roosevelt had wanted with the French; his failure to obtain it was the reason that he had lost the key stage of his duel with de Gaulle.

Rumours of the Committee's, and de Gaulle's, attempts to bring Giraud to heel reached Murphy in early September. He reported to Roosevelt that 'the extreme elements of the Gaullist faction have, it seems clear, decided that the time has come to make a further effort to lessen Giraud's power as CinC as well as to strengthen de Gaulle's own control.' Murphy's language, equating Gaullism with extremism, was typically alarmist. Roosevelt reacted predictably, cabling Churchill: 'I have very distinct feelings that we should not send further equipment or munitions to the French Army in North

Africa if our prima donna is to seize control of it from the old gentleman.'

De Gaulle's intentions were not as crude as this. He was more than happy to leave Giraud as Commander-in-Chief but sought ruthlessly to take advantage if Giraud acted behind the Committee's back. The invasion of Corsica by French forces in mid-September gave him an opportunity. Giraud conducted the operation with dash and nerve but, without consulting the Committee and without fully realizing the internal politics of the Corsican underground, he had collaborated with the Communist-controlled branch of the resistance, giving it effective control of the island. With good reason, de Gaulle saw a genuine need for Giraud to take political advice before launching into military operations and the Committee began to agree with him. It was something of an irony that de Gaulle, castigated at Washington in May as a Communist sympathizer, should have to take a stand against Giraud who unwittingly had encouraged Communist control.

Churchill, like Roosevelt, was determined to stop de Gaulle gaining sole control and instructed Macmillan to warn de Gaulle that 'very grave danger' would be created by any fundamental change in the character of the Committee. Macmillan knew that, whatever he did, he was damned. If he delivered the message, de Gaulle would get 'very excited over another "Allied intervention in French affairs"'. If he disobeyed orders and suppressed the message, 'I should be told that it was all my fault for disobeying my orders and that the delivery of the "intervention" would have saved the situation.' To Macmillan, it all seemed thoroughly unnecessary, as, with increasing confidence, de Gaulle was beginning to assume human shape: 'He is still shy, sensitive, and very prone to take offence. But he has a sense of humour (rather Puckish) and he can relax in company where he is at ease.' Meanwhile, antagonism towards de Gaulle, and anyone who dared to support him, was provoking some weird ideas in Roosevelt. On 30 October, Margaret Suckley recorded: 'Anthony Eden, he thinks, is the Dictator type. He wouldn't trust him. It is he who is backing de Gaulle, and if the Allies should land in France, both Anthony Eden and de Gaulle would at once establish a dictatorship . . . How strange it would be if FDR and Stalin were to have to enforce their democratic ideas on England! But stranger things have happened before!'

In early November, the inevitable happened. Under pressure from the Committee Giraud resigned from the joint Presidency, although he retained his job as Commander-in-Chief. Churchill expressed his infuriation to Roosevelt: 'The body we recognised was of a totally different character, the essence being the co-presidency of Giraud and de Gaulle. I suggest we maintain an attitude of complete reserve until we can discuss the position together.' The weakness of his response betrayed Churchill's powerlessness. A few days later, at the Cairo conference, Macmillan recorded that, while Churchill was 'incensed' at Giraud's departure, he knew in his heart that the dual leadership was 'only a temporary expedient'.

Immediately after de Gaulle assumed sole power, there was a further crisis with the British. In the summer, General Catroux, de Gaulle's plenipotentiary in the Levant, had finally agreed that elections should be held, in accordance with the promises given at the time of the invasion in 1941. In Lebanon, they resulted in an overwhelming victory for the Nationalist and anti-French parties, who proposed a series of constitutional amendments that would inevitably lead to full independence and an end to the French mandate. De Gaulle was furious with the British, believing that Spears had done everything in his power to support the pro-independence parties. The French Delegate-General in Lebanon, Ambassador Helleu, protested at the suggested amendments, but on 8 November the Lebanese Chamber voted for them by 48 votes to 0.

Three days later, Helleu, probably acting on his own initiative, ordered French forces to arrest the Lebanese President and senior ministers, dissolved the Chamber, and suspended the new constitution. It was yet another reason for Churchillian fury. He wrote to Roosevelt about these 'lamentable outrages' committed by the French in Syria: 'There is no doubt in my mind that this is a foretaste of what de Gaulle's leadership of France means.' Helleu's action was indefensible but de Gaulle, instead of repudiating him, said it was all a British provocation. It was one of the few occasions on which de Gaulle was clearly in the wrong and tried to bluster his way out of it. Eventually under threat of British forces enforcing martial law, Catroux released the ministers and reinstated the President. It also transpired that Helleu was a drunkard and may have been under the influence when he issued his explosive orders.

Such contretemps did nothing to prevent de Gaulle's power and support growing more credible by the day. He had established a consultative assembly in Algiers and Macmillan believed that a genuinely democratic resistance movement was emerging: 'The new arrivals from France, both to the Committee and to the Assembly representing the resistance movement, are by no means slavish or adulatory supporters of de Gaulle. They represent all sorts and types – aristocrats, bourgeois, workmen and peasants ... the "resistance" has (temporarily at any rate) bound them together in a fierce spiritual unity – not to be neglected.' Roosevelt was fully informed of the gathering forces in a series of memorandums by the OSS Chief, William Donovan. In December, Donovan wrote: 'the majority of the French people consider de Gaulle the personification of all French resistance.'

Yet Roosevelt's hostility to de Gaulle was unabated. His grandson, Curtis Roosevelt, maintains that it continued to be driven throughout by an idealistic view that it was wrong to recognize any French leader before a liberated France had the chance to vote in free elections: 'He had nothing to gain politically from holding out strongly for the French nation choosing its leaders after the war. There was no constituency for this. He wasn't going to win or lose votes in the United States. This was a totally idealistic position that the French people had to decide their own future. And he saw de Gaulle as a potential despot and as possibly, maybe even likely, an impediment to the French people deciding their own future politically.' However several observers were beginning to believe that Roosevelt was indulging in a personal vendetta. The British Ambassador, Lord Halifax, found his motives incomprehensible: 'It would seem that the President, encouraged perhaps by Leahy, is alone responsible for our difficulties. It is perhaps again worth noting that his attitude does not correspond to any current of opinion in Congress or among the American public so that it seems to be a purely personal one.' The Secretary of War, Henry Stimson, who was in a position to observe Roosevelt at close quarters, recorded in his memoirs his disappointment at 'the degree of personal feeling which seemed to enter into the thinking of Mr. Roosevelt.'

Churchill's loathing was expressed more viciously than Roosevelt's. In November, Churchill appointed Duff Cooper to succeed Macmillan as his representative to de Gaulle. He warned that de Gaulle 'is a man Fascist-minded, opportunist, unscrupulous, ambitious to the last degree and his coming into power in the new France would lead to great schisms there and also to a considerable estrangement between France and the Western democracies.' However, the difference remained that, despite his rancour, Churchill still remembered 1940 and the British Government saw that there was no alternative to de Gaulle and the FCNL. Vitriol had to give way to policy.

This did not stop sporadic explosions. In December, Boisson, Peyrouton, and a third former Vichy collaborator, Pierre Etienne Flandin, were arrested on the orders of the Committee. The first two had been offered the protection of the Americans when they changed sides after 'Torch' and Flandin was a friend of Churchill's son, Randolph. The arrests were mainly due to pressure from the resistance. However Churchill and Roosevelt seized on it as a last gasp means of ejecting their monster. Macmillan noted, 'we are about to enter upon another first-class row', and that 'the P.M. was in a most excited mood, roaring like an excited bull down the telephone. The next day Churchill 'was in such a passion on the telephone that I thought he was going to have an apoplectic fit.'

Churchill protested to Roosevelt about the arrests and, in his own handwriting Roosevelt replied: 'It seems to me that this is the proper time effectively to eliminate the Jeanne d'Arc complex and to return to realism. I too am shocked by the high-handed arrests at this time.' Roosevelt cabled Eisenhower: 'Please inform the French Committee as follows: In view of the assistance given to the Allied Armies during the campaign in Africa by Boisson, Peyrouton and Flandin, you are directed to take no action against these individuals at the present time.' The only interpretation of this overbearing telegram was that Roosevelt was once again intent on provoking a break with de

Gaulle. His commanders and officials on the ground found such interference infuriating and counter-productive. In particular Edwin Wilson, who had succeeded Murphy and was now American Ambassador to the French Committee, protested to the State Department at such an order being given over his head. Macmillan judiciously summed up the tangled web of relationships: 'The President hates de Gaulle and the French Committee. He would seize on any excuse to overthrow them and restore Giraud. The PM's sentiments are more complex. He feels about de Gaulle like a man who has quarrelled with his son. He will cut him off with a shilling. But (in his heart) he would kill the fatted calf if only the prodigal would confess his faults and take his orders obediently in future.'

Under pressure from his people on the ground, Roosevelt toned down his telegram to the Committee and the crisis was resolved when de Gaulle informed Wilson that the three Vichy officials would not be tried until a representative French government was in place. In the meantime they would be housed in comfortable accommodation. Once again the common sense of their officials and commanders had saved Churchill and Roosevelt from rash and destructive action. It was all very annoying for the President. On New Year's Eve 1943, he wrote to Churchill: 'When you and I look back eleven months we realise that de Gaulle and his Committee have most decidedly moved forward by "the process of infiltration" – in other words, here a little, there a little.' Quite so.

America and Britain threw their massive weight into the liberation of France in 1944; yet the standard bearer of his nation's liberty remained an outcast. Much of the problem remained de Gaulle's personality. In early January, Macmillan wrote an acute memorandum analysing its intensity and complexity. He believed that de Gaulle's undeniable patriotic fervour took the form of 'that particular *orgueil* for which there is no real English equivalent.' The nearest translation of *orgueil* is 'pride' but, in de Gaulle, it also produced an arrogance which 'makes him from time to time almost impossible to deal with; but it is, as no doubt modern psychologists would agree, the reverse side of an extreme sensibility. I have never seen a man at once so ungracious and so sentimental . . . the smallest act of courtesy or special kindness touches him with a deep emotion.' Macmillan concluded that 'the terrible mixture of inferiority complex and spiritual pride are characteristic of the sad situation into which France has fallen. I have often felt that the problems here could not be dealt with by politicians. They are rather problems for the professional psychiatrist.'

Churchill and Roosevelt had neither the time nor the inclination to be de Gaulle's analyst. Roosevelt's bottom line view, expressed later in the year, was that de Gaulle was a 'nut'. Churchill never believed that and, though loathing had become his prominent sentiment, the admiration of 1940 still lurked. In January, he went to Marrakech to recover from illness and, after invitations had been offered, refused and resurrected with mutual displays of suspicion and amour propre, de Gaulle came to lunch with him on 12 January. A stiff beginning melted away by the late afternoon into shows of warmth and affection; de Gaulle made the friendliest possible gesture of inviting Churchill to inspect French troops with him the following morning and Churchill gladly accepted. It did not stop Churchill reporting to Roosevelt an exchange with one of de Gaulle's generals, who told him: 'De Gaulle might seem unreasonable to us but felt the humiliation of his country so deeply that he had an inferiority complex, to which I replied sententiously that to have suffered

great disasters was no excuse for committing great follies.'
Nevertheless, Churchill could not help expressing his admiration
of de Gaulle, remarking in French to a colleague: "C'est un
grand animal!"

Macmillan reported that de Gaulle departed 'in a very good
mood, delighted with his visit to PM at Marrakech. He thanked
me most generously and even emotionally for all I had done for
France.' By now Eisenhower had also grown to admire de Gaulle.
Above all, he was clever and efficient. Stimson noted in mid-
January: 'Eisenhower has now reported to us that de Gaulle had
changed; that he is easier to work with than even Giraud; and
also the Committee is apparently getting more sedate and, while
it is very anxious to be recognized as the ultimate government of
France, it is no longer anti-American in its demonstrations.'

If great egos had not been at stake, now would have been the
time for the British and Americans to cement their alliance with
de Gaulle and the FCNL and collaborate in the battle for France.
French troops were proving themselves in Italy, the Committee
and Consultative Assembly in Algiers appeared a credible provisional government, and de Gaulle burned with a desire that, for
the honour of France, French forces should play their full part in
battle. It was not to be; the accumulated baggage was too much
and Roosevelt's mistrust was ineradicable. He wrote to Edwin
Wilson that 'certain French elements ... have diverted themselves from the main task and have devoted themselves to political activities which retard and are a constant threat to the Allied
military effort.' The latter half of his remark was simply untrue
and bore the stamp of Leahy, the unwavering Gaullophobe. In
early February, Halifax sent a revelatory dispatch to London in
which he reported that the Assistant War Secretary, John
McCloy, had told him: 'Within the last week Admiral Leahy had

advised the President that when Allied troops enter France, the most reliable person to whom we could look for help in rallying the French was, in his view, Pétain.' Such an assessment from one of Roosevelt's most trusted advisers, and the man who had spent over a year at Vichy, beggars belief.

On 15 March, Roosevelt sent Churchill the final draft of the crucial directive he intended to give Eisenhower on the administration of France after the liberation. In essence, it dumped the problem in Eisenhower's lap, with the proviso that nothing he did should be construed as recognition of the FCNL or any other group 'as the government of France even on a provisional basis.' While he was allowed to consult with them and use his discretion in authorizing them to select and install administrative personnel, he was also authorized to deal with any other groupings or individuals in France as long as they had not 'wilfully collaborated with the enemy.' It was a far cry from the FCNL's request to be considered the provisional government and it was also a recipe for anarchy amongst competing groups. Leahy did not see it this way, advising Roosevelt at the end of March that de Gaulle would cause civil war in France. The threat remained in the back of Roosevelt's mind for many months. However, because of either Leahy's bad advice or his own misjudgement, he failed to understand that the best protection against civil war would be the unified strength of de Gaulle and the FCNL, while its most likely ignition was his own preference for localized and potentially rival administrations set up by the occupying powers. Eisenhower felt beleaguered by the lack of direction: 'We are going to need very badly the support of the Resistance Groups in France and it is our general opinion that these can be brought into full play only through the agency and leadership of the French Committee.'

An absurd scenario had now been created for the weeks leading up to D-Day. Churchill arranged for General Leclerc's armoured division to be part of the Allied force though it would not go ashore until early August, but de Gaulle was to be given no information about the date or place of landings. While he remained in Algiers, General Pierre Koenig, the hero of Bir-Hakeim, headed the French Mission in London and was co-ordinating with Eisenhower. On military matters, there was easy collaboration. However, because of Roosevelt's attitude to the FCNL, Koenig was not allowed by de Gaulle to discuss any political matters concerning the administration of France with Eisenhower. This presented Eisenhower with a huge problem; how was he to govern and communicate with the French people without the help of French-speaking officials from the organization, to which, it seemed increasingly clear, most of those people looked upon as their government-in-waiting?

Throughout May, documents in Eisenhower's war papers betray his worries. On 11 May, he told the Combined Chiefs-of-Staff: 'The limitations under which we are operating in dealing with the French are becoming very embarrassing and are producing a situation which is potentially dangerous.' Another message comments on the further problems which had been caused by the black-out on communications between London and Algiers, which had been imposed because of the distrust of de Gaulle: 'Right now one of our chief headaches is the French situation. The so-called Mission here is cut off from Algiers because of lack of communication and de Gaulle has given the Mission orders, therefore, to do nothing. Yet if our planning does not get ahead we are going to be sadly embarrassed.' Eisenhower felt keenly that a closer relationship with the FCNL would help in alleviating resentment inside France against the Allied bombing of key installations. Three days later he was bewailing 'the friction and bad atmosphere' created by Roosevelt's policy.

Churchill had originally been just as unwilling as Roosevelt to deal with the FCNL. At the end of January he told Eden that he was not in favour of the Committee taking over civil administration in any parts of liberated France as there was no guarantee that de Gaulle and 'his vindictive crowd' would not 'hoist the Cross of Lorraine over every town hall.' However, as D-Day approached, pressure from his ministers and the press, as well as his own understanding of the operational necessities, told him that the exclusion of de Gaulle was becoming a nonsense.

The most hopeful way to break the deadlock was to encourage Roosevelt to invite de Gaulle to Washington. Churchill and de Gaulle had often managed to defuse tensions in face-to-face meetings. However de Gaulle had a tendency to decline invitations, sometimes because he was smarting from the latest insults from his Allies, at other times through sheer bloody-mindedness. Not unnaturally Roosevelt was wary. While he was happy for de Gaulle to come and see him, he was not happy to issue an invitation without a guarantee that it would be politely accepted. Churchill sympathized: 'Obviously you must know where you are with a man like this before you send an invitation.'

De Gaulle, of course, had no intention of going to Washington unless he received an invitation from the President which reflected his status as head of a provisional government. Churchill continued to press the idea of a meeting, only provoking Roosevelt to climb on his high horse: 'Circumstances are so often misconstrued later that I will not ever have it said by the French or by American or British commentators that I invited him to visit me in Washington. If he asks whether I will receive him if he comes, I will incline my head with complete suavity and with all that is required with the etiquette of the 18th Century. This is farther than the Great Duke would have gone don't you think so.' Despite the joke, Roosevelt's rancour remained. On 4 May, Halifax reported on a meeting with Hull in which 'he spoke very strongly about the President feeling hostile to de Gaulle.'

With three weeks to go to D-Day, the impasse with de Gaulle and the Committee was causing acute discomfort in London. On 12 May, Churchill proposed to Roosevelt that de Gaulle should be invited to Britain the next week for military and political talks. Roosevelt concurred with the invitation but insisted that de Gaulle should remain in Britain until the landings were over; more importantly Eisenhower should not be allowed to discuss political matters with him. In Algiers, de Gaulle, goaded by the continuing prevarications, had made a speech condemning the delays in his conversations with the Allies and calling for a permanent French alliance with 'dear Russia'. In a further tightening of the ratchet, the Consultative Assembly now declared that the Committee would henceforward be called the Provisional Government of France. At a meeting with Churchill, Eden, and Eisenhower's deputy, General Bedell-Smith, Alexander Cadogan noted: 'Bedell-Smith evidently expects violent reaction from President against French provisional Government. So we don't get anywhere. P.M. says, as usual, "Don't ask me to quarrel with President over de Gaulle." No one asks him to but we do wish he would reason with President. He won't.'

Meanwhile, one million men prepared for the greatest amphibious operation in history. As Eisenhower expressed his concerns over the French to General Marshall, Roosevelt retorted: 'I still think Eisenhower does not quite get the point. He evidently believes the fool newspaper stories that I am anti-de

Gaulle, even the kind of story that I hate him etc. All this, of course, is utter nonsense. I am perfectly willing to have de Gaulle made President or Emperor or King or anything else so long as the action comes in an untrammelled and unforced way from the French people themselves.'

On 26 May, after strident criticism in Parliament of the Government's refusal to recognize the FCNL, Churchill sent a less compliant cable to Roosevelt. He reported that, after the valiant fighting by French troops in Italy, there was a very strong feeling in Britain in favour of the French: 'The feeling is that she should be with us in this. But who is "She"? When this works out in the person of de Gaulle, all those difficulties which you and I know so well emerge.' Churchill had already decided to send his invitation to de Gaulle to come to Britain: 'He has lately shown some signs of wishing to work with us and after all it is very difficult to cut the French out of the liberation of France.' Roosevelt curtly responded: 'I am hopeful that your conversations with General de Gaulle will result in inducing him to actually assist in the liberation of France without being imposed by us on French people as their Government.' Churchill pleaded again with Roosevelt to send a cabinet-level minister to London so that there might be some prospect of opening a political dialogue with de Gaulle. 'No-one will understand their being cold-shouldered', he wrote.

Of course, in the inevitable unfolding of their relationship, Roosevelt was now calling the shots and Churchill had, on more than one occasion, to retreat into unwelcome compliance. Apart from de Gaulle, there had been a running disagreement over the bombing of French railways in the run-up to D-Day. The prospect deeply worried Churchill because of the likely civilian casualties and potentially harmful long-term effect on Franco-

British relations. However, when the military commanders persisted in their request for the bombings, Roosevelt brusquely overruled Churchill and he was forced to submit.

On 31 May, Roosevelt showed that he would not be budged. He intended only to send General Marshall: 'We cannot give him plenary powers to negotiate with de Gaulle singly or with you and de Gaulle jointly, because this is wholly in the political and not in the military field. Marshall can, of course, talk about all military matters . . . I think I can only repeat the simple fact that I cannot send anyone to represent me at the de Gaulle conversations.' On 1 June, Churchill told Roosevelt of the strong feeling in the War Cabinet that de Gaulle and leading FCNL members had to be told about D-Day before it happened: 'Otherwise it may become a very great insult to France.' Concerns about insults to France were not high on the Presidential agenda.

Roosevelt had now cast the die. On 3 June, after some hesitation that he was being drawn into another British and American trap, de Gaulle accepted Churchill's urgently expressed request to fly to Britain. On the same day, Churchill drove down to Portsmouth where a special train had been dispatched to serve as his office and home. He visited the harbour, watching troops embark on their cross-Channel transports, and cruised down the Solent, stopping to board several ships. His ministers were less impressed with his railway headquarters which, to the consternation of Eden, had only one bath, in which Churchill always seemed to be, and one telephone which was monopolized by his Chief-of-Staff, General Ismay. Churchill liked his new base, telling Roosevelt: 'I am here near Ike's headquarters in my train. His main preoccupation is the weather. There are wonderful sights to see with all these thousands of vessels.'

Eisenhower was still worrying about the resistance groups

who seemed only to recognize de Gaulle. He wrote on 3 June: 'De Gaulle is, of course, now controlling the only French military forces that can take part in this operation . . . He, however, takes the attitude that military and political matters go hand-in-hand and will not cooperate militarily unless political recognition of some kind is accorded him . . . the whole things falls into a rather sorry mess.' This was not quite correct; de Gaulle wanted his forces to be used but he would not discuss the administration of France after the invasion, the very time when Eisenhower would need help from his French allies. De Gaulle had, however, agreed that 200 French liaison officers should accompany the invasion to ease contact with liberated areas.

The next day, 4 June, de Gaulle landed in Britain and a welcoming letter from Churchill invited him down to lunch at the railway carriage. As de Gaulle arrived, Churchill was waiting on the platform and greeted him with arms outstretched. Eden, who arrived at the same time, recalled that 'de Gaulle did not respond easily to such a mood.' Moods were mellowed by lunch. Churchill outlined the scale of the armada and its timing and objectives for de Gaulle. In thanking him for the explanation, de Gaulle restrained from any comment on the short notice at which it was given. Instead he expressed his genuine admiration for Churchill, telling him that the invasion with such tremendous forces 'was the striking justification of the courageous policy which he himself had personified since the war's darkest days.' Churchill explained that a series of broadcasts was to be made to Europe on D-Day by Eisenhower and the rulers of the nations that were to be liberated. He invited de Gaulle to speak to France; de Gaulle accepted.

At dessert, Churchill and Eden attempted to turn the conversation to the political matters and particularly the administration of France. De Gaulle, sensing a trap, promptly indicated that he had not travelled to discuss these; it was best for now to concentrate on fighting the war. Churchill insisted that the FCNL and the British should try to come to a political agreement, after which de Gaulle should go to Washington and try to sell it to Roosevelt face-to-face. After all, despite Roosevelt's refusal to extend an official invitation, the door had been opened to an approach and a political agreement with the Americans might follow soon after. Eden said Britain would regret it if de Gaulle refused the offer to open political talks. The Labour Minister, Ernest Bevin, who had joined the party for lunch, added that the Labour Party would be 'hurt'.

At this provocation, de Gaulle exploded in fury. "Hurt!" he retorted, " you say that you will be hurt. Had it not occurred to them that France was hurt?" He recalled that the Committee had tried to initiate political discussions with the Americans as far back as September 1943, but there had been no reply. The only response had come six months later, in Roosevelt's directive to Eisenhower of March, which had snubbed the Committee. In the face of such ill-treatment, de Gaulle derided the idea that he should go as a supplicant to Washington: 'Why do you think that I need to submit my candidacy for the authority in France to Roosevelt? I have nothing to ask in this respect of the United States of America nor of Great Britain.' Further raising the temperature, de Gaulle said that he had just discovered that the Americans intended to issue so-called French currency to occupying troops without even consulting him. He told Churchill: 'I expect that tomorrow General Eisenhower, acting on the instructions of the President of the United States and in agreement with you, will proclaim that he is taking France under his authority. How do you expect us to come to terms on this basis? *Allez, faites, la guerre, avec votre fausse monnaie!*'

There was now a crucial exchange that would have long-lasting effects on Britain's future relations with de Gaulle. Churchill said, "I must tell you bluntly that, if after every effort has been exhausted, the President is on one side and the French National Committee on the other, I will almost certainly side with the President. Anyhow no quarrel will ever arise between Britain and the United States on account of France." To which de Gaulle replied, "I quite understand that in case of a disagreement between the United States and France, Great Britain will side with the United States." A miserable Eden shook his head at Churchill's threat, and Bevin said that the Prime Minister had only spoken for himself, not the British Cabinet. De Gaulle would never forget it and, in later years, it would be repeated over and over again. As the lunch and the argument drew to an end, Churchill sadly raised his glass: "To de Gaulle, who never accepted defeat." De Gaulle replied: "To England, to Victory, to Europe."

Churchill and Eden drove de Gaulle to see Eisenhower at his headquarters in a nearby wood. The diplomatic Commander-in-Chief took de Gaulle through the invasion plans and even asked for de Gaulle's advice on whether the invasion should be postponed because of the bad weather. De Gaulle was flattered and replied "Don't delay." Eisenhower raised the question of the broadcasts and showed the text of his own speech to de Gaulle. De Gaulle was horrified. It made no mention of the FCNL or himself and simply told French people to carry out American orders. Eisenhower said that it was only a draft and he was prepared to alter it to meet de Gaulle's objections. As the briefing ended, Churchill offered de Gaulle a lift back to London in his car. De Gaulle brusquely declined, saying that he would prefer to travel with French officers. Churchill said to Eden: "I feel chilled."

The following day, 5 June, both men were back in London. Cadogan believed that de Gaulle had had little option at the lunch: 'He refused to discuss civil affairs, in absence of Americans. This, from his point of view, quite sensible and not incorrect. That is where we have landed ourselves!' Sensitivities now multiplied. As agreed, de Gaulle sent Eisenhower his amendments to his speech, but he was told that, with D-Day now confirmed for the following day, it was too late to change the text. De Gaulle was then informed by the Foreign Office that his broadcast would be relayed immediately after Eisenhower's. De Gaulle believed that this would manoeuvre him into appearing to condone Eisenhower's words. He replied that he would agree to broadcast but only independently of any other speeches and with words of his own choosing. After the previous day's confrontation, and with all the anxieties of the forthcoming invasion, Churchill was in an emotional state. At the 6.30pm Cabinet meeting, Cadogan recorded: 'So de Gaulle refuses to broadcast! We endured the usual passionate anti-de Gaulle harangue from P.M. On this subject, we get away from politics and diplomacy and even common sense. It's a girls' school. Roosevelt, P.M. and – it must be admitted de Gaulle – all behave like girls approaching the age of puberty. Nothing to be done.'

Then came a further bombshell. De Gaulle decreed that the 200 French liaison officers assigned to accompany the invasion would not be allowed to go, because there was no political agreement on their duties. 'Well, that puts the lid on it', noted Cadogan: 'We always start by putting ourselves in the wrong, and then de Gaulle puts himself *more* in the wrong. He deserves to lose the rubber.' Churchill told the Cabinet that if de Gaulle refused to lift his ban on the liaison officers, 'it would not be possible for us to have any further discussions with General de Gaulle on civil or military matters. It might even be necessary to indicate that an aeroplane would be ready to take him back to Algiers forthwith.' When General Marshall heard of de Gaulle's decision, he was outraged, remarking that 'no sons of Iowa would fight to put up statues of de Gaulle in France.' At 9pm Churchill was informed that de Gaulle had not actually refused to broadcast; rather he had insisted that he would only do so on his own terms. It made no difference to Churchill, who demanded that de Gaulle should do as he was told.

As the invasion fleet set sail for France, de Gaulle's Ambassador to London, Pierre Vienot, was called to the Foreign Office. The following day Vienot dictated a detailed account of the astonishing events of that night to an assistant. Eden remonstrated with him about the broadcast and de Gaulle's refusal to send the liaison officers. Vienot explained that the broadcast was being drafted and that de Gaulle's action on the liaison officers was justified because of the Americans' high-handed view of themselves as an occupying force. Just before midnight, Vienot arrived at the Connaught Hotel where de Gaulle was staying. De Gaulle had worked himself up into a violent rage against Britain and America. He told Vienot that the suggestion that he should offer to visit Roosevelt in Washington was a trap; he had been made a prisoner in England, and Churchill was a gangster trying every sort of disgusting tactic: 'They're out to get me, but no-one will! I refuse to let them know whether I'm going to give the speech or not. It is my business and my business only!'

At 1am on the morning of D-Day, as the first parachutists landed in France, Vienot scuttled back to the Foreign Office. He was told that Eden had gone to see Churchill. Vienot crossed over to 10, Downing Street to find Churchill in bed, with Eden standing beside him. Vienot explained the misunderstanding over the radio speech. Eden seemed relieved to hear that some form of speech would go ahead, but Churchill, who, in this tensest of moments, had drunk a great deal, let forth a barrage of invective. He accused de Gaulle of 'treachery in battle' and, according to Vienot, charged him again and again with 'not understanding the monstrous sacrifice of young English and Americans who were going to die for France . . . "It is blood that has no value to you," he cried. "De Gaulle has only ever been a problem between the democracies. He is devoured by his own personal ambition, like a ballerina in a theatre. He thinks only of his own political future." Vienot declared that he would not be spoken to in this way; French soldiers would fight one hundred per cent. Churchill threatened to expose de Gaulle in front of Parliament.

At 3am Vienot left. Churchill immediately issued an instruction to a private secretary that de Gaulle should be put into a plane and sent to Algiers 'in chains if necessary. He must not be allowed to re-enter France.' Vienot returned to de Gaulle whom he found to be 'calm and serene'. He listened with great and apparently perverse satisfaction to Vienot's account of the conversation and told him: 'Everything turns violent when you want to speak to Churchill.' Vienot reminded him that this was the most important night in Churchill's life; he had the right to be nervous. His highly emotional state resulted not just from disappointment at de Gaulle's attitude, but also from 'a 70-year-old's incomprehensible love for France.' Now calm and, in a curious way, pleased with what he had provoked, de Gaulle was happy to agree.

D-Day dawned. After the blazing rows of the night de Gaulle

issued a public declaration affirming his admiration for Britain and her leader: 'Here I am in Great Britain under the invitation of the Prime Minister and His Majesty. How could I not be here at the place from which France, at the most crucial and difficult time, sees the Liberation armies coming, the shores of this old and dear England?' But there still remained the hurdle of de Gaulle's broadcast. Eisenhower's speech had been transmitted and French people might begin to wonder what had happened to the self-proclaimed leader of their provisional government. De Gaulle bided his time. According to Cadogan, Vienot was 'too frightened to ask for his script. He was to record at 12.30.' Duff Cooper was sent to dissuade de Gaulle from carrying out his order on the liaison officers, but de Gaulle declined to see him. The Foreign Office decided that they had no choice but to allow the broadcast to go ahead without vetting: 'It was agreed we should have to check de Gaulle from the disc and stop it if it was too bad.'

Of course, it was not. De Gaulle made one his most magnificent speeches of the war. As so often had happened before, a blazing row behind the scenes was followed by the fulfilment of his duty. "The supreme battle has been joined", he proclaimed: "For the sons of France, wherever they are, whatever they are, the simple and sacred duty is to fight the enemy by every means in their power." But de Gaulle gave no quarter to his Allies' notion of control: "The orders given by the French Government and by the leaders which it has recognized must be followed precisely." However, de Gaulle gave his heartfelt thanks to the British for their effort in the liberation of France. On hearing him, tears welled up in Churchill's eyes. Noticing a certain scepticism in General Ismay, he said: "You great tub of lard! Have you no sentiment?"

To Eden, Churchill glowered. 'He said that nothing would induce him to give way, that de Gaulle must go,' Eden recorded. 'Said I had no right to 'bully' him at a time like this and much more. There would be a Cabinet tomorrow. House of Commons would back him against de Gaulle and me and any of Cabinet who sided with me, etc etc. FDR and he would fight the world.' Late on D-Day a conciliatory message came through to Churchill from Roosevelt; the President had told de Gaulle that he would be glad to see him in Washington at the end of June or the beginning of July. Thought Churchill did not know it, Roosevelt, with the Presidential election of November looming, was preparing a purely political U-turn. The next day, Churchill innocently replied: 'I think it would be a great pity if you and he did not meet. I do not see why I should have all the pleasure.'

On the afternoon of 7 June, Duff Cooper finally persuaded de Gaulle to rescind his order on the French liaison officers. De Gaulle wondered why it should always be he who made the concessions. At dinner with Eden, he lamented the baleful state of his relations with the British. Eden noted: 'He was personally trying, I think, to make himself pleasant, but politically stiff. He is convinced that this is the only way to get anything out of the Americans and ourselves, whereas so far as W. is concerned the tactics could not be worse. It is my failure that I have never been able to persuade de Gaulle of this.' It was something of a tragedy that de Gaulle could not bring himself to surrender the small amount of pride that would have been enough to evoke Churchill's emotional core of Francophilia. But it would have been like asking the Arctic to melt. Cadogan believed that the two leaders of the free world had diminished themselves by their inability to rise above it all: 'Of these critical 72 hours, I suppose about 40 have been occupied by all the High-Ups wrangling about purely imaginary and manufactured grievances against de Gaulle! President is so odd on this question that I think he must have made secret agreement with Pétain and/or Laval!'

For several days Churchill continued to rage against de Gaulle. Roosevelt, beginning to see the odds, was more coolly detached, offering Churchill the blandishment that, when de Gaulle arrived in Washington, 'I will do my best to attract his interest to the Allied war effort.' Finally, after the customary soothings of Eden and bewilderment in the House of Commons at the treatment of de Gaulle, Churchill agreed that he should be allowed to visit France on 14 June. The evening before, Eden tried to persuade de Gaulle to write Churchill a letter of thanks. Unfortunately, de Gaulle had gained wind that Churchill, at the last minute, had told the Cabinet that he wanted to stop the trip; no letter was written.

On 14 June, de Gaulle crossed the Channel on the French ship, *La Combattante*, and was driven into liberated Bayeux. After four years of exile, his reception would finally determine whether he was a returning hero or a self-promoted phantasm. The verdict was unequivocal. The people acclaimed him and Allied intelligence reported to London and Washington that de Gaulle seemed to be the name on every Frenchman's lips. The American magazine, *Newsweek*, reported that, 'everywhere he was welcomed by cheers, tears, and hastily organized demonstrations.' Perhaps the people of France did not understand the intricacies of the real de Gaulle but there was no doubt that he was the symbol they had been waiting for. De Gaulle installed his former aide de camp, François Coulet, as Commissioner of the Republic for the liberated territory of Normandy. The British Commander-in-Chief, General Montgomery, went out of his way to call on Coulet and was exceedingly polite. He understood the value of the Free French in the local administration and liaison with the Resistance. As De Gaulle said to one of his generals: 'You see, we just had to present the Allies with an accomplished fact. Our administration is now in place. You'll see that they will say nothing.' And, more or less, he was right. He had won.

CHAPTER FOURTEEN
ENDGAME

As the towns and villages of Normandy were liberated, de Gaulle's advance men secured the local administration without a struggle. Churchill's fear that he would hoist the Cross of Lorraine over every town hall was amply fulfilled, but there was no need for de Gaulle to force himself on the people of France; they wanted him. Eisenhower's worries of chaos and Roosevelt's policy that local administrations should be set up by the Allies on a case-by-case basis vanished in the sweep of events. For Eisenhower, it was an enormous relief; he could concentrate on fighting the battle, knowing that the Gaullists were securing his rear.

In the days after D-Day Roosevelt had begun to be overwhelmed by a flood of advice on the emerging realities. On 13 June, de Gaulle had left for Bayeux. The heads of the American Army, Air Force and Navy, General Marshall, General Arnold, and Admiral King had jointly put their names to a warning about the danger of hostility from the French resistance, which was playing a useful role in disrupting the movements of German forces, if de Gaulle were to continue to be frozen out. They also told Roosevelt that Churchill was isolated within his Government in his opposition towards de Gaulle. On the same day, the O.S.S. office in Bern warned that, in denying recognition to the FCNL, the Americans were 'delivering a dangerous weapon to the enemy, since such a refusal is construed as an indication that the French resistance is not trusted.' On 30 June, O.S.S. reported that 'a campaign of unheard-of violence has been started in various resistance groups against Roosevelt and against the Americans.'

At this time Stimson wrote a long entry in his diary, analyzing Roosevelt's policy which, he believed, was now 'dealing with unrealities.' While he shared the distaste for de Gaulle, he thought it was manifestly impossible for the United States to act as the moral arbiter of how France should govern itself and arrange its elections. It was far more productive not to quarrel with de Gaulle, even though he was inching his way to power, and get on with fighting the war. His analysis led Stimson to conclude: 'The President's position is theoretically and logically correct, but as I said in the beginning, it is not realistic. The present situation I have come to believe requires for its solution an immediate reconciliation between the British and American governments even if we provisionally recognize de Gaulle.' Roosevelt still refused to take that final plunge; indeed he told Stimson that de Gaulle would crumple and his British supporters would be confounded by the progress of events. Stimson wryly noted: 'This is contrary to everything that I hear.' Even while he clutched at such straws, Roosevelt was slowly softening. On 14 June he wrote to Churchill that he was now in favour of making 'full use' of any organisation or influence de Gaulle might have.

Another senior American, Admiral Stark, was also trying to interpret de Gaulle's mood. On 20 June, he astutely judged that, while de Gaulle had many signs of incipient dictatorship, 'he is intelligent, so he may see France's dislike of regimentation, and he is genuinely devout, while most dictators are cynics on religious matters. My tentative and intuitive guess is that the worst danger of a xenophobe de Gaulle dictatorship has passed.' The most brilliant insight of all came from an O.S.S. report: 'Whether the French over the future will want this man who apparently considers himself today as the male incarnation of Joan of Arc as their future leader, I do not know, but I do feel that, short of an accident, the first government of liberated France will be headed by de Gaulle. There is no other choice, and also he will be chosen because, by doing so, the French, in some subtle way which is hard to explain, can fulfil what is almost a psychic impulse – a soul craving – to be able to tell their children that France was never defeated, that it kept fighting on till victory.' It was an extraordinarily accurate prophecy of the legacy de Gaulle would create for his people, a legacy which would prevent them, until quite recent times, from acknowledging the sordid history of collaboration.

Churchill, his fury at de Gaulle now taking second place to reason, added his voice, telling Roosevelt that de Gaulle and the Committee represented most of the elements who wanted to help the Allies: 'The energising factor of de Gaulle must not be forgotten in our treatment of the French problem.' Churchill suggested exploring 'whether there is a basis for an agreement with the French Committee provided it gives nothing away which you and we do not wish to give away.' De Gaulle was now set to visit Washington in July and Roosevelt replied that he would not wish to be saddled with any *fait accompli* before his arrival. Churchill assured him that he would not be, but he would soon find that the President was playing a crafty game.

On 6 July, the game of invitations and requests that had begun in April at last resulted in de Gaulle touching down, for the first time, on American soil. Roosevelt had ordered that he should only be given a 17-gun salute, befitting a general, rather than the 21-gun salute appropriate for a head of state. To the world beyond, the ceremony of his greeting, and the way it was reported in the newsreels, made it seem more like the descent of a monarch. Only five days before Roosevelt had made his remark to his private secretary, William Hassett, that de Gaulle was a nut, but he now welcomed him like an old friend, saying in French "I am so happy to see you." Roosevelt was a clever loser, so clever that anyone unfamiliar with the accumulation of insults and jokes would never have realized that he had ever been anything but de Gaulle's most ardent admirer.

Curtis Roosevelt remembers the mood at the White House: "FDR, being the politician, simply saw the reality, had to face it, did a complete flip-flop, rolled out the red carpet, couldn't have been nicer. And there's a lovely picture of my mother standing behind FDR receiving de Gaulle, all smiles and charm." Banquets were laid on, and de Gaulle was introduced to all the men who had tried so hard to destroy him. Offering drinks, Roosevelt quipped to Leahy that Vichy water might be appropriate for him. De Gaulle did not see the joke. Nevertheless Leahy recorded: 'At our meeting I found him more agreeable in manner and appearance than I had expected . . . I had a better opinion of him after talking to him.' In the light of three and a half years of undiluted prejudice, it was a breathtaking admission.

Margaret Suckley was all agog to know how things were going: 'The President saw de Gaulle yesterday – will have lunch with him today – The President said he would call me up about it, some time over the week-end – I can't wait to hear how the Prima Donna behaves! Whether "she" is Jeanne d'Arc or Clémenceau or both!!' Margaret was to be disappointed by the lack of gossip. In their meetings both men behaved with the utmost civility, Roosevelt deigning to give de Gaulle a lengthy description of his vision of the post-war world which would be policed by America along with Russia, China and Britain. He even discussed the future of the British Empire which, in such places as India and Singapore, would have to bow to American authority. Gleefully, de Gaulle later reported this back to Duff Cooper who passed it on to Churchill. Churchill was naturally angry that Roosevelt should have spoken so much more frankly to de Gaulle than himself about the future of his nation but, suffering under the burden of being Roosevelt's junior partner, sought to blame the messenger rather than the message. He wrote to Eden: 'I think it would be a good thing to let the President know the kind of way de Gaulle interprets friendliness. I have now had four years' experience of him, and it is always the same.' Such a message, of course, was also a way of conveying his upset to Roosevelt. Eden wisely advised him to let the matter drop as de Gaulle had only been acting as an ally should. 'As you will,' replied a beaten Churchill.

Churchill was also about to be outmanoeuvred. At a press conference on 10 July, Roosevelt announced that he would accept the FCNL as the de facto authority for civil administration in France. Legalistically, it was not quite the same as recognizing the Committee as a provisional government, but there was no doubting the message. Roosevelt cabled his decision to Churchill, but only after it had been made, and London first heard about it from the Reuters news agency. Eden took the Reuters report round to Downing Street. Churchill, he recorded, 'didn't like it, the more so since it was so close to what I forecast would happen.' Eden returned after dinner and found himself embroiled in a late night conversation with Churchill: 'He was in a mellow mood, in part I think because he felt I had been right about the French. Finally escaped at 2am, W. remarking "You and I have some heavy burdens to bear together."' The British Embassy had no doubt about Roosevelt's motives, reporting that his carefully staged performance with de Gaulle would allow him 'to go to the Polls with a shining diplomatic record from which earlier stains of appeasement and opportunism would largely have been washed.'

On the day of Roosevelt's volte-face, Stark tried to explain de Gaulle's appeal to James Forrestal, the newly appointed Secretary for the US Navy. Once again the comparison with the maid of Orleans was rolled out: 'He is, I would say, rather filled with the Joan of Arc Mission to save France. The British say he also has Joan's feelings towards England . . . I think he feels that he is the only one who can bear the torch. He has always played for high stakes. He has staked all on practically every throw. For one who has finally arrived where he has, I think it is only fair to say that he must have shown considerable diplomatic skill while at the same time being apparently so rigid.' Of all the Americans, Stark had always had the most perceptive understanding of de Gaulle.

From Washington de Gaulle travelled on to a hero's reception in New York, where he was fêted by Mayor LaGuardia, who had been a loyal supporter from the beginning. He wrote an effusive letter to Roosevelt, thanking him 'for the kind reception you gave me and the warm hospitality the American Government bestowed on me;' he said that he and the French people were 'unanimous in friendship and determined to continue fighting and working beside our Allies for victory and peace.' On Roosevelt's side, any such sentiments remained skin-deep. A few days later, de Gaulle received, from an anonymous source, a photocopy of a letter Roosevelt had written to a Congressman, Joseph Clark Baldwin, in which he said of de Gaulle: 'I suspect that he is essentially an egoist.' In his memoirs de Gaulle wryly noted: 'I was never to know if Franklin Roosevelt thought that in affairs concerning France Charles de Gaulle was an egoist for France or for himself.'

As the Allies approached Paris, de Gaulle faced his final moment of truth. He was understandably nervous. As the Paris insurrection against the remaining Nazis brought chaos to the streets, he knew that the two extremes of France were plotting their own uprisings. In a last ditch effort to hold on to power, Laval was trying to reconstitute the pre-armistice National Assembly of 1940 as the legitimate government with himself at his head; at the other extreme, the Communist resistance was planning a *putsch*. On 24 August the United States 4th Infantry Division and General LeClerc's 2nd Armoured Division, which had been allowed to join in the liberation of Paris for obvious symbolic reasons, entered the city. A sensible collaboration between the Allied commanders, initiated by Churchill's insistence on sending LeClerc's division to France, had allowed the French to be seen to have an important success. It was in marked contrast to the squabbles of the political leaders. The next day, after the German surrender, de Gaulle arrived. As he marched from the Arc de Triomphe to Notre Dame Cathedral on 26 August, shots from a sniper's rifle crackled through the air; tension and danger both physical and political, hung over the city. Eisenhower wrote later that de Gaulle called for American assistance to keep the peace, a supremely ironic request from the proud and independent Frenchman; de Gaulle hotly denied the claim. Ironically, Roosevelt, not Churchill, had been instrumental in building up de Gaulle's army. In mid August the landings in the South of France, Operation 'Dragoon,' which had initially been envisaged as a D-Day feint, finally took place. Churchill had protested against them right from the beginning, partly because it would distract from the possibility of a British-led success in Italy, but to no avail. Roosevelt's insistence on 'Dragoon' led directly to the American rearmament of General de Lattre de Tassigny's French Army B comprising some 250,000 men who were needed as infantry for the operation. Roosevelt thereby played a vital role in restoring France as a military power, whereas, if Churchill had had his way, this would, at the very least, have been delayed.

De Gaulle moved rapidly to amalgamate the resistance into the French army, offering in return places for the Communist leaders in his provisional government. Roosevelt continued to believe that France would be overwhelmed by revolution. In early September he told Stimson that he wanted American forces to be protected from it 'by having some other nation than the United States occupy the territory of Germany nearest to France.' A few days later Stimson found out that the main prophet of revolution was Leahy and noted with asperity: 'Leahy is not a very acute person and, although he has had the advantage of being stationed in Vichy for several years, I don't think his advice is good.' Even though it was becoming increasingly evident that de Gaulle was the bulwark against revolution, Roosevelt still held out against final recognition of the FCNL as the provisional government of France.

When recognition finally came, the trickery of July repeated itself. At the second Quebec conference in September, Roosevelt and Churchill were advised by Eden and Hull, who had now completed an about turn, that the time was ripe. The two leaders responded, according to Eden with 'a tirade against de Gaulle.' In a succession of memorandums, Hull kept up the pressure, drawing Roosevelt's attention to newspaper articles which said that the United States was out on a limb. Eden also worked on Churchill, and on 14 October, Churchill cabled Roosevelt that he was now in favour of recognition. On 19 October, Roosevelt was still counselling delay: 'I think until the French set up a real zone of interior that we should make no move towards recognising them as a provisional government.'

Two days later, the Foreign Office heard out of the blue that the American Ambassador in Paris had been instructed by the State Department to prepare to recognize. In the light of Roosevelt's last message, Cadogan could hardly believe it: 'God help us! Is this simple inefficiency and crossing of wires or are the US trying to do us down?' On 23 October, Roosevelt again told Churchill that he was not ready; by then, in Paris, the deed had already been done by his Embassy. Churchill instantly complained to Roosevelt about 'the very sharp turn taken by the State Department'. Roosevelt lamely replied with regrets that 'my absence from Washington resulted in more precipitate action by State Department than was contemplated.' Whether or not he was being ingenuous is unclear. Once again in danger of being beaten to the draw, the British Government rushed through its own announcement. Cadogan recorded his displeasure: 'We have *all*, thank God, Americans, British and Russians, recognised de Gaulle. At *last*! What a fuss about nothing! Due to that spiteful old great-aunt Leahy. Hope he's feeling pretty sick.' De Gaulle found it all irrelevant. He simply responded: 'The French government is satisfied to be called by its name.'

On 7 November, Roosevelt won his fourth Presidential election. The recognition of de Gaulle was hardly a major electoral factor but his timing was as acute as ever. Political recognition, of course, did not mean friendship. Churchill had been invited to Paris to celebrate Armistice Day on 11 November. That day

Oliver Harvey noted: 'We all tremble for the result. P.M. being still violently anti-deG ... De G. on other hand, is believed to be in a nasty and clamorous mood.' Lo and behold, three days later, Harvey recorded: 'P.M.'s visit to Paris an outstanding success and all our forebodings dispelled.'

De Gaulle and, indeed, the French people had laid out the red carpet, the Champs Elysées teeming with cheering crowds, spectators waving from every window. Churchill's report to Roosevelt described a remarkable change of heart: 'I re-established friendly private relations with de Gaulle, who is better since he has lost a large part of his inferiority complex. Giraud was at the banquet apparently quite content. What a change in fortunes since Casablanca. Generally I felt in the presence of an organised government, broadly based and of rapidly-growing strength, and I am certain that we should be most unwise to do anything to weaken it in the eyes of France at this difficult, critical time. I had a considerable feeling of stability in spite of Communist threats, and that we could safely take them more into our confidence. I hope you will not consider that I am putting on French clothes when I say this.'

It was too much to hope that the story would have a happy ending. A summit between Roosevelt, Churchill and Stalin had been arranged for February 1945 at Yalta and de Gaulle believed that he was entitled to be present. Churchill tried gently to persuade Roosevelt that he could at least attend meetings when French affairs were under discussion. Roosevelt replied sharply that de Gaulle's inclusion would 'merely introduce a complicating and undesirable factor.' Despite a visit by de Gaulle to Moscow in December and his oft-expressed pro-Russian sentiments, Stalin also dismissed the idea, wondering with withering contempt what the French had done in the war to deserve a seat at the victors' high table. By January, Churchill, back on the love-hate switchback, had also changed his mind, writing to Eden: 'I cannot think of anything more unpleasant and impossible than having this menacing and hostile man in our midst, always trying to make himself a reputation in France by claiming a position far above what France occupies, and making faces at the Allies who are doing the work.'

Despite that, Churchill, helped by the ailing Harry Hopkins, energetically defended France's position at Yalta, ensuring that she would have a place on the Allied Control Commission for Germany and become a permanent member of the United Nations Security Council. Though he required persuasion, such a concession could not have been granted without Roosevelt's agreement. If he expected any thanks, he was mistaken. Before Yalta, the American Ambassador had given de Gaulle a personal message from Roosevelt suggesting that they meet at Algiers on his return. De Gaulle gracelessly refused, attempting to draw an unwarranted parallel with Roosevelt's inability to accept an invitation to visit Paris in November. Churchill's doctor, Lord Moran, noted: 'The dreary story of de Gaulle's gaucherie came to its melancholy climax.' However, de Gaulle's refusal was backed by the majority of his cabinet and the French press. Perhaps by now Roosevelt and his advisers should have realized that an invitation to the head of the provisional French Government to meet on French soil, with its echo of the summons to Casablanca, was hardly a model of tact.

On his return to Washington, Roosevelt, reporting to Congress on his trip, referred to "prima donnas" whose whims had prevented a valuable discussion. It is the last recorded reference he made to de Gaulle; on 12 April, he was dead. De Gaulle believed that, had Roosevelt lived longer, 'he would have understood and appreciated the reasons that determined my actions as Chief of State . . . it was with all my heart that I saluted his memory with regret and admiration.' Perhaps Roosevelt's death really did induce in de Gaulle that streak of extreme sentimentality which Macmillan had once noticed. However, it is hard to believe that Roosevelt could ever have come to think the same of the French General whom he had alternately ridiculed and despised. In the end, as his grandson Curtis Roosevelt puts it, 'politics was a game to FDR' and de Gaulle just another politician to whom 'he lost a skirmish.'

De Gaulle's triumph was short-lived. When the war was over, the French people voted for a new French Constitution and members of the new Assembly voted unanimously for de Gaulle as its first President. However the elections also brought back all the old parties and old squabbles. De Gaulle, wearied by the return of coalition politics, resigned as President in 1946. Although he expected the clamour for his return to come much sooner, he had to wait until the crisis in Algeria twelve years later for his summons. France finally acknowledged the need for a strong leader and gave de Gaulle the Constitution of the Fifth Republic with which to exercise presidential power. For eleven years he led France, much in the autocratic manner with which Roosevelt came to lead America. Perhaps then, the two men might have recognized each other as similar types of players on the world stage.

Churchill lived to see de Gaulle's eventual apotheosis. His passions towards him were undiminished until the very end of the war and after. In the closing days of the fighting, French troops were sent by de Gaulle to occupy the province of Cuneo in north-west Italy. Eisenhower instructed them to withdraw to make way for occupation by the Allied Military Government in

Italy. De Gaulle ordered them to stay put, and told his local commander to threaten the Allies that any action taken against his forces 'could have grave consequences.' The new American President, Harry Truman, retaliated by ordering that no further issues of equipment or munitions would be made to French forces. De Gaulle backed down, but not before Churchill had cabled Truman that de Gaulle 'after five long years of experience I am convinced is the worst enemy of France in her troubles . . . I consider General de Gaulle one of the greatest dangers to European peace.' It turned out to be Churchill's parting shot at the Frenchman who had provoked such contrasting feelings. On 26 July, the votes were counted in the British general election and he resigned from office.

Militarily, the agonies over de Gaulle meant little. The war would have been won without the Free French, and without the former Vichy army for that matter. However de Gaulle, viewed for so long by Roosevelt as the potential dictator who would bring civil war to France, turned out to be the strong man who ensured that it did not happen. Politically, Roosevelt lost rather more than a 'skirmish'. His besting by de Gaulle was his most significant personal defeat of the war. Furthermore, although the problem of de Gaulle was not the greatest in magnitude, it brought a longer and greater tension into Churchill's relationship with Roosevelt than any other. In addition, it produced sometimes savage disharmony between Churchill and his ministers, as Churchill hung on to his overriding policy that he must not allow it to cause a breach with Roosevelt.

Although it is impossible to know exactly what passes in the minds of men, it is hard to believe that the bruising de Gaulle received at the hands of his Allies did not leave a legacy. At the beginning of the war he had no reason for hostility to the United

States; de Gaulle knew his history and America was the historic friend of France, going right back to the War of Independence against the British. However, as President of France in the 1960s, although at the moments of greatest crisis (like Cuba in 1962) he stood by his Western Allies, he used every other opportunity to criticize America. The Vietnam War was an ideal opportunity. In 1966 de Gaulle described it in a major speech in Phnom Penh as a "detestable war, since it leads a great nation to ravage a small one."

As foretold in the Special Branch report of February 1943, he sought an axis with Germany through which France, as the senior partner, would dominate Europe, and an alliance with Russia. In 1963 he vetoed Britain's attempt to join the European Common Market, claiming that she would be America's Trojan horse in Europe. After all, had not Churchill himself said at that railway station that, when it came to the crunch, Britain would always side with America?

Two years after de Gaulle's rejection, Churchill died. As they grew older, the two men made their peace, rediscovering the mutual admiration of June 1940 and even some of the warmth. In 1958, Churchill went to Paris where de Gaulle, hovering like a benevolent guardian over the stooped old man, hung the Cross of the Liberation around Churchill's neck. It was an intensely moving sight; two titanic figures, both possessed of great passions which, during the war, had brought them so near to total rupture. De Gaulle himself was finally broken by the French people, resigning in 1969 after defeat in the referendum he had called to re-establish his authority after the riots in Paris of May 1968. He died in November 1970.

On 8 May 1945, de Gaulle wrote to Churchill: 'As the cannons stop firing over Europe, I am writing to tell you of my sincere friendship and admiration. What happened, would not have happened without you. I am sure that I share your hopes that our two magnificent countries will walk together in harmonious and glorious peace.' There was indeed glory at the end for the three allies at war, even if Roosevelt did not live to see the final victory. Sadly, harmony between them had not been a part of it.

NOTES ON SOURCES

The documents and books listed in the bibliography have all played a part, some substantial, others supplying a piece of information, a pointer, or a story. The most consistently used archive sources are the Public Record Office at Kew and the *Foreign Relations of the United States* (FRUS). In addition Warren Kimball's *Complete Correspondence between Churchill and Roosevelt* is a sine qua non. Apart from these, most direct quotations come from the listed diaries and papers. Churchill and de Gaulle both wrote highly readable and often exciting war memoirs, which are sometimes most interesting for their omissions. Roosevelt died too early to leave us his account but, unlike Churchill and de Gaulle, he was never an enthusiastic writer anyway. There are particular further debts where the sources are not obvious or where I have used quotes from secondary sources which I would like to acknowledge in this brief résumé.

Chapter One

Randolph Churchill's account of the encounter with his shaving father is told in Vol 2 of Martin Gilbert's *Churchill's War Papers*. Milton Viorst's *Hostile Allies* gives the detail of Roosevelt's exchanges with Reynaud. General Edward Spears's *Assignment to Catastrophe* and *Two Men who saved France* contains a dramatic account of these days and the first sightings of de Gaulle. Philip Bell's *A Certain Eventuality* has been of paramount use in the detail of the events throughout 1940.

Chapter Two

Warren Kimball's *Forged in War* and David Stafford's *Roosevelt and Churchill*, which includes Joseph Kennedy's unpublished diplomatic memoir, contain excellent background on their relationship. Curtis Roosevelt told me the story about Aunt Dora. The State Department analysis on de Gaulle is quoted in Rossi's *Roosevelt and the French* which is an admirable analysis of the cultural conflict between Roosevelt and de Gaulle. Francois Kersaudy's *Churchill* and de Gaulle's superbly detailed study of their relationship, tells the Gladwyn Jebb story. Pierre Messmer and Claude Bouchinet Serreulles gave television interviews for *Allies at War*. The 'bar of soap' story is told in Jean Lacouture's de Gaulle, *The Rebel*.

Chapter Three

The story of de Gaulle and the tropical kit comes from Charles Williams's highly entertaining biography, *The Last Great Frenchman*. Jimmy Green's *Naval Diaries of an Ordinary Sailor 1936–1948* give an exciting account of the shelling of the *Cumberland*. I am indebted to Julian G. Hurstfield's *America and the French Nation 1939–1945*, a richly detailed analysis of its subject, for the subtleties of the reporting of Dakar in the United States. Maurice Schumann's quote is reported by Lacouture.

Chapter Four

Robert Murphy's *Diplomat Among Warriors* is a vital source, despite the risks when it is the only account. Hitler's attitude to Vichy is quoted by Rossi from *Ciano's Diplomatic Papers*, ed. Malcolm Muggeridge. Roosevelt's press conference on Martinique is quoted in Hurstfield. Parr is quoted in Bell's *A Certain Eventuality*. Philip Bell has recounted the story of de Gaulle and the Royal Thames Yacht Club.

Chapter Five

The Attorney-General's criticism of M.I.5 comes from new PREM 3 documents obtained by Marc Tiley. Sherwood's *Roosevelt and Hopkins* gives a full account of Hopkins's mission to Churchill. Henri de Kerillis is quoted by Hurstfield.

Chapter Six

Spears's *Fulfilment of a Mission* is a key book on Syria, both eloquent and splenetic. Kersaudy gives a fully rounded picture and Lapie told him the story about too many English during an interview in 1979.

Chapter Seven

Raoul Aglion's *Roosevelt and de Gaulle* quoted de Gaulle's 16 July memorandum. Colville's lovely account of the Churchill / de Gaulle meeting is given in *Footprints in Time*. For background on St Pierre I am indebted to *Over by Christmas* by Richard Doody and also to the delightful and hospitable local people.

Chapter Eight

The snub to the Free French on Memorial Day is recorded in detail by Aglion. The Foreign Office record of Churchill's bad-tempered meeting with de Gaulle is a paradigm of diplomacy for which its author should be congratulated.

Chapter Nine

Arthur Funk's *The Politics of Torch*, a superb day-by-day account, was a vital source for this chapter. Mark Clarks *Calculated Risk* is a stirring and frank first-hand account. Donovan's suggestion to Roosevelt about Darlan is quoted in Hurstfield. I feel indebted to the huge achievement of Alfred D. Chandler in compiling and editing Eisenhower's papers which I have found fascinating.

Chapter Ten

Billotte's remark is quoted by Kersaudy. The remark about kissing Darlan's stern is quoted in *My Three Years with Eisenhower*, the diaries of Harry Butcher. Jean Cremieux Brilhac was interviewed for the television programme, *Allies at War*, as was Philippe Raguenau.

Chapter Eleven

Churchill's Conditions most agreeable quote is taken from Kimball quoting Howard, *Grand Strategy*, IV. Eliot Roosevelt's *As He Saw It* is most enjoyable, but considered not entirely reliable by some academics and, indeed, Curtis Roosevelt. Hopkins's descriptions are taken from Sherwood. Etienne Burin de Roziers was interviewed for the television programme, *Allies at War*. De Gaulle's remark to an aide after the meeting with Roosevelt is quoted in Kersaudy. Robert Hopkins was interviewed for *Allies at War*. De Gaulle's press conference of 9 February is quoted by Kersaudy. The King's warning to Churchill is in J.W. Wheeler-Bennett, *King George VI*. My main source for the Richelieu story is Aglion. The revelation that Churchill was prepared to use force against de Gaulle and that, on his orders, M.I.5 bugged de Gaulle's private phone is contained in new PREM 3 documents obtained by Marc Tiley.

Chapter Twelve

Jose Aboulker told his story about the meeting with de Gaulle in an interview for *Allies at War*. Like John Colville's diaries in the earlier part of this story, Harold Macmillan's war diaries contain some wonderful and beautifully written descriptions.

Chapter Thirteen

Churchill's venomous warning to Duff Cooper is quoted by Kersaudy. Roosevelt's warning to Edwin Wilson and retort to Marshall are quoted in Rossi. De Gaulle's remark about 'hurt' in the railway carriage is from Pierson Dixon's diary quoted in G. E. Maguire, *Anglo-American Policy towards the Free French*. Maguire's penetrating book first alerted me to the importance of reading the *Eisenhower Papers*. The 'great tub of lard' story is told by Kimball quoting from an interview Ismay gave to Forrest Pogue, the official historian of SHAEF, in 1946. The "c'est un animal" story is from Martin Gilbert, *The Road to Freedom*.

Chapter Fourteen

The O.S.S. reports are quoted in Rossi. I am grateful to Philip Bell for pointing me to the irony of 'Dragoon.'

ARCHIVE SOURCES

Public Records Office, Kew

CAB   *(Cabinet Papers)*
      CAB 21/1464, CAB 65/35, CAB 65/38, CAB 106,/771,
      CAB 118/39, CAB 120/539, CAB 120/10, CAB 163/10,

PREM *(Prime Minister's Files)*
      PREM 3/174/2, PREM 3/120/2, PREM 3/120/4, PREM
      120/10, PREM 120/539, PREM 3/121/4, PREM
      3/121/1, PREM 3/181/3, PREM 3/121/5, PREM 3/377

FO   *(Foreign Office)*
      FO 371/24345, FO 371/28545, FO 371/31873, FO
      371/36047, FO 371/36083, FO 371/28436, FO
      371/28320, FO 954/8, FO 954/9, FO 660/85, FO
      660/86

ADM   *(Admiralty)*
      ADM 1/15626, 1/13140, ADM 97-100

AIR   *(Air Ministry)*
      75/11

CO   *(Commonwealth Office)*
        CO 323/179, CO 968/30/1

HS   *(Special Operations Executive)*
        6/311

HW   *(Government Communications Head Quarters)*
        HW 1/1352, HW 1/1467,

INF   *(Ministry Of Information)*
        INF 1/970,

KV   *(Security Service)*
        KV 4/45

WO   *(War Office)*
        WO 106/5416

Middle East Centre, Oxford
Spear Papers, 1941–45

Churchill College, Cambridge
Spears Papers, 1940
Vansittart Committee Minutes

National Archives, Washington DC
State Department files

United States Embassy, London
FRUS *(Foreign Relations of the United States)*
Volumes – 1940:2, 1941:2, 1942:2, Washington
Conference, Casablanca Conference, 1944: 3

Franklin D. Roosevelt Library, Hyde Park, New York
PSF Diplomatic, France
Map Room, Special File

Dwight D. Eisenhower Library, Abilene
Eisenhower's correspondence

Library of Congress, Washington DC
Admiral William Leahy Diaries

Yale University Library
Henry Lewis Stimson Diaries

US Navy Library, Washington D.C.
Admiral Harold Raynsford Stark Diaries

Teyssot Estate, Paris
Leon Jon Teyssot Diaries

BIBLIOGRAPHY

Aglion, R, *Roosevelt and De Gaulle*, Macmillan, London (1984)

Bell, P.M, H. *A Certain Eventuality*, Saxon House (1974)

Bell, P.M, H. *France and Britain 1940–1994*, Longman, London (1997)

Bell, P.M.H, *France and Britain 1900–1940*, Longman, London (1996)

Berle, A, *Navigating the Rapids*, Harcourt Brace, New York (1973)

Blum, J.M (ed), *The Diary of Henry A. Wallace 1942–46*, Houghton Mifflin, New York (1973)

Blum, JM, *From the Morgenthau Diaries 1941–45*, Publisher: Houghton Mifflin Co. (1967).

Bouchinet-Serreulles, C, *Nous Etions Faits Pour Etres Libres*, Grasset, Paris (2000)

Bullitt, O.H, *Correspondence between Franklin D. Roosevelt and William Bullitt*, Houghton Mifflin, New York (1972)

Butcher, H.C, *My Three Years with Eisenhower*, Simon & Schuster (1946)

Campbell, T, *Diaries of Stettinius*, Franklin Watts, New York (1975)

Catroux, *Dans la bataille de Mediterranée*, Julliard, Paris (1949)

Chandler, A.D (ed), *The Papers of D.D. Eisenhower – The War Years,*

Churchill, W.S, *The Second World War. Vols 1–6,* Houghton Mifflin (1948)

Clark, M, *Calculated Risk,* Harper, New York (1950)

Colville, J, *Downing Street Diaries,* 1939–1955, Hodder & Stoughton, London (1985)

Colville, J, *Footprints in Time,* Collins, London (1976)

Cooper, D, *Old Men Forget,* Davis, London (1953)

Cremieux-Brilhac, J-L, *La France Libre,* Gallinard (1996)

De Gaulle, C, *Lettres, Notes et Carnets, vols 1–3,* Plon, Paris (1972)

De Gaulle, C, *The Complete War Memoirs,* Simon & Schuster, London (1960)

Dilks, D, (ed), *Diaries of Sir Alexander Cadogan,1938–45,* Cassell, London (1971)

Eden, A, *The Reckoning,* Cassell, London (1965)

Eisenhower, D.D, *The Papers of D.D. Eisenhower. Vols 1–5,* Hopkins, London (1970)

Ferrel, R.H, (ed), *The Eisenhower Diaries,* Norton & Co, London (1981)

Foot, MRD, *The SOE in France,*

Freedman, M, *Roosevelt and Frankfurter,* Little, Brown & Co, Boston (1967)

Freidel, F, *Roosevelt,* Little Brown, Boston (1990)

Funk, A.L, *The Politics of Torch,* Kansas UP (1974)

Gellman, IF, *Secret Affairs- Roosevelt, Hull and Sumner Welles* (1995)

Gilbert, M, *The Churchill War Papers,* Heineman, London (1994)

Green, J, *Naval Diaries of an Ordinary Sailor,* Greenwood, Kent (1996)

Harriman, W.A, *Special Envoy to Churchill and Stalin,* Random House, New York (1975)

Harvey, J (ed), *War Diaries of Oliver Harvey, 1941–45*, Collins, London (1978)

Hassett, W.D, *Off The Record with FDR*, Rutgers, New Jersey (1958)

Horne, A, *Macmillan*, Macmillan, London (1988)

Hull, C, *The Memoirs of Cordell Hull*, Hodder and Stoughton (1948).

Hurstfield, J.G, *America and the French Nation, 1939–1945*, North Carolina University Press (1986)

Ickes, H, *The Secret Diary of Harold L. Ickes,* Simon & Schuster, New York (1954)

Ismay, H, *Memoirs*, Heinemann, London (1960)

Israel, F.L (ed),*The War Diary of Breckinridge Long*, Nebraska University Press (1966)

Kersaudy, F, *Churchill and de Gaulle,* Collins, London (1981)

Kimball, W.F, *Forged in War – Roosevelt and Churchill,* William Morrow, New York (1997)

Kimball, W.F, *Churchill and Roosevelt, The Complete Correspondence, vols 1–3,* Princeton, New Jersey (1987)

Kimball, W.F, *The Juggler,* Princeton University Press, New Jersey (1991)

Lacoutre, J, *De Gaulle: The Rebel 1890–1944,* Norton, New York (1990)

Lash, J.P, *Roosevelt and Churchill 1939–41,* Norton, New York (1977)

Lash, J.P, *The Diaries of Felix Frankfurter,* Norton, New York (1975)

Leahy, W, *I Was There: a personal story based on notes and diaries*, Gollancz, London (1950)

Leutze, J, *The London Observer: The Journal of General R.E. Lee*

Lukacs, J, *The Duel,* Oxford University Press, (1992)

Macmillan, H, *War Diaries,* Macmillan, London (1984)

Maguire, G.E, *Anglo-American Policy towards the Free French,* Macmillan, London (1995)

Marnham, P, *The Death of Jean Moulin,* Murray, London (2000)

Moran, Lord, *Winston Churchill,* Constable, London (1966)

Murphy, R, *Diplomat Among Warriors,* Doubleday, New York (1948)

Nicholson, N, *Diaries of Harold Nicholson,* Collins, London (1967)

Ousby, I, *Occupation,* Pimlico, London (1997)

Passy, *Souvenir Vol. 1&2,* Raoul Solar, Paris (1947)

Pendar, K, *Adventures in Diplomacy,* Cassell, London (1966)

Peterson, N.H, *From Hitler's Doorstep,* Pennsylvania State University Press (1996)

Peyrefitte, A, *C'était de Gaulle,* Fayard, Paris (2000)

Pimlott, B, (ed), *The Second World War Diary of Hugh Dalton,* London (1986)

Renwick, R, *Fighting With Allies,* Times Books, London (1996)

Roosevelt, E, *An Autobiography of Eleanor Roosevelt,* Da Capo, New York (1992)

Roosevelt, E, *As He Saw It,* Duel, Sloane & Pearce, New York (1946)

Roosevelt, F.D, *The Public Papers and Addresses of FDR,* (1950)

Rossi, M, *Roosevelt and the French,* Praeger, London (1993)

Sherwood, R, E, *Roosevelt and Hopkins, vols 1–2,* Bantam, London (1948)

Soames, M (ed), *Speaking For Themselves,* Black Swan, London (1998)

Soames, M, *Clementine Churchill*, Cassell, London (1979)

Spears, E .L, *Assignment to Catastrophe*, Heinemann, London (1954)

Spears, E.L, *Fulfillment of a Mission*, Leo Cooper, London (1977

Spears, E.L, *Two Men Who Saved Pétain*, Stein and Day (1966)

Stafford, D, *Roosevelt and Churchill*, Little Brown, London (1999)

Stimson, H.L, *On Active Service*, Hutchinson, London (no date)

Thody, P, *French Caeserism*, Macmillan, London (1989)

Viorst, M, *Hostile Allies*, Macmillan, New York (1965)

Ward, G.C, *Closest Companion*, Houghton Mifflin, Boston (1995)

Webster, P, *Pétain's Crime*, Dee, Chicago (1991)

Wheeler-Bennett, J.W (ed), *Action This Day*, Macmillan, London (1958)

Wheeler-Bennett, J.W, *King George VI*, London (1958)

Williams, C, *The Last Great Frenchman*, Little Brown, London (1993)